T0205531

# Corpora and Intercultural Studies

## Volume 11

**Series Editors**

Kaibao Hu, Institute of Corpus Studies and Applications, Shanghai International Studies University, Shanghai, China

Hongwei Ding, School of Foreign Languages, Shanghai Jiao Tong University, Shanghai, China

This book series publishes original monographs and edited volumes in the investigations of different types of corpora (including text, speech and video) with a particular focus on intercultural studies. The differences in language use expressed in comparable corpora can be analyzed from an intercultural perspective. The emphasis is on excellence and originality in scholarship as well as synergetic interdisciplinary approaches and multicultural perspectives. Books exploring the role of the intercultural studies in the research fields of translation, linguistics, and culture, with a corpus-based approach will be especially welcome. The series publishes books that deal with emerging issues as well as those that offer an in-depth examination of underlying issues.

The target audiences of this series include both scholars and professionals who are interested in issues related to intercultural communication across different cultures and social groups, which are reflected by the investigation in comparable corpora.

Corpora and Intercultural Studies book series is published in conjunction with Springer under the auspices of School of Foreign Languages (SFL), Shanghai Jiao Tong University (SJTU). The first series editor is the Dean of SFL at SJTU, and the book series editorial board consists of leading scholars in the research field of corpora and intercultural studies in the world.

Michelle Lam Sut I

# A Corpus-assisted Multimodal Analysis to Policy Addresses of Macao SAR Government

Two Decades of Change in Macao

 Springer

Michelle Lam Sut I ⓘ
Faculty of Languages and Translation
Macao Polytechnic University
Macao, China

ISSN 2510-4802 ISSN 2510-4810 (electronic)
Corpora and Intercultural Studies
ISBN 978-981-99-1197-4 ISBN 978-981-99-1195-0 (eBook)
https://doi.org/10.1007/978-981-99-1195-0

This Springer imprint is published by the registered company Springer Nature Singapore Pte Ltd.
The registered company address is: 152 Beach Road, #21-01/04 Gateway East, Singapore 189721,
Singapore

# Contents

**1 Introduction** .................................................... 1
  1.1 General Scientific Background .......................... 2
  1.2 Specific Background .................................... 5
    1.2.1 Socio-Economic Context of Macao .................... 5
    1.2.2 Political and Socio-Cultural Context of Macao ........... 6
    1.2.3 Macao's Stories in Academic Research ................. 8
    1.2.4 Macao's Stories in Policy Addresses .................... 9
  1.3 Research Aims, Objectives and Questions ..................... 11
  1.4 Organization of the Book .................................. 12
  References ................................................... 13

**2 Literature Review** ............................................. 17
  2.1 Social Approach to Discourse Analysis ...................... 17
    2.1.1 Critical Discourse Analysis .......................... 18
    2.1.2 Fairclough's Discursive Change
      and Socio-Cultural Change ......................... 21
    2.1.3 Halliday's Meta-Functions of Language ................ 24
  2.2 Potential Semiotic Constituents for Analysis .................. 27
    2.2.1 Linguistic Resources .............................. 27
    2.2.2 Non-verbal Resources ............................. 31
  2.3 Translation Shifts ........................................ 42
  2.4 Summary ............................................... 47
  References ................................................... 47

**3 Methodology** ................................................. 53
  3.1 Data and Tools ......................................... 53
  3.2 Analytical Framework .................................... 57
  3.3 Summary ............................................... 59
  References ................................................... 59

**4  Case Analysis** ...................................................... 61
    4.1  Identifying Key Words ........................................ 61
         4.1.1  Key Words with Reference to Policy Foci ................ 64
         4.1.2  Key Words with Reference to Actions ................... 66
         4.1.3  Key Words with Reference to Social Groups
                and Institutes ........................................ 67
    4.2  Contextualizing Key Words ................................... 69
         4.2.1  Key Words with Reference to Policy Foci ................ 69
         4.2.2  Key Words with Reference to Actions ................... 75
         4.2.3  Key Words with Reference to Social Groups
                and Institutes ........................................ 84
    4.3  Translating Key Words ....................................... 88
         4.3.1  Key Words with Reference to Policy Foci ................ 88
         4.3.2  Key Words with Reference to Actions ................... 97
         4.3.3  Key Words with Reference to Social Groups
                and Institutes ........................................ 100
    4.4  Multimodal Analysis ......................................... 109
         4.4.1  Analysis of the Visual Presentation of the Policy
                Addresses ............................................. 109
         4.4.2  Analysis of the Infographics of the Policy Addresses ...... 123
    4.5  Summary of Finding .......................................... 136
    References .................................................... 141

**5  Discussion** ...................................................... 143
    5.1  Ideology Constructed in Discourse ........................... 144
         5.1.1  Discourse Constructing Changes of the Condition
                for Governance ........................................ 144
         5.1.2  Discourse Constructing Changes of the Image
                of the Gaming Industry ................................ 146
         5.1.3  Discourse Constructing Changes of the Economic
                System ................................................ 147
         5.1.4  Discourse Constructing Changes of the Image
                of the Government ..................................... 149
         5.1.5  The Role of Translation in Ideology Construction ......... 151
    5.2  Dialectical Relationship Between Policy Addresses and Society ... 156
         5.2.1  Discourse and General Social Background ............... 156
         5.2.2  Discourse and Socio-Economic Structure ................ 157
         5.2.3  Discourse and Political & Cultural Identities ............. 160
         5.2.4  Discourse, Knowledge and Power ....................... 164
    5.3  Summary .................................................... 166
    References .................................................... 167

**6  Conclusion** .................................................... 169
    6.1  Summary of the Research .................................... 169
    6.2  Implications ................................................ 171
         6.2.1  Theoretical Implications .............................. 171

        6.2.2   Empirical Implications ............................... 172
        6.2.3   Practical Implications ............................... 172
    6.3   Perspectives for Future Work ............................... 173
    References   .................................................. 174

# About the Author

**Michelle Lam Sut I** is a lecturer of Faculty of Languages and Translation, Macao Polytechnic University. She has published book chapters in Routledge and Springer and papers on academic journals related to translation studies, linguistics and Macao studies. Her current research interests include discourse analysis, multimodal analysis and corpus-based analysis to translation studies.

# List of Figures

Fig. 2.1    Hallidayan model of language, adapted from Munday (2016, 90) .......................................... 24

Fig. 2.2    Fairclough's three-dimensional conception of discourse (1992, 73) ........................................... 25

Fig. 2.3    The English person categories (Halliday and Matthiessen 2014, 384) .......................................... 29

Fig. 2.4    System network of the distinctive feature of letterforms (van Leeuwen 2006, 151) ................................. 37

Fig. 2.5    Relationship between texts and contexts (based on Eggins (1994/2004)'s model) ................................. 42

Fig. 3.1    AntConc 3.5.7 (Anthony 2018) ........................... 56

Fig. 3.2    Nvivo 12 plus ........................................ 56

Fig. 3.3    Overall research framework of the study .................... 58

Fig. 4.1    Keyness of 民生 (LT: people's lives) in the investigated period ..................................... 64

Fig. 4.2    *Keyness* of 博彩 (LT: gambling) in the investigated period ..... 65

Fig. 4.3    *Keyness* of 非博彩 (non-gambling) in the investigated period ... 65

Fig. 4.4    *Keyness* of 多元 (LT: diversification) in the investigated period ..................................... 66

Fig. 4.5    Different naming of the speaker ........................... 68

Fig. 4.6    Example of visual presentation of policy addresses in CHPAC ........................................... 110

Fig. 4.7    Visual presentation of PA2000c and PA2008c .............. 111

Fig. 4.8    Example of visual presentation of policy addresses in CCPAC ........................................... 112

Fig. 4.9    PA2005 in Chinese and English .......................... 120

Fig. 4.10    PA2019 in Chinese and English .......................... 120

Fig. 4.11    The top/top-left headings of general policy objectives ......... 121

Fig. 4.12    The use of colors on pages of the infographics of the policy addresses ........................................... 124

Fig. 4.13   Biological and cultural categorisation of social actors
            represented in PA2015p .................................   129
Fig. 4.14   Simple figures in PA2016p ..............................   130
Fig. 4.15   Cartoon figures in PA2016p .............................   130
Fig. 4.16   Special narrative representation in PA2016p .................   131
Fig. 4.17   Narrative representation in PA2017p ......................   131
Fig. 4.18   Narrative representaion in PA2018p ......................   133
Fig. 4.19   Narrative representaion in PA2019p ......................   134
Fig. 4.20   Images related to gaming industry in infographics
            of the Policy Addresses .................................   135

# List of Tables

Table 2.1   Transtivity for realizing ideational meaning . . . . . . . . . . . . . . .   25
Table 2.2   Representation in visual grammar (based on Kress
            and van Leeuwan 1996a, b/2006/2021) . . . . . . . . . . . . . . . . . .   33
Table 2.3   Color dimensions and meaning potentials . . . . . . . . . . . . . . . .   35
Table 2.4   Presentation of basic principles of *salience* . . . . . . . . . . . . . . .   38
Table 2.5   Kinds of composition for creating *information value* . . . . . . . .   38
Table 2.6   Framing and connectivity devices . . . . . . . . . . . . . . . . . . . . . . . .   39
Table 3.1   Data of the study . . . . . . . . . . . . . . . . . . . . . . . . . . . . . . . . . . . . .   54
Table 4.1   Top ten *Keywords* of CCPAC and CHPAC . . . . . . . . . . . . . . . .   62
Table 4.2   Key words identified in CHPAC and CCPAC . . . . . . . . . . . . . . .   63
Table 4.3   Frequency of apparent keywords denoting participants
            in CHPAC and CCPAC . . . . . . . . . . . . . . . . . . . . . . . . . . . . . . . . .   67
Table 4.4   Collocates of 博彩 (LT: gambling) in CHPAC and CCPAC . . .   70
Table 4.5   Collocates of 民生 (LT: people's lives) in CHPAC
            and CCPAC . . . . . . . . . . . . . . . . . . . . . . . . . . . . . . . . . . . . . . . . . .   72
Table 4.6   Collocates of 多元 (LT: diversification) in CHPAC
            and CCPAC . . . . . . . . . . . . . . . . . . . . . . . . . . . . . . . . . . . . . . . . . .   74
Table 4.7   Significant nouns co-occurring with the common key verbs . . .   76
Table 4.8   Categories of the significant nouns co-occurring
            with the common key verbs (improving/refining) . . . . . . . . . . .   76
Table 4.9   Significant goals being improved/refined in CHPAC
            and CCPAC . . . . . . . . . . . . . . . . . . . . . . . . . . . . . . . . . . . . . . . . . .   77
Table 4.10  Significant lexical collocates of 確保 (ensure) in CHPAC . . . . .   81
Table 4.11  Significant lexical *Collocates* of distinctive key verbs
            in CCPAC . . . . . . . . . . . . . . . . . . . . . . . . . . . . . . . . . . . . . . . . . . .   83
Table 4.12  Apparent Collocates of 我們 (*we*) in CHPAC and CCPAC . . . .   85
Table 4.13  Translations of key word 博彩 (LT: gambling) . . . . . . . . . . . . .   89
Table 4.14  *Collocates* of *gambling*, *gaming* and *casino* . . . . . . . . . . . . . . .   91
Table 4.15  Translations of key word 多元 (LT: diversification) . . . . . . . . . .   93
Table 4.16  Word choices in translating 民生 (LT: people's lives) . . . . . . . .   96

Table 4.17   Top three word choices in translating key verbs
             with referent to improving/refining .....................   99
Table 4.18   Normalised frequency of the word choices in translating
             key verbs denoting improving/refining ...................   99
Table 4.19   Top lexical Collocates of *improve, enhance, raise*
             and *promote* .........................................   100
Table 4.20   Frequency of 我們 *(we, us, our, ours)* in ST and TT ........   101
Table 4.21   Frequency% of We in CHPAE, CCPAE and CSOTU .........   104
Table 4.22   Collocates of *we* in CHPAE and CCPAE .................   105
Table 4.23   Salient Lexical Collocates of We ........................   105
Table 4.24   Significant *Collocates* of We representing epistemic
             warranty ..............................................   107
Table 4.25   Significant *Collocates* of We representing boulomaic
             commitment ...........................................   108
Table 4.26   Elements provide visual weight to items included in texts ....   113
Table 4.27   Sub-headings of the general policies objectives in theme
             position on content pages .............................   119
Table 4.28   Colors used as visual rhyme in infographics ..............   123
Table 4.29   Social actors in infographics ..........................   126

# Chapter 1
# Introduction

Macao is a city with unique political, historical, and cultural background. It is recently well-known to the World with its gaming industry's flourishing and revenue surpassing Las Vegas as the top in the market in the past decades. It is a former Portuguese Colony, a special administrative region at the periphery of the People's Republic of China, and an international tourism city with foreign investment and a sizable imported workforce.

In 1999, the sovereignty over the city returned to China, and a new government, Macao Special Administrative Region Government, was formed to implement "one country, two systems" in the city's governance. Annually, the Chief Executive of the Macao Special Administrative Region (Macao SAR) Government presents the government report named "Policy Address" on behalf of the whole administrative office to announce to the public the policies and the work plan that are set for the coming year.

The Policy Addresses serve as the most significant government reports of the Macao SAR Government, reflecting the social reality and the social change of the city. The printed version of this critical category of government reports is the documents with different linguistic resources and non-verbal resources.

This study sets out to investigate the discursive construction of the Policy Addresses released by the Macao Special Administrative Region Government in the first two decades of the post-handover period (2000–2019) to explore how the Policy Addresses and their translations reflect and construct the social ideologies and social change of the city. This chapter introduces the study with the general scientific and specific research backgrounds, research aims, objectives, and the research questions to be answered in the examination, as well as the book's structure to provide an overview of the study for the readers.

© The Author(s), under exclusive license to Springer Nature Singapore Pte Ltd. 2023    1
M. Lam Sut I, *A Corpus-assisted Multimodal Analysis to Policy Addresses of Macao SAR Government*, Corpora and Intercultural Studies 11,
https://doi.org/10.1007/978-981-99-1195-0_1

## 1.1   General Scientific Background

Language is presented as a collection of words and characters that we choose when we write or speak. When selecting certain words, we convey our perspectives on and experience of what happens. For example, we can find differences in the following sentences: (1) A teacher is talking to the students in class. (2) Students are concentrating in class.

These two sentences contrast in the actions as well as the participants. Regarding the actions, two different sorts of actions are represented by the present participles as "talking" in Sentence (1) but "concentrating" in Sentence (2). With "talking", Sentence (1) represents the physical action of "A teacher" as giving a speech. With "concentrating", Sentence (2) represents the mental action of "Students" as directing their attention and efforts toward a particular activity. For the participants, while mentioning "A teacher" and "the students in class" to involve both the agent of the action ("A teacher") and the one affected by the action ("the students in class") in Sentence (1), there is only the agent of the action ("Students") involved in Sentence (2).

These two sentences could be two versions of linguistic presentation that guide different interpretations of the same reality. These are examples of situation in that we use language to construct meaning with our perspective and experience.

When we use language, we also choose words that make us feel we are a part of a particular community. For instance, a person from another region who speaks in a group can make himself a stranger or a foreigner. Thus, language is not neutral and often contains values, attitudes, and assessments toward something. This is the situation in that we use language to create social relationship. In addition, when we use language, we will join sentences and ideas together with our composition to provide proper information flow in the use of language. With all these features, the use of language is a form of communicative event, which is the social approach to language.

According to Halliday's (1994, 1985; Halliday and Matthiessen 2004, 2014) Systemic Functional Linguistics (SFL), there are three meta-functions of language: ideational function, interpersonal function and textual function. When we use language, we are describing to represent the World, building relationships with people we are communicating with, and joining ideas together to make cohesive or coherent texts. More than representing, interacting, and composing as mentioned before, how a subject is talked about can change our view of the subject. This is to show that language helps create changes in realities and can be used to change behaviors as well, which makes language a powerful tool. Hence, language is the discourse conveying values and opinions to characterise our attitude rather than a collection of words and characters only.

Furthermore, the norms and conventions of the particular language context directly or indirectly shape our use of discourse somehow (Fairclough 1992, 64). The investigation of discourse with all these particular foci is understood as the social approach to discourse analysis, which involves the consideration of the relationship between the language and the context with its particular social and cultural setting (Paltridge 2012). These lead to the discussion of how discourse is produced to contribute to the construction of particular views of the World and people, which makes discourse a practice with ideological effects.

In Translation Studies, with the view of positioning translations not purely the passive transfer between languages, with the perspective on the social approach to discourse analysis, the socio-cultural context of translations is an interesting concern to further investigate the role of translation in reflecting and constructing or supporting social ideologies. Building on Halliday's Systemic Functional Grammar, discourse analysis attained popularity in Translation Studies since 1990s. In one of Munday's (2001/2016/2022) influential works, which serves as a significant text-book for the students in Translation Studies all over the World, discourse analysis is conjointly illustrated as one of the major research areas in this discipline. Discourse analysis turns the prominence of Translation Studies from the traditional debate of literal translations or free translations, from the nature of "equivalence" and from the consideration of the cultural environment of translations, to the socio-cultural context of translations as the primary concern.

There are some leading works on Translation Studies that have employed Halliday's Systemic Functional Linguistics model, includes House's (1997), Baker's (1992/2011/2018), and Hatim and Mason's (1990, 1997). Hatim and Mason go beyond register analysis to consider translation's pragmatic and semiotic dimensions and the sociolinguistic and semiotic implications of discourses and discourse communities (1990, 1997).

Under the social approach to discourse analysis integrated with the investigation of the role of translation, corpus-assisted approach allows us to go beyond the examination of a small number of texts to investigate a large number of texts and compare them with other selections of texts which are produced under similar or different circumstances. With the capability of probing into a large selection of data, the corpus-assisted approach provides us with opportunities to conduct the analysis with some degree of objectivity.

Since the mid-1990s, researchers have attempted to integrate the methodology suggested by the corpus-assisted approach to discourse analysis, such as Hardt-Mautner (1995, 2000), Koller and Mautner (2004), O'Halloran and Coffin (2004), Baker (2004, 2006, 2009), and Orpin (2005). Corpus analysis refers to the methodology of identifying linguistic patterns of variation automatically generated by using interactive computer programs in a collection of texts of the target language variety. It has been a fruitful research method in Translation Studies as well. See Baker (1993, 2000), Tymoczko (1998), and Laviosa (1996, 2002).

Coming from Latin, "corpus" means "body". A corpus-assisted investigation of language could be understood as studying the body of the language, which refers to "the quantity and representativeness of data being of paramount importance in data collection" (Tuominen et al. 2018, 8). However, focusing only on verbal resources may result in discounting codes from other semiotic resources in the meaning-making process (Baños et al. 2013, 488). In this case, acknowledging the need for the analysis to consider both linguistic elements and other non-verbal aids, the study of "the use of several semiotic modes in the design of a semiotic product or event" which is termed as "Multimodality" (Kress and van Leeuwen 2001, 20) was hence developed.

After years of development, challenges remain in integrating multimodality into corpus investigations. A few researchers attempt to solve this problem by building up multimodal corpora and resources, such as Baldry and O'Halloran's (2010) MCA Web Browser, Adolphs and Carter's (2013) Nottingham Multi-Modal Corpus, and Jimenez Hurtado and Soler Gallego's (2013) multimodal annotation software *Taggetti*.

Nevertheless, these multimodal resources are often unachievable due to their complex design and construction, which requires the constant support from specialist technical expertise (Baños et al. 2013). Since multimodal corpora are not yet widespread, other alternatives exist for integrating multimodal analysis into corpus-linguistic research. For example, Salway and Graham (2003) and Salway (2007) use the information presented in scripts, transcripts, or audio descriptions for insights into the representation of gaze directions, locations, actions, etc. Multimodality is considered as a sort of resource and meanwhile a challenge for scholars in Translation Studies (O'Sullivan 2013).

The notion of incorporating multimodal analysis into Translation Studies is embraced by some scholars, such as Pérez-González (2007), Borodo (2015), and Ketola (2018) in their research. However, the interplay between the verbal and non-verbal resources in translation still seems to be an area awaiting exploration (Yu and Song 2016). Other scholars hesitate for the reasons that "multimodality oriented corpus-based translation research still has some open questions related to the alignment of modes, the segmentation of units of analysis and the need for a tagging system that takes account of the different modes" (Tuominen et al. 2018).

Recognizing the high threshold of the multimodal corpora and regarding the existing alternative approaches to multimodal translated discourse studies, the present study attempts to present a workable framework that has the potential to make up for the deficiencies as mentioned above under the limitation of accessing multimodal corpora.

First, to ensure the alignment of modes, draw on the same theoretical basis across different modes, i.e., Systematic Functional Grammar (SFG) (Halliday 1994) with the specific steps including an initial corpus-assisted analysis with the verbal resources to offer insights for a subsequent multimodal analysis toward the visual resources, and to uncover how the information of verbal mode is translated into different modes for creating meanings and to explore the interplay between modes.

Secondly, to systemize the tagging system for different modes, Systemic Functional Grammar serves as the same theoretical basis for the analytical framework for anlyzing the resources of different modes. While lexicogrammar developed by Halliday is to analyze linguistic configurations systematically, visual grammar evolved from it by Kress and Van Leeuwen (1996/2006) can be applied to the analysis of the visual modes.

This study positions itself as falling into the research field of discourse analysis in Translation Studies with a corpus-assisted multimodal approach. With this general scientific background, the present study implemented discourse analytical methodology with a corpus-assisted approach and multimodal approach to Translation Studies, allowing the discussion with sociocultural context of the multimodal discourse with large verbal data in examination.

## 1.2  Specific Background

After a brief introduction of the general scientific background, this section introduces the specific research background of this study. It situates at the specific background of the city, Macao, in the time of the two decades after Portugal returned the exercise of sovereignty over the city to the People's Republic of China. The following includes the social and cultural context of Macao and Macao's stories in academic research and Macao's stories in Policy Addresses.

### *1.2.1  Socio-Economic Context of Macao*

As mentioned above, Macao Special Administration Region is a city well-known to the World for the blooming development of its gaming industry. Before the handover in 1999, Macao, this city had been a place with the gambling sector legalized as the attractions for people from other regions to come over. In 1842, the British started to exercise their sovereignty over Hong Kong and developed it as an essential trading port between the Western and China. Macao's role at the time was replaced by Hong Kong. To sustain the tax income, Macao's Portuguese Government legalized gambling activities in the city in 1847, and the gambling activities at the time were the stalls named "Fan-tan".

"Fantan" is the general name of one category of traditional Chinese games of chance. This particular type of gambling activity was considered as a synonym of all kinds of Chinese gambling-related table games in the nineteenth century. In the mid-nineteenth century, there were more than two hundred stalls of "Fan-tan" operating in the city. This traditional type of gambling activity serves as the beginning of the long gaming history of Macao. "Fan-tan" is the oldest game of chance in operation today. Toward the late nineteenth century, this city earned the appellation "Monte Carlo of the Orient" due to its development of the industry with gambling activities, which became a significant source of tax income for the Government.

Throughout the early development, this particular industry of the city has experienced the period with a monopoly system dominated by the local operators Hou Heng Company, Tai Heng Company, and the operator formed by Hong Kong and Macao business people, Sociedade de Turismo e Diversões de Macao (S.T.D.M), respectively.

After the handover of sovereignty over Macao to China in 1999, to end the monopoly system of the gambling sector in the city for further development, the

SAR Government opened this market to foreign investment and granted three casino operating concessions in 2002 to start the dynamic change to the growth of this traditional sector of the city. The three operating concessions later allowed three more sub-concessions. With the gaming liberalization, the industry was injected with new dynamics for the Government to reinforce the policy direction as "with the gaming sector as its 'head', and the service industry as its 'body' [to drive] the overall development of other industries" (Macao SAR Policy Address 2002).

The liberalization did bring prosperity to the development of the related economic activities. The gross gaming revenue was 28,673 million MOP in 1996, and it rocketed to 360,748 million MOP in 2013. The gaming tax revenue, which as a percentage of the government revenue rises year by year, increased from 37% in 2000 to over 64% in 2004 and up to 80% in 2014.[1] The gaming industry in Macao acts as the industry that dominates the economy of the city.

The domination of the gaming industry in the economy of Macao has brought an unprecedented economic boom to the city, yet, it meanwhile creates instability to the economy of the city due to the nature of this special industry. The growth of the gaming industry depends on the prosperity of the economy of other regions. It is susceptible to changes of the economic climate and financial policies of other regions, especially the ones in Asia. It is also radically affected by the attitude of the Chinese Central Government. The independence of the nature of this industry is evident in the considerable fall to the gaming revenue after 2014 due to the China's aggressive anti-corruption policy announced (Sheng and Gu 2018) and after 2019 due to the Covid-19, which brought crisis to the economy of the city.

## 1.2.2   Political and Socio-Cultural Context of Macao

Aside from being the most prominent gaming hub in the World with the notable development of the gaming industry, Macao is a city with unique historical and cultural background. Portuguese arrived in Macao in the sixteenth century, and their extended stay in this city with different political statuses over time created the long-established interaction of cultures, which created the peaceful coexistence of Chinese and Western cultures in this special region. This historical background has created a multicultural context for the city with the unique culture blended with Eastern and Western ones. This coexistence and interaction of cultures are "based on mutual respect and tolerance, harmony instead of conflict, and stability in plurality" (Kaeding 2014, 185).

Macao's unique cultural identity is prominently formed by three cultures: the Chinese culture, the Portuguese culture and the culture of the Macanese. The developments of language and civic education, as well as the presence of Luso legacy in daily life, indicate that the colonial regime concentrated more on the cultural aspects

---

[1] *DESC statistics database*. DSEC. (n.d.). Retrieved July 22, 2022, from http://www.dsec.gov.mo/TimeSeriesDatabase.aspx?KeyIndicatorID=15.

of identity, which has now contributed to the construction of the unique cultural identity of Macao.

In terms of the language use of the city, Macao is a language museum (Wong 1998). As a former Portuguese colony, a special administrative region at the periphery of the People's Republic of China, and, more recently, an internationalized tourism city with foreign investments and a large, imported workforce, these varieties of roles create the multilingual context of the city, with a predominantly Cantonese speaking Chinese community, a Portuguese speaking community (with an even smaller community with Creole, named Macanese Patois or Patuá, created by the colonized history), and an imported community with English as the medium in communication. This social background provides Cantonese an absolute advantage, English the practical value, Mandarin the potential space, and Portuguese a historical origin (Su 2014).

Portuguese has been the official language of Macao since the start of the colonial period while Chinese was first offered the official position in 1991 which is in the transitional period between the date of the entry into force of the Joint Declaration on Question of Macao. In addition to the two official languages, English has been with its surprisingly high application before 1999 and is widely used in the fields of the city, such as politics, economy, education, media, etc., which enjoys a "de facto status" within government agencies in the city (Moody 2008, 4). The mentioned varieties of roles provide the city the language community with the rich application of languages, which offers translation an influential role in the development of the city, markedly between Portuguese and Chinese. With the research limitation, in terms of interlingual translations, this study focuses on Chinese and English.

Macao, which is a city with remarkable political and unique cultural background, started experiencing an era of dramatic development in the first two decades of the post-colonial period. In addition to the instability of the economy, as mentioned before, the rapid development of the city due to the booming of the gaming industry has posed challenges to the tourist carrying capacity, human resources, social order affected by gambling addiction, etc. which lead to public concerns over the locals' wellbeing (Sheng and Gu 2018).

The Chinese Central Government has mentioned that the development of Macao is with different work plans related to these social needs created by the social development and city's resources due to its special political and cultural background. Related to the economy of the city, in the 11th Five-Year Plan for National Economic and Social Development of the People's Republic of China released in 2006, the Chinese Central Government first mentioned that the development of the economy of Macao should be diversified. The Outline of the Plan for the Reform and Development of the Pearl River Delta released in 2008 by the National Development and Reform Commission further positioned Macao as the city to be developed as a World Centre of Tourism and Leisure, which was also mentioned in the 12th Five-Year Plan released by the Chinese Central Government in 2011. In 2016, the 13th Five-Year Plan of the country further assured this positioning as the strategic objective of the development of Macao.

In the similar vein, Macao SAR Government set up a committee to advance the work of transforming Macao to a World Centre for Tourism and Leisure since 2015, which is chaired by the Chief Executive of Macao. The committee is responsible for drafting a blueprint plan for tourism development and to set up a mechanism for annual revision of the plan. The studies and formulation work of the mentioned plan, which was afterwards named as Macao Tourism Industry Development Master Plan (hereafter referred to as the "Master Plan"), started in the same year, the final version of which was released to the public by Macao Government Tourism Office (MGTO) in September 2017 to unveil the blueprint for the development of Macao tourism industry in next 15 years and a relevant guideline for future actions.

Later in 2017, the Tourism Federation of Cities in Guangdong, Hong Kong and Macao Bay Area was established. Macao, as one of the members of the scheme, works together with other members to push forward tourism cooperation and interchanges between the three destinations and to build up their joint branding as one international tourism destination and forging a new tourism benchmark as a World-class bay area, creating a strong momentum for the tourism development of the entire area of Guangdong, Hong Kong and Macao as well as the national tourism development.

All these policies show that the city, Macao, has developed as a prominent tourist city in Chinese-speaking regions and has even played a significant role in national tourism development. As described by Macao Trade and Investment Promotion Institute (IPIM), "Macao is currently positioning itself as the World Centre of Tourism and Leisure as it develops into a quality international tourist destination".[2] Macao has gone through history from a city with the legalized traditional Chinese gambling activities, "Fantan", to an international gaming market that is well-known to the World with noticeable gaming revenue and to a city that is positioned as the World Centre of Tourism and Leisure. The image of Macao has been changing in the first two decades of the post-handover period. With the strategic objectives of the city development guided by the national and regional policies, the Government has spared no effort to build Macao as "a quality international tourist destination" with its diversified historical and cultural resources, which leads to a series of changes in Macao's social ideologies.

### 1.2.3  Macao's Stories in Academic Research

Macao has been a subject arousing scholar's research interests due to its special political and cultural identities. In the history of the development of Macao's Studies, it has moved forward from the research on history to the interdisciplinary studies regarding the research subject, Macao (Lam 2018). Studies of Macao start with the studies on its history with the first influential work in Chinese published in 1751 and the first influential one in a foreign language published in 1832 (Jin and Ng 2002, 1). This is also the research area with relatively more significant results in Macao's

---

[2] *Tourism: About Macao.* Macao Trade and Investment Promotion Institute. Retrieved December 15, 2022, from http://www.ipim.gov.mo/en/macao-exhibition-and-conference/information-on-exhibition-and-conference/tourism/.

studies (Ng 2019, 8). The influential works include *Aomen Shi Xin Bian* (澳門史新編, A new history of Macau) (Wu et al. 2008) and the *Chronicle of Macao* (澳門編年史) (Ng et al. 2009), which are the monumental co-authored by renowned experts in the related field to vividly depict the unique and eventful history of Macao over the past in nearly 500 years.

The start of Macao's studies with particular attention paid to history, is followed by scholars' research interests in the economy of the city in the 1980s, with research centres established particularly for this field of studies (Lam 2018, 8). Since late 1980s, 'Macaology' was formally suggested by the founding members Mr. Chan Su Weng and Mr. Wong Han Keung (Chan 1995; Wong 1989, 2001). Mr. Wong worked actively with some other well-known scholars for the foundation of Institute of Social Sciences of Macau to promote the studies of the filed. The Institute of Macau Studies established the academic journal *Macao Studies* in 1988, which is the first interdisciplinary academic journal with Macao as the core research subject (Lam 2018, 9). Over time, there are more and more local academic journals established for Macao Studies, such as *Review of Culture* published by Cultural Affairs Bureau Macao (ICM), *Administração* published by Public Administration and Civil Service Bureau Macao (SAFP), *Journal of One Country Two Systems Studies* published by Macao Polytechnic Institute and *Macau Journal of Linguistics* published by Linguistic Society of Macau.

In the past thirty years, there have been published papers regarding Macao as the research subject falling on the research areas in the industry, the economy, and management, law, social development, literature, and linguistics, etc., with the majority of the research fields falling in the economy of Macao in CSSCI index and hospitality leisure sport tourism in international core journals (Lam 2018). Lam's (2018) paper, honouring the thirty-year development of the first local academic journal on Macao Studies, presented a detailed description of the path of the studies of Macao in the past thirty years, which is a route from the studies of history to the interdisciplinary studies.

## *1.2.4  Macao's Stories in Policy Addresses*

Government work reports are essential documents for conveying the government's voice and publicizing the tasks it sets for the region. "Policy Address" is the name used by the Macao Special Administrative Region Government for this category of important government work reports, which summarizes the Government's work in the past year and publicizes its work plan set for the coming year. The Policy Addresses carry essential information about social and economic developments of the region at the same time.

As a particular type of institutional discourse, the Policy Addresses are with ideological effects on the city. As mentioned, the social approach of discourse analysis involves the consideration of the relationship between language and social context and cultural setting. Discourse is socially constitutive and socially shaped (Fairclough and Wodak 1997, 258). The policy addresses, as the important documents produced by the institution which governs the city, are the discourse type which demonstrate the corelation among discourse, power and institutions.

"Institutions' power and politics are frequently exercised through discourse of their members" (Mayr 2008, 1). A Policy Address is a particular type of government document with its unique characteristics of text production and consumption. Macao' Policy Addresses are a type of governmental documents which are produced by a group of authors, and it addresses all relevant social agents. They are written by the consultants of the Office of the Chief Executive of the Macao Special Administrative Region of the People's Republic of China (Gabinete do Chefe do Executivo) with the Chief Executive, who presents the Policy Addresses to the public as a leading figure of the Special Administrative Region Government on behalf of the whole team of administrations. The Chief Executive's presentation of the Policy Addresses is to clarify the vision of the governance and explain in detail the Government's vision and measures in various policy areas. After the presentation, the relevant addressees would have to take action to get the Policy Addresses into practice.

Throughout the first two decades of Macao SAR Government, four offices have been led by two Chief Executives respectively. Mr. Edmund Ho Hau Wah took the first office of the new Government and was sworn in as the first Chief Executive of Macao SAR Government on 20 December 1999. He presented the first Policy Address of Macao SAR Government, Policy Address of 2000, on 29 March 2000 with the leading role of the whole administration of the new Government at the time. Mr. Ho took the offices in the first and the second term of Macao SAR Government, from 1999 to 2008, and presented Macao Policy Address 2000 to Macao Policy Address 2009. Mr. Ho's Policy Addresses started with the strategic objective as "creating the foundations for achieving firm development by consolidating the existing basis" (Policy Address 2000) to the organizational priorities as the coordination of the development of the economy with that of the society, the sustainable development of both the economy and the society, as well as the progressive enhancement of the holistic quality of life of Macao's residents (Policy Address 2005), and end with the administrative outlines as (1) "modifying economic strategies and enhancing adequate economic diversification", (2) "dedicated to safeguarding people's wellbeing and building a good society", (3) "deepening human development and raising standards", (4) "committed to fulfilling Government duties and multiplying the effects of reform" (Policy Address 2009).

On 20 December 2009, Dr. Fernando Chui Sai On was sworn in as the Chief Executive of the third term of Macao SAR Government and started his ten-year governance of the city. He presented his first Policy Address with the governance vision of "Coordinate development in harmony" (Policy Address 2010) on 16 March 2010. Dr. Chui later continued his leading role in the administration in the fourth term of Macao SAR Government. He started his second term of governance of the city with the governance vision as "boosting the economy, focusing on livelihoods, and ensuring stable development" (Policy Address 2016). Dr. Chui presented the Policy Addresses of Macao from 2010 to 2018, which include Policy Address 2010 to Policy Address 2019. He ended his terms of governance of the city with the policy vision of "seize opportunities for balanced development" (Policy Address 2019) in the last Policy Address he presented.

There is existing literature from the perspective of discourse analysis that investigates how this particular text type functions in the social practice of specific regions, such as Zhu's (2011) and Qian and Tian's (2014) analysis of the government work reports of China, Agnieszka's (2013) analysis of the addresses of the US (Agnieszka 2013), and Wang and Li's (2013) analysis of Policy Addresses of Hong Kong. After the first two decades of a new government, this study probes into the Policy Addresses of Macao SAR Government with the entry points of the ideological effects of discourse from the perspective of Critical Discourse Analysis, the meaning-making process involving verbal and visual modes from the perspective of multimodality, and the objectivities of dealing with large set of data in the study with corpus-assisted approach.

## 1.3  Research Aims, Objectives and Questions

With the role of a type of crucial governmental document, Policy Addresses reflect the policy foci of the governments in a historical period of time. Meanwhile, with the role of institutional discourse, they are with features of this discourse type as their participation in social practice (Qian and Tian 2011, 40). These features demonstrate how an institution is shaped by discourse and how it, in turn, have the capacity to create and impose discourses, which provide it considerable control over the shaping of our experience of the World and the way we classify the World (Mayr 2008, 1). Thus, analyzing the Policy Addresses as a discourse type of institutional discourse in a period of time enables the researchers to figure out the policy foci of the administrations of different periods of time, the path of change in the social realities in the investigated period as well as how the Policy Addresses as a discourse type function in the social changes.

Given the specific features of the particular discourse type of policy addresses, this study investigates the Policy addresses in two decades from the beginning of Macao's post-handover period, with corpus-assisted multimodal approach from the perspective of Critical Discourse Analysis. It is to explain the relationship between the discursive construction of Policy Addresses in the role a particular discourse type and the socio-cultural context of Macao Special Administrative Region. The corpus-assisted analytical approach enables the study to investigate the discourse prosodies with the analysis of key words and their collocations of a large set of data. In contrast, the multimodal approach allows the study to probe into the visual configurations to avoid discounting codes of other semiotic resources in meaning-making process when focusing on only one mode of resources. With the corpus-assisted multimodal approach, the study aims at identifying changes in the government plans and achievements in the investigated period and exploring how the policy addresses as a discourse type function in the social changes of Macao SAR through discussing the social factors to the production and consumption of Policy Addresses.

To be more specific, the study aims to attain the following objectives: (1) To depict the specific verbal and visual configurations in the discourse which functions in representing the changes in government plans and achievement; (2) To describe the shifts in the interlingual translation from the Policy Addresses in Chinese texts to their English translations, as well as the shifts in the inter-semiotic translation process from the verbal version of the Policy Addresses to the infographics of the Policy addresses. (3) To interpret how verbal and visual realizations construct social ideologies. (4) To discuss the social and cultural factors influencing discursive construction and the interplay between the discourse and the socio-cultural context.

With the research aims and objectives mentioned above, this study attempts to answer the following key questions: (1) What are the verbal and visual configurations in the selected data contributing to the representation of the changes in the Government's plans and achievements in the investigated period? (2) In what way do the linguistic and semiotic realizations of the selected data reflect the social realities and social structure of Macao? (3) What are the relationship between the discursive construction of Policy Addresses as a particular discourse type and the socio-cultural context of Macao?

The research questions are to be answered in the detailed analysis with the theoretical foundation developed in the following chapters to fulfill the mentioned objectives. It is hoped that this study will carry the significance as the following: (1) With the integrated analytical framework developed, the study proposes an applicable framework for investigating multimodal discourse with large data set of verbal resources. (2) With the analytical framework proposed, it offers possible tools to analyze semiotic configuration (with both verbal and non-verbal resources) to avoid discounting codes of other modes in meaning-making process. (3) By positioning itself as the study falling into the research field of discourse analysis in translation studies with corpus-assisted multimodal approach, the examination and the interpretation of the shits in both interlingual and inter-semiotic translation processes amplify the role of translation in discursive construction, which is to arouse interests from scholars to contribute to the field that is relatively less discussed in Translation Studies. (4) With the city arouses research interests from scholars due to its unique political and cultural identities, it is hoped that this study serves to complement the research field of Macao Studies integrated with the entry points of *Translation Studies*, *Multimodal Analysis*, as well as the *Discourse Analysis* toward the Policy Addresses of Macao to study the social ideologies of city in the post-handover period.

## 1.4   Organization of the Book

This book is with six chapters. This chapter provides a comprehensive introduction to the study by presenting the general scientific and specific research background, describing the research aims, objectives, and significance, and listing the research questions to offer the general setting of the study.

Chapter 2 presents an overview of the theoretical framework for the study revision of the related theoretical concepts. It first reviews Fairclough's three-dimensional *Critical Discourse Analysis,* followed by elaborating the theories related to the analysis of verbal and non-verbal resources in the theoretical foundation of Halliday's Systemic Functional Linguistics. The revision ends with the elaboration of relevant translation theories. The chapter offers the following analysis the theoretical basis with the systemic variables for detailed examination, as well as the theoretical foundation for discussion of the results of the analysis.

Chapter 3 presents the descriptions of the data for examination and the tools implemented to conduct the investigation, followed by the elaboration of the analytical framework built for the study.

Chapter 4 moves forward to the case analysis. It presents a detailed analysis with the theoretical basis depicted and the analytical framework built on the data introduced in the previous chapters. There is the examination of the large data set of verbal resources with corpus-assisted approach, the multimodal analyzes of the visual resources, and the investigation of the translation process, including interlingual translations and inter-semiotic translations. At the end of the chapter, the findings of the analysis are summarized for discussion in the next chapter.

Chapter 5 is a discussion of the analysis conducted. It interprets and explains the results of the analysis within the discursive and socio-cultural context to reveal the social changes in the city in the first two decades of Macao SAR Government.

Chapter 6 presents the conclusion of the study by summarizing the findings of the study, stating the implications of the study, as well as suggesting the possibilities for relevant future works.

# References

Adolphs, S., and R. Carter. 2013. *Spoken corpus linguistics. From monomodal to multimodal.* London and New York: Routledge.

Agnieszka, S. 2013. A critical discourse approach to the analysis of values in political discourse: The example of freedom in President Bush's State of the Union addresses (2001–2008). *Discourse & Society* 24 (6): 792–809.

Baker, Mona. 1992/2011/2018. *In other words*, 3rd ed. London and New York: Routledge.

Baker, Mona. 1993. Corpus linguistics and translation studies: Implications and application. In *Text and technology: In honour of John Sinclair*, ed. Mona Baker, Gill Francis, and Elena Tognini-Bonelli, 233–250. Amsterdam/Philadelphia: John Benjamins.

Baker, Mona. 2000. Towards a methodology for investigating the style of a literary translator. *Target* 12 (2): 241–266.

Baker, Paul. 2004. "Unnatural acts": Discourses of homosexuality within the House of Lords debates on gay male law reform. *Journal of Sociolinguistics* 8 (1): 88–106.

Baker, Paul. 2006. *Using corpora in discourse analysis.* London: Continuum.

Baker, Paul. 2009. The BE06 corpus of British English and recent language change. *International Journal of Corpus Linguistics* 14 (3): 312–337.

Baldry, Anthony, and Kay O'Halloran. 2010. Research into the annotation of a multimodal corpus of university websites: An illustration of multimodal corpus linguistics. In *Corpus linguistics in language teaching*, ed. T. Harris, 177–210. Bern: Peter Lang.

Baños, R., S. Bruti, and S. Zanotti. 2013. Corpus linguistics and audiovisual translation: In search
    of an integrated approach. *Perspectives: Studies in Translatology* 21 (4): 483–490.
Borodo, Michał. 2015. Multimodality, translation and comics. *Perspectives* 23 (1): 22–41. https://
    doi.org/10.1080/0907676X.2013.876057.
Chan, Shu Weng. 1995. Develop Macaology, promote Macao studies. *Macao Daily*, 1995, "學海".
Fairclough, Norman. 1992. *Discourse and social change.* Cambridge, England: Polity.
Fairclough, Norman, and Ruth Wodak. 1997. Critical discourse analysis. In *Discourse as social
    interaction*, ed. Teun A. van Dijk, Discourse studies: A multidisciplinary introduction, 258–284.
    London: Sage.
Halliday, Michael. 1985. *An introduction to functional grammar*, 1st ed. London: Edward Arnold.
Halliday, Michael. 1994. *An introduction to functional grammar*, 2nd ed. London: Edward Arnold.
Halliday, Michael, and Christian Matthiessen. 2004. *An introduction to functional grammar*, 3rd
    ed. Great Britain: Hodder Arnold.
Halliday, Michael, and Christian Matthiessen. 2014. *Hallidays introduction to functional grammar*,
    4th ed. London and New York: Routledge.
Hardt-Mautner, G. 1995. How does one become a good European: The British press and European
    integration. *Discourse and Society* 6 (2): 177–205.
Hardt-Mautner, G. 2000. *Der britische Europa-Diskurs: Methodenreflexion und Fallstudien zur
    Berichterstattung in der Tagespresse.* Wien: Passagen-Verlag.
Hatim, Basil, and Ian Mason. 1990. *Discourse and the translator.* London and New York: Longman.
Hatim, Basil, and Ian Mason. 1997. *The translator as communicator.* London and New York:
    Routledge.
House, Juliane. 1997. *Translation quality assessment: A model revisited.* Tübingen: Gunter Narr.
Jimenez Hurtado, C., and S. Soler Gallego. 2013. Multimodality, translation and accessibility: A
    corpus-based study of audio description. *Perspectives: Studies in Translatology* 21 (3): 577–594.
Jin, Guoping, and C. L. Ng. 2002. *Research on the history of Macao.* Macao: Association for Adult
    Education.
Kaeding, Malte Philipp. 2014. Post-colonial Macao's changing identity. In *China's Macao trans-
    formed: Challenge and development in the 21st century*, ed. Eilo W. Y. Yu and Ming K. Chan.
    Hong Kong: City University of Hong Kong Press.
Ketola, Anne. 2018. *Word-image interaction in technical translation: Students translating an
    illustrated text. Acta Universitatis Tamperensis 2364.* Tampere: Tampere University Press.
Koller, V., and G. Mautner. 2004. Computer applications in critical discourse analysis. In *Applying
    English grammar: Corpus and functional approaches*, ed. C. Coffin, A. Hewings, and K.
    O'Halloran, 216–228. London: Arnold.
Kress, Gunther, and Theo van Leeuwen. 1996/2006. *Reading images: The grammar of visual design*,
    2nd ed. New York and London: Routledge.
Kress, Gunther, and Theo van Leeuwen. 2001. *Multimodal discourse: The modes and media of
    contemporary communication.* UK: Arnold.
Lam, Iok Feng. 2018. From chronicle narrative to the multidisciplinary development: A review of
    development of Macau studies from the regional studies approach. *Journal of Macao Studies*
    90 (3): 7–23.
Laviosa, Sara. 1996. *The English Comparable Corpus (ECC): A resources and a methodology for
    the empirical study of translation.* Manchester: The University of Manchester.
Laviosa, Sara. 2002. *Corpus-based translation studies: Theory, findings, application.* Amsterdam:
    Rodopi.
Mayr, Andrea (ed.). 2008. *Language and power: An introduction to institutional discourse*, ed. Sally
    Johnson, Advances in sociolinguistics. London and New York: Continuum.
Moody, Andrew. 2008. Macau English: Status, functions and forms. *English Today* 24 (3): 3–15.
Munday, Jeremy, Sara Ramos Pinto, and Jacob Blakesley. 2001/2016/2022. *Introducing translation
    studies: Theories and applications*, 5th ed. London and New York: Routledge.
Ng, C.L. 2019. Macaology and Macao's development path. *South China Quarterly* 9 (1): 4–12.

Ng, C.L., H.K. Tong, and G.P. Kam. 2009. *Chronicle of Macau*. Guang Zhou: Guangdong People Press.

O'Halloran, Kay L., and C. Coffin. 2004. Checking overinterpretation and underinterpretation: Help from corpora in critical linguistics. In *Applying English grammar: Corpus and functional approaches*, ed. C. Coffin, A. Hewings, and K. O'Halloran, 257–297. London: Arnold.

O'Sullivan, Carol. 2013. Introduction: Multimodality as challenge and resource for translation. *The Journal of Specialized Translation* 20: 2–14.

Orpin, D. 2005. Corpus linguistics and critical discourse analysis: Examining the ideology of sleaze. *International Journal of Corpus Linguistics* 10 (1): 37–61.

Paltridge, Brian. 2012. *Discourse analysis*, 2nd ed. London: Bloomsbury.

Pérez-González, Luis. 2007. Intervention in new amateur subtitling cultures: A multimodal account. *Linguistica Antverpiensia* 6: 67–80.

Qian, Yufang, and Hailong Tian. 2011. Discourse and social change in China: Taking government working reports for example. *Foreign Languages and Their Teaching* 3 (258): 40–43.

Qian, Yufang, and Hailong Tian. 2014. A decade of change in China: A corpus-based discourse analysis of ten government work reports. In *Discourse, politics and media in contemporary China*, ed. Qing Cao, Hailong Tian, and Paul Chilton, 77–96. Amsterdam/Philadelphia: John Benjamins Publishing Company.

Salway, Andrew. 2007. A corpus-based analysis of audio description. In *Media for all: Subtitling for the deaf, audio description and sign language*, ed. J. Díaz-Cintas, P. Orero, and A. Remael, 151–174. Amsterdam and New York: Rodopi.

Salway, Andrew, and Mike Graham. 2003. Extracting information about emotions in films. In *Proceedings of the eleventh ACM conference on multimedia*.

Sheng, Mingjie, and Chaolin Gu. 2018. Economic growth and development in Macau (1999–2016): The role of the booming gaming industry. *Cities* 75: 72–80. https://doi.org/10.1016/j.cities.2018.01.003.

Su, Jinzhi. 2014. The socio-cultural meaning and its theoretical value of "Research on the application of Mandarin in Macao". *Applied Linguistics (Yuyan Wenzi Yingyong)*.

Tuominen, Tiina, Catalina Jiménez Hurtado, and Anne Ketola. 2018. Why methods matter: Approaching multimodality in translation research. *Linguistica Antverpiensia, New Series: Themes in Translation Studies* 17: 1–21.

Tymoczko, Maria. 1998. Computerized corpora and the future of translation studies. *Meta: Journal des traducteurs* 43 (4). https://doi.org/10.7202/004515ar.

Wang, Jialin, and Yukun Li. 2013. An analysis of the HK governments' policy addresses. *Journal of GuangDong University of Foreign Studies* 4: 88–91.

Wong, Han Keung. 1989. Thoughts regarding establishing Macaology. *Hong Kong and Macao Economy* 2: 12–13.

Wong, L. 1998. *Macao: Language museum*. Hong Kong: Hoi Fong Press.

Wong, Han Keung. 2001. Thoughts regarding subject and methodology of "Macaology." *Academic Research* 7: 34–36.

Wu, Zhiliang, Guoping Jin, and Kaijian Tang (eds.). 2008. *A new history of Macau*. Macau: Macau Foundation.

Yu, Hailing, and Zhongwei Song. 2016. Picture–text congruence in translation: Images of the Zen master on book covers and in verbal texts. *Social Semiotics* 27 (5): 604–623. https://doi.org/10.1080/10350330.2016.1251104.

Zhu, Xiaomin. 2011. A corpus-based critical discourse analysis of the English translation of report on the work of the government: First person plural pronouns. *Foreign Languages Research* (3): 73–78+112. https://doi.org/10.13978/j.cnki.

# Chapter 2
# Literature Review

This chapter presents an overview of the related theories and concepts to build a theoretical framework for the study. As mentioned in Chap. 1, this study aims to investigate the discursive construction of Macao SAR Policy Addresses in the post-handover period to explore how the Policy Addresses as a discourse type function in the construction of social ideologies and the change of social realities of city as well as the role of translation in the same processes. The study positions itself as falling into the research field of Discourse Analysis in Translation Studies. With the specific concerns to reveal the interplay between discourse and social change and discuss the role of translation in the construction of social ideologies and social change, *Critical Discourse Analysis* is implemented as the macro analytical perspective with *Systemic Functional Grammar* (SFG) as the micro analytical framework, and the concept *Translation Shifts* as the framework for translation-oriented analysis.

## 2.1   Social Approach to Discourse Analysis

The study of discourse has become a significant focus of research in many different disciplines. Discourse analysis means different things to scholars in different fields of study. Discourse analysis is an umbrella term covering various approaches to analyzing linguistic practice in social reality, with the assumptions of defining "discourse" differently. Descriptions of the term 'discourse' vary in different time periods, different disciplinary fields and different systems of thought, which are abundant as the survey in many books of Linguistics with collections of classic papers in discourse analysis disclosed, such as Jaworski and Coupland (1999, 29) and Schiffrin (1994, 23–43). Schiffrin et al. (2003/2015, 1) summarized the previous definitions of discourse into three general categories as "(1) anything beyond the sentence, (2)

© The Author(s), under exclusive license to Springer Nature Singapore Pte Ltd. 2023     17
M. Lam Sut I, *A Corpus-assisted Multimodal Analysis to Policy Addresses of Macao SAR Government*, Corpora and Intercultural Studies 11,
https://doi.org/10.1007/978-981-99-1195-0_2

language use, and (3) a broader range of social practice that includes non-linguistic and non-specific instances of languages".

The first category, **beyond sentence level**, is the formal approach to discourse from the linguistic tradition which originated with the linguists back in the 1950s to try to understand how sentences are put together to form texts. The second category, **language use**, is the functional approach to discourse from the perspective of sociolinguistics, with which the analysis focuses on how language is used to get things done in specific contexts. The third category, **social practice**, is the social approach to discourse, with which the analysis leads to the exploration of how language is used to advance certain versions of reality and certain relationships of power, as well as how beliefs, values, and social institutions are constructed through discourse and supported by discourse. With this definition in particular, as Paltridge (2012) puts, in his socially oriented views on discourse analysis,

> *Discourse analysis examines patterns of language across texts and considers the relationship between language and the social and cultural contexts in which it is used. Discourse analysis also considers the ways that the use of language presents different views of the World and different understandings. It examines how the use of language is influenced by relationships between participants as well as the effects the use of language has upon social identities and relations. It also considers how views of the World, and identities, are constructed through the use of discourse.*

(Paltridge 2012, 2)

This branch of discourse analysis involves the consideration of the elements consisting social and cultural contexts, ideologies, relationships between discourse participants and social identities, as well as the interplay between discourse and these elements.

### 2.1.1  Critical Discourse Analysis

Going beyond language use with the assumption that discourse is used to do things in different situations, such as making requests, issuing warnings and apologizing as the functional approach to discourse suggests, the social approach to discourse conceives that the way which discourse is used is bound to issues of what we believe to be right and wrong, who has power over whom, and what we have to do and say to conform with the social context (Jones 2012, 36). The concerns with all these elements are termed as **critically** analyzing discourse by critical discourse analysts.

*Critical Discourse Analysis* deviates from other perspectives toward discourse analysis due to not only its different views of discourse, but also the involvement of its distinctive concepts as **Critical** and **Trans-disciplinary**. The term **Critical** doesn't mean to foreground the negative dimension as in its common usage. Instead, it is associated with two major concerns as the *dialectical relation* between discourse and society, as well as the social practice to *social change*.

To be critical, Critical Discourse Analysis aims to uncover the connections between texts, power and society. It considers how texts function in the social relations regarding power and domination, how texts work ideologically, and how texts negotiate the personal and social identities with their linguistic and semiotic resources (Fairclough 2001, 230). To Critical Discourse Analysts, discourse is not just a product or reflection of social processes, but it is itself seen to contribute toward the (re-) production of these processes (Teo 2000, 11). This is understood as the dialectical relationship between a particular discursive event and the situation(s), institution(s) and social structure(s).

Meanwhile, Critical Discourse Analysis is critical given that it has an emancipatory "knowledge interest" (Habermas 1971). The analysis itself is to encourage the social change (See Fairclough 1989/2001; Locke 2004; Scollon 2001; Wodak 1999, 2001). Critical Discourse Analysis puts emphasis on this emancipatory knowledge interest of discourse rather than analysis at linguistic and semiotic aspects only. It begins with social issues and is with the critical goal of dealing with power, dominance and social inequality as social practice.

In addition to **critical**, **interdisciplinary** acts as the other distinctive feature of Critical Discourse Analysis. With the aim to uncover the connections between semiosis and society, Critical Discourse Analysis opens a dialogue between "disciplines concerned with the linguistic and semiotic analysis, and disciplines concerned with theorizing and researching social processes and social change" (Fairclough 2001, 230). To summarize, Critical Discourse Analysis is problem oriented, and it addresses social issues and aims to bring about social change through critically analyzing discourse.

Regarding the theoretical origins, Critical Discourse Analysis is with its roots in *Critical Linguistics*, which is a branch of discourse analysis developed in the 1970s (See Fowler et al. 1979; Kress and Hodge's 1979). It initiates the analytical perspectives as marrying linguistic text analysis with the social theory of the functions of language, which "goes beyond the description of discourse to an explanation of how and why particular discourse are produced" (Teo 2000, 11).

Fowler later published the paper which is with the leading role of the field, *On Critical Linguistics* (1996). This paper was first published in 1989, in which Fowler summarized the research aims, research significance and research methodology in the disciplinary field of Critical Linguistics, which were further explored in the relevant literature in the decades followed.

In 1992, supported by University of Amsterdam, a small symposium which was attended by notable scholars in the relevant filed, such as Teun van Dijk, Norman Fairclough, Gunther Kress, Theo van Leeuwen and Ruth Wodak, took place in Amsterdam upon its completion with a discussion of theories and methodology among the attended well-known critical discourse analysts. Later in 1993, a special issue of the dominating academic journal in the relevant field, established by van Dijk, *Discourse and Society*, was published with the prominent paper of the renowned scholars mentioned above to explore some of the contemporary issues concerned in a critical endeavor after the small two-day symposium in 1992 mentioned before.

In the following development of Critical Discourse Analysis, different approaches with particular foci emerged. They are summarized into eight methods by Fairclough and Wodak (1997), namely Foucault's French Discourse Analysis, Kress and Fowler's Critical Linguistics, Kress and van Leeuwen's Social Semiotics, Fairclough's socio-cultural change and change in discourse, van Dijk's socio-cognitive studies, Wodak's discourse-historical method, Maa's reading analysis and Jager's dispositive analysis. All these methods demonstrate the variations in the perspectives toward the role of discourse in the process of shaping the social realities as well as the process of being shaped by the social realities.

Taking a relatively marginal role when compared to mainstream research (Dijk 1993), Critical Discourse Analysis has been meeting various criticism against its notion and methodology, which are represented by three significant debates (Tian and Zhao 2012). The first debate started with Widdowson's (1995) "Discourse Analysis: A Critical Review", which argues that there is conceptual confusion in the field of Critical Discourse Analysis. They fall into two main arguments as "the uncertainty of the scope of description" and "the tendency to equate social and linguistic theory with political commitment" (ibid.). They raise the questions of distinction between text and discourse, and the relationship between interpretation and explanation.

In the same issue of the *Journal Language and Literature*, Fairclough (1996) publishes his reply to Widdowson's by clarifying that the distinction between text and discourse has been argued in at least Fairclough's early work, which has illuminated that the process of "interpretation" is 'making meanings through an interplay between features of a text and the varying resources which [people] bring to the process' (Fairclough 1996, 49), and the process of "explanation" (Fairclough 1989,) is 'seeking to show connections between both properties of texts and practices of interpretation in a particular social space' (Fairclough 1996, 50), which is to say the relationship in between is that the explanation process is to investigate how authentic practices of interpretation are socially, culturally and ideologically conditioned.

The second debate involves Blommaert's work (Blommaert 2005), *Discourse: A Critical Introduction.* In this chapter of the work, there is a particular section named *Pros and Cons of Critical Discourse Analysis* (Blommaert 2005, 31–37), in which Blommaert summarizes other works to point out the critical comments of methods, methodology and analytical approaches of Critical Discourse Analysis, and states from his own points of view on it to criticize the potential offer of Critical Discourse Analysis as becoming a critical study of language. To illustrate, Blommaert criticizes the emphasis of Critical Discourse Analysis on linguistic analysis which causes the neglect of the unseen discourse influencing the text in its production and consumption processes. He also criticizes the research scope as limited to the social context of Britain and European, the descriptions of the interplay between discourse and society developed from which are with limitation to be applied in understanding the discourse Worldwide. The last main category of criticism he drew falls into the question of the lack of diachronic analysis in the linguistic aspect.

Wodak later replied to Blommaert's comments by claiming that the criticisms tend to point to the unsolved problems, integrate some aspects but elaborate others, reduce or even distort relevant dimensions via polemical debates, and not to mention necessary research of the relevant field at all (Wodak 2006, 603).

The third debate began with Biling's (2008) paper which examines how critical discourse is written by considering the concept of nominalization. Biling censured critical analysts' abuse of the very forms of language whose ideological potentiality they are warning against, such as deleting agency, using passives and turning processes into entities, and being suggested to use simpler and less technical prose which can clearly represent agency and processes (Biling 2008, 783). In the same issue of the Journal in which Billing's paper was published, Martin (2008), Fairclough (2008b) and van Dijk (2008) respond to Biling's comments. In the replies, it is claimed that critical analysts arrange the grammatical metaphors differently to construct different discourses for different readerships, and there is a need in the use of nominalizations when critical analysts have no question of hiding the negative role of powerful actors but just to present their analytical discourse as any other scientific discourse (Dijk 2008; Fairclough 2008a; Martin 2008).

## 2.1.2  Fairclough's Discursive Change and Socio-Cultural Change

As mentioned above, there are different positions within Critical Discourse Analysis. As one of the representing paradigms, Fairclough's perspective between sociocultural change and change in discourse is to be elaborated in this section. Western Marxism views language as a consciousness that "only arises from the need, the necessity, of intercourse with other men" (Marx and Engels 1964/1978, 158). This is in line with Critical Discourse Analysis's view of discourse as social practice. As Fairclough puts, "[c]ritical discourse analysis can be seen as an application of the sort of critical analysis which has developed within 'Western' Marxism to language in particular" (Fairclough 2001, 232). 'Western' Marxism moves away from the 'economics' of classical Marxism and highlights cultural aspects of social life.

In accordance with Gramsci (1971), capitalism is combined with 'political society' and 'civil society'. The former one is associated with the practice of persuading the public to do things by force or threat. In contrast, the latter one is associated with 'hegemony', which is the control or power over the economic, political and ideological domains of society. Garmsci's (1971) concept of hegemony provides Fairclough's model the views of how power relations influence the production of discourse practice and how discourse practice reproduces, reconstructs and challenges existing power relations (Forgacs 1988).

Drawing on Althusser (1971), Fairclough (1992, 87) views ideologies as constructions of the physical World, social relations and social identities, which are built into various dimensions of the forms/meanings of discursive practice and contribute to the production, reproduction or transformation of relations of domination. That is to say, ideologies create a shared Worldview among people in particular groups to provide models of how the World is supposed to be, and position people in particular ways as social 'subject', and discourse is one way that ideologies are constructed, maintained and challenged (Baker and Ellege 2011, 57).

Both Gramsci (1971) and Althusser (1971) stress the significance of ideology for modern societies to sustain and reinforce their social structure and relations. Drawing upon Althusse's theory of ideology and Grasci's hegemony, Fairclough develops his model by "[discussing] discourse in relation to ideology and to power, and place discourse within a view of power as hegemony, and a view of the evolution of power relations as hegemonic struggle" (Fairclough 1992, 86).

In addition to Western Marxism, the Foucaultian view of discourse (dialectical relations) and the Bakhtinian emphasis on intertextuality also contribute to Fairclough's model of Critical Discourse Analysis. Challenging the common notion of power as being possessed by individuals or institutes via domination or coercion, Foucaultian view claims that power is everywhere and comes from everywhere. It is not deployed by the subjects but by constituting them. Power is embodied in discourse, knowledge and regimes of truth (Foucault 1991; Rabinow 1991). Discourse is manipulated by power, which is termed as "an effect of power" by Foucault, and meanwhile constituting power, which is termed as "an instrument of power" by Foucault (1988). This Foucaultian view of power correlates with knowledge. What we know governs how we can shape something via discursive practice (knowledge creates power). However, we only know what we are allowed to know or what is considered as legitimate knowledge (power creates knowledge). With Foucault's view of power, discourse is described as a vehicle for social and political processes with the interplay among power, knowledge, and discourse. Similarly, Fairclough's model pays attention to dialectical relation as that discourse is socially constituted and socially constitutive.

Bakhtin (1986)'s emphasis on intertextuality is another vital influence on Fairclough's model of Critical Discourse Analysis. 'Intertextuality' is a term coined by Kristeva (1986) as "ways that texts refer to or incorporate aspects of other texts within them" (Baker and Ellege 2011, 64). Bakhtin's work places emphasis on Kristeva's dialogical properties of texts as any text is 'in dialogue with' other existing or anticipated texts explicitly or implicitly, which constitute its 'intertexts', and texts are connected to react to, draw in and transform each other. Bakhtin's work also accentuates the genre of texts, claiming that texts are shaped by the existing types of genre or even mixed with genres. Employing Bakhtin's foci, Fairclough concerns 'intertextuality' in his model in terms of production, distribution and consumption in discourse practice as that texts contribute to the constitution of the existing 'intertexts' and repertoire of the genre, texts move along or transform in the predictable network in accordance with their intertextuality, and intertexts are involved in the process of interpreting the discursive meaning of the texts.

In Fairclough's model, he distinguishes 'manifest intertextuality' and 'constitutive intertextuality' (Fairclough 1992, 117). The former refers to the use of actual content from one text in another, and the latter involves the use of structures from existing texts. The concept of intertextuality stresses the historicity of texts as transforming the existing convention into the present, which happens as naturalizing texts into conventions and routines or creatively configuring new modes of intertexts (Fairclough 1992, 100). Fairclough later places discourse into the broad context of political and economic globalization to investigate the function of discourse in the processes of globalization (Fairclough 2006). His claim of recontextualization which contributes to the social change and the concept of intertextuality are inter-related. Foucaultian view of power and discourse and Bakhitinian's emphasis on the texture of texts point to the way in which orders of discourse structure are restructured by discourse practice.

With the theoretical origins of the social theories mentioned above, Fairclough develops his critical views on discourse by exploring the discursive change in relation to socio-cultural change. Halliday's Systemic Functional Linguistics provides a prominent linguistic theoretical foundation for Fairclough's approach to Critical Discourse Analysis. According to Halliday, "language is as it is because of its function in the social structure, and the organization of behavioral meanings should give some insight into its social foundations" (Halliday 1973, 65). Only by placing language into the socio-cultural environment, the function and nature of language can be explained. Halliday's view of language is in line with the socio-cultural view of discourse in Critical Discourse Analysis.

Halliday's model is a top-down analytical framework in which the elements affect and determine the others according to the hierarchy with socio-cultural environment at the top, followed by genre, register, discourse semantics and lexico-grammar respectively, as presented in Fig. 2.1. The rank of discourse semantics refers to the meta-functions of language as ideational function, interpersonal function and textual function. With the insights of Halliday's view of discourse, Fairclough suggests three aspects of the constrictive effects of discourse as ideational (texts signifying the World and its processes, entities and relations), identity (discourse setting up social identities) and relational (enacting and negotiating social relationships between discourse participants) functions. Identity and relational functions of languages are combined in Halliday's model as the 'interpersonal' function. Halliday's 'textual' function, which concerns how information is foregrounded or backgrounded, is also considered as "usefully added" to Fairclough's list (Fairclough, 1992, 65).

Fairclough claims that discourse is a mode of representation that reflects a more profound social reality, meanwhile, discourse is a source of the social tool with which people take action toward the World and to each other. This is the dialectical relationship between discourse and social structure that is emphasized in Fairclough's approach (1992, 1995a, b, 2001, 2006, 2009). The approach analyzes discourse in a three-dimensional model by viewing discourse as text, discursive practice and social practice, to investigate the discursive change in its relationship with social and cultural change.

As Fairclough puts, the three-dimensional conception of discourse is to correlate three important analytical conventions of discourse analysis. They are the close textual and linguistic analysis, the analysis of social practice in line with social structures ("macrosociological tradition"), and the view of social practice as what people actively produce with their shared Worldview (ideologies) (Fairclough 1992, 72). This approach is presented as a diagram in Fig. 2.2.

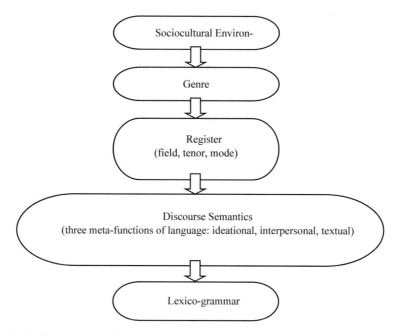

**Fig. 2.1** Hallidayan model of language, adapted from Munday (2016, 90)

In the three dimensions of the approach, the level that deals with the analysis of texts refers to describing the existing semiotic phenomena of discourse, while the part which covers discursive practice analysis is to interpret the textual phenomenon. The producers and distributors of texts are united by their shared purpose to attract attention of the texts audience who are the consumers of the texts, which offers texts the quality as a certain communicative event as discourse. Thus, to attain the interpretation of texts, the analysis required in this dimension is associated with processing of the text within its particular discursive context with specific production, distribution and consumption. Since it is rare for us to consider the features of a text without any reference to the text production and/or interpretation, the line between the analysis of texts and the analysis of discursive practice is blurred (Fairclough 1992, 73), with the semiotic features of texts (i.e., vocabulary, grammar, cohesion and text structure) as the focus in text analysis but the process of production and interpretation of texts in discursive practice analysis.

In addition to text analysis and discursive practice analysis, the major concern of the social practice dimension is to explain why texts are put together and interpreted, why texts are produced, distributed and consumed in particular ways with their socio-cultural context, and to contribute to social structures and social struggles. When describing and interpreting texts, as mentioned, Halliday's meta-functions of language offer a concrete framework for the analysis.

**Fig. 2.2** Fairclough's three-dimensional conception of discourse (1992, 73)

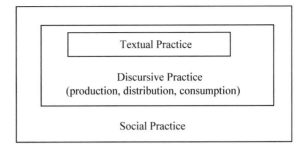

## 2.1.3 Halliday's Meta-Functions of Language

As mentioned, in accordance with Halliday's functional approach to language (1994; Halliday and Matthiessen 2004, 2014), whenever we use language, we are always doing three things at once: we are representing the World with language to describe events, states, and entities involved (ideational function); we are creating, ratifying or negotiating our relationships with the people with whom we are communicating (interpersonal function), as well as joining sentences and ideas together in particular ways to form cohesive and coherent texts (textual function). With Halliday's top-down model, the meta-functions of language are further realized by lexico-grammar. The lexical and grammatical parameters which contribute to discourse semantics are categorized with the rank scale as *morpheme* at the bottom, followed by *word*, *group* or *phrase* and *clause* at the top.

For representing the World, which is termed as ideational function in Halliday's Systemic Function Grammar, it is our experience of reality that is captured in terms of word denotation at word level and transitivity at clause level. The configuration of a process, and participants are the grammatical resources for construing the experience of the World provided by the transitivity system. The processes are the types of contents representing of happening, doing, sensing, meaning, being and becoming, which are termed differently and with different participants in Systemic Fucntional Grammar as listed in Table 2.1, namely *material*, *mental*, *verbal*, *relational*, *existential* and *behavioural* processes.

Material processes represent doing an action or actions with participants as *actors* and *goals*; Mental processes represent a desiration or thinking with the participants as *sensors* and *phenomena*; Verbal processes represent the content of what is said or indicated with the only type of participants as *sayers*; Relational processes represent being, possessing, or becoming, with the participants as *carrier* and *attributes*, or *token* and *value*; Existential processes represent existential constructions with the only type of participants as *existent*; Behavioural processes represent material and mental process with the only type of participants as *behavers*. All these processes are introduced by the vector in the clause.

For creating, ratifying or negotiating our relationships with other discourse participants, which is termed as interpersonal function in Halliday's Systemic Function Grammar, it is the aspects of texts which work to portray the authors of the texts as

**Table 2.1** Transtivity for realizing ideational meaning

| Process | Representing … | Participant |
| --- | --- | --- |
| Material | Doing an action or actions | Actor, goal |
| Mental | A desideration or thinking | Sensor, phenomenon |
| Verbal | The content of what is said or indicated | Sayer |
| Relational | Being, possessing, or becoming | Carrier/token, attribute/value |
| Existential | Existential constructions | Existent |
| Behavioural | Material and mental process | Behaver |

certain kinds of people and at the same time, construct the readers of the texts as certain kinds of people. Texts make available certain "reading positions" (Hodge and Kress 1988) that situate readers in relation to the authors of the text, the topic that the test deals with and other people or institutions relevant to the topic. As Halliday (Halliday and Matthiessen 2014, 29) puts, "while construing, language is always also enacting." The interpersonal function is with two foci: "inter-" and "people". With "inter-", it indicates the meaning which occurs in the process of interaction or exchange; with "people", it refers to the persons who are involved in the process of interaction or exchange (Wang 2016, 36). This is the function of enacting (or helping to enact) interaction which is characterized by specific social purposes and specific social relations (Kress and van Leeuwen 1996a, b/2006/2021, 228). It is reflected by language as its modality which influences or explains speakers' attitudes or opinions of the truth of a proposition conveyed in the discourse or even their attitudes toward particular situations or events.

Simpson (1993) summarizes the modal system with four major categories, namely *denotic, boulomaic, epistemic* and *perception*. By *denotic*, Simpson refers to the modal system of duty. It concerns a speaker's attitude to the degree of obligation attaching to the performance of certain actions, as the differences between a. *You are permitted*, b. *It is possible* and c. *It is necessary*. By *bouomaic*, it refers to the modal lexical verbs which indicate the wishes and desires of the speaker, such as *I hope, I wish, I regret, it is hoped, it is regrettable, hopefully, regrettably,* etc.. *Epistemic* is about the speaker's confidence or lack of confidence in the truth of a proposition expressed. For instance, with a modal auxiliary, the certainty in a. *You could be right* is lower than b. *You are right*. However, with a modal lexical, the situation will be diversed as in *I think, I suppose, I believe, You're sure, It's certain, It's doubtful*, etc. For *perception*, it is regarded as a subcategory of epistemic modality. It is distinguished by the fact that the degree of commitment to the truth of a proposition is predicated on some reference to human perception, usually visual perception, such as the elements in the bold form in the following examples: a. ***It is clear that** you are right*. and b. *You're **clearly** right*.

For joining sentences and ideas together in particular ways to form cohesive and coherent texts, which is termed as textual function in Halliday's Systemic Functional Grammar, it is how the speakers construct their messages in a way which makes them fit smoothly into the unfolding language event, interact with their listeners and say something to them about the World. Speakers constantly organize the way their message fits in with other parts of a communicative event. *Cohesion* and *thematization* are the main ways in which textual meanings are constructed (Thompson 1996/2004/2014, 141).

Thematization relates not only to how individual components are expressed but also to structuring the clause itself. It concerns the order of the linguistic constituents that appear in the clause. An author's selection of the linguistic items in the first positions of clauses determines the informative flow of the text. A clause, which is basically in two segments, with the first as theme and the second as rheme, has the structure of a message as that it says something (the rheme) about something (theme) (Baker 1992/2011/2018, 136).

For *cohesion*, Halliday and Hasan (1976) identify five prominent cohesive devices in English as *reference, substitution, ellipsis, conjunction* and *lexical cohesion. Reference* is the set of grammatical resources which allow the speaker to indicate whether something is being repeated from somewhere earlier in the text or whether it is newly mentioned in the text (i.e., it has not yet appeared in the text to the readers). Unlike *reference* as the semantic relationship, *substitution* and *ellipsis* are grammatical relationships. *Substitution* involves the cases that another linguisitc token replaces the wording to be repeated from elsewhere. *Ellipsis* involves the cases of leaving something unsaid, which however, is understood. Readers are signaled that they should repeat the wording from a previous clause. *Conjunction* is the signal to show how different parts of a text are related. With conjunction, the specific relationship between linguistic constiuents is revealed, such as additive, adversative, causal, temporal and continuative. *Lexial cohesion* refers to the repetition of lexical items in clauses to indicate that they are related, as well as the involvement of a pair of lexical items which are associated with each other in the language in some way (Baker 1992/2011/2018, 194–227).

## 2.2 Potential Semiotic Constituents for Analysis

With the theoretical root of Halliday's Systemic Functional Grammar, the lexico-grammar system (Halliday and Matthiessen 2014, 64) presents various semiotic constituents at different ranks which are with potential in meaning construction. This system offers Critical Discourse Analysis a set of parameters for the textual description and discursive interpretation. Some resources related to this study are elaborated in the following.

## 2.2.1  Linguistic Resources

The elaboration of the parameters starts with the linguistic resources. The resources in the verbal form under investigation in this study include keywords, pronouns, discourse prosody and nominalization.

### Keywords

Corpus-assisted approaches help attain the general view of corpora. Oakes (1998) points out, "in corpus analysis, much of the data is skewed." Words don't just occur as random collections. "No terms are neutral. Choice of words expresses an ideological position" (Stubbs 1996, 107). We can interpret that examining the skewed use of the words in a corpus can help to reveal the possible implicit elements of the texts. One of the corpus tools, a *keyword* list, which is determined by the *keyness* of words, can help researchers better reveal the lexical choice of the corpora. Keyness is the frequency of a word in the text compared to its frequency in a reference corpus.

Williams (1976/1983) associates keywords with the speaker's ideological awareness. A keyword list shows words with significant differences in the frequency when compared with a reference corpus. "[Therefore, it] gives a measure of saliency, whereas a simple word list only provides frequency" of the corpus under examination (Baker 2006, 125). Thus, the keywords, in this study, are believed to be one of the tools to reveal social changes and institutional ideology. Scott (1999) says that keyword lists tend to present three types of words. They are proper nouns, "aboutness" keywords and grammatical words with significantly high frequency. The "aboutness" keywords are the lexical words that include nouns, verbs, adjectives and adverbs. In accordance with Scott (1999), the "aboutness" keywords are generally the group that is the most interesting to analyze and the noticeably frequent grammatical words can probably indicate the style of a text.

### Pronoun

The modal commitment of discourse can be indicated by grammatical means in verbal resources, such as modal auxiliaries, modal adverbs (or sentence adverbs), evaluative adjectives and adverbs, generic sentences and verbs of knowledge, prediction and evaluation (Simpson 1993, 43). As Halliday and Matthiessen put, "[with] pronouns, the referent is defined interpersonally, by the speech situation. With proper names, it is defined experimentally." (Halliday and Matthiessen 2014, 84) The personal pronouns represent the World in accordance with the speaker in the context of speech exchange. The selection of personal pronouns is likely limited by the interpersonal relationship between the two communicators regarding social relationships and familiarity (Xin 2005, 75). They are closely "[associated] with two dimensions fundamental to the analysis of all social life—the dimension of power and solidarity" (Brown and Gilman 1960, 252). With these theoretical beliefs, personal pronouns are considered as one sort of linguistic resource which conveys language modality.

The fundamental distinction of English personal pronouns is into speech roles, as *I, you*; and other roles as *he, she, it* and *they*. There is also a generalized one as *one*.

They are with the distinction of 1st, 2nd or 3rd person, singular or plural, specific or general. Figure 2.3 presents these categories of English personal pronouns. There is existing literature about the analysis of personal pronouns with a corpus-assisted approach which aims at investigating the truth of proposition as well as disclosing the social relationships between the communicators, such as Lakoff (1990)'s, Paul Baker (2006)'s, Zhu (2011)'s and Hue et al. (2018)'s. Generally, the 1st person plural pronouns are with inclusive and exclusive use. The inclusive use of 1st person plural pronouns is proposed to shorten the social distance between listeners and speakers (Fowler et al. 1991, 203), and one text may have more than its fair share of the first-person pronouns when compared to other texts. Thus, the comparison between the use of 1st person plural pronouns of texts is a valuable way of revealing discourse semantic prosodies (Baker 2006, 143).

### *Discourse Prosody*

The elaboration of the concept, *discourse prosody,* should start with the linguistic phenomenon, *Collocation,* which refers to the occurrence of two or more words within a short space of each other in a text (Sinclair 1991, 170). As lexical items are with honest representation when they are working with different words in different contexts, more specific meanings can be interpreted in the lexical items with particular collocations. The corpus-assisted analysis, *Keyword* analysis, supplemented by the *Collocate* and *Concordance* search, is believed to enable the close examination of the keywords with their contexts in use. All the linguistic phenomena attained with the help of the corpus tools are believed to be the evidence to explore how a discourse type functions in social changes. Stubbs (2001, 100) also believes that studying typical collocations of keywords may shed light on an author's "cultural connotations".

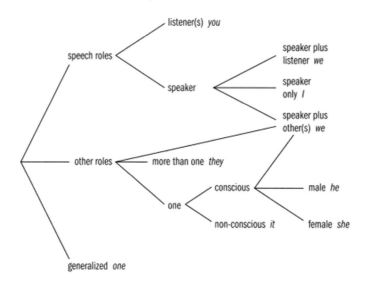

**Fig. 2.3**  The English person categories (Halliday and Matthiessen 2014, 384)

Noting the ideological effects of collocations, the analysis of collocations helps to 'show the associations and connotations they have, and therefore the assumptions which they embody' (Stubbs 1996, 172). The analysis of collocations can stretch to the analysis of the relation, not between individual words, but between a lemma or a word form and a set of semantically related words, which is termed *Semantic Preference* (Stubbs 2001, 65). For example, when analyzing the collocations of the word, *cup*, in the British National Corpus, it is found that the lemma, *cup* (which includes the singular form and the plural form of the word), is with the semantic preference as collocating with the words related to drinking and sports matches (Baker and Ellege 2011, 125–126).

More than *Semantic Preference*, *Semantic Prosodies* similarly focus on the relationship between single words but further reveal the language users' attitudes as well. This concept is popularized by Louw's (1993) paper on irony. It is mentioned that irony tends to rely on a collocative clash. In other words, a writer will deviate from using expected collocates for ironic effect.

To reveal the *Semantic Preference* and *Semantic Prosodies*, an analysis of *Collocations* can be implemented with corpus software. It is because, as Paul Baker and Ellege (2011, 17–18) mentioned, there are many collocations which are not noticeable, particularly to non-native speakers, which can only be revealed by corpus-assisted methods. As Paul Baker (2004a)'s investigation of gender-related discourse, collocation analysis helps to reveal the focus of the discourse. Kempannen's (2004) analysis of the discourse in Finnish and translated Finnish, the investigation of collocations reveals the particular political image constructed in the translation process. Other existing literature on collocation analysis to reveal discourse prosodies includes Laviossa (2000), Kenny (2001), Dayrell (2007), Kim (2013), Zhu (2011), Lu (2016) and Hu, Li and Meng (2018), etc.

*Nominalization*

As suggested by Halliday (Halliday and Matthiessen 2014), one of the primary resources to extend the semantic potential of language is grammatical metaphors. For a metaphor, it generally means that the meaning of which is different from its literal meaning. As in the following examples, the two sentences, (1) *John is undecided.* and (2) *John is sitting on a fence.* are with the same meanings but distinct wordings. Comparing these two sentences, *undecided* in the first sentence is the congruent wording while *sitting on a fence* in the second sentence is the metaphorical wording, the meaning of which is extended to be different from its literal meaning as taking the physical action of sitting. The use of congruent wording expresses the meaning which is intuitively closer to the physical and mental events in the external World that are being represented. While the use of metaphorical expressions creates a difference from the usual assumption. The non-congruence can happen not only in lexical terms but also in grammatical expressions, such as nominalization, which is labeled as one of the forms of grammatical metaphors.

**Nominalization** is the use of nouns or nominal groups to express a process meaning. As in the following examples, the two sentences (3) *The newly announced policy received widespread criticism.* and (4) *Many people criticized the newly* *announced policy.* are with word groups in similar meanings as underlined in the sentences. The nominal group *widespread criticism* in Sentence (3) is derived from the verbal form *criticized* as presented in Sentence (4). Nominalization represents not only the narrative processes as in *widespread criticism*, but also conceptual processes meanings. For example, in the following two lines, *The ambivalence toward literacy...* and *People are ambivalent toward literacy...*, they are with similarly meaning but again distinct wording. The noun phrase *the ambivalence* in the first line is with the relational process as being ambivalent as presented in the second line *People are ambivalent*. The major function of this particular form of grammatical metaphor is its encapsulation. Broadly speaking, new meanings are usually introduced in the form of clauses since they are negotiable. The readers can then reject, in principle, the writer's claims represented in the clauses. In contrast, with a nominal group, the new meanings represented are referred to an abstract "thing" that has existence. Meanwhile, when represented as a 'thing', it can function as a participant in another process in a clause, which means that it can function as the **Theme** of a clause. In this way, the represented process in nominalization is expressed without other participants. Furthermore, nominalized processes are non-finite. They are not tied to any specific time in relation to the time of speaking, which is attuned to the aim of science discourse to establish timeless truths. The deletion of the agents of actions and other participants, as well as the temporal, the spatial and the modal adjuncts of the processes represented in nominalization, enhances the objectivity, formality and professionality of discourse (Fairclough 2008a, 813). With all these qualities of nominalization, the analysis of this sort of linguistic resource can help to reveal the ideology of discourse (Hu et al. 2018, 29).

### 2.2.2  Non-verbal Resources

Language is an abstraction until it is materialized or expressed through either speech or writing. When language is expressed through speech, it is presented by phonology. When language is materialized as writing, it is presented by graphology in the case of a handwritten text or typography in the case of a printed text. Lim (2004) proposed the Integrative Multi-Semiotic Model (IMM model) to illustrate the three planes of meaning, namely the expression plane (which is referred to the phonology, graphology and typography, etc.), the content plane (which is divided into grammar and discourse semantics) and the context plane (which consists of register, genre and ideology). This scheme states that choices made from the systems on the expression plane contribute to the meanings made through systems operating on the content plane and meanwhile are manipulated by the systems operating on the context plane.

This type of communication with "[the] use of several semiotic modes in the design of a semiotic product or event" is systematically termed as *Multimodality* (Kress and van Leeuwan 1996a, b/2006/2021, 20). The word "modality" here means the mode of communication, such as speech, writing or music (or sometimes called the medium of communication). From the perspective of multimodality, all the modes are independent semiotic resources, which are with their own grammar generated from their own means for producing meaning. As Forceville and Urios-Aparisi (2009, 4) mention, "one mode's potential to render 'meaning' can never be completely 'translated' into that of another mode". For instance, teacher's facial expressions, gestures, hand-writing of the board or different realia involved in the classroom lead to radically different teaching effects (Kress and van Leeuwen 2001) and different advertising effects can be interpreted from the analysis of the combination of both linguistic elements and other visual aids (Cook 2001; Forceville 1996). Scholars in the field of multimodal approaches attempt to investigate the 'more' meanings conveyed by the combination of all modes involved in the communication rather than linguistic forms only.

Jewitt (2009/2017) summarizes three main perspectives of multimodal approaches as social semiotic approach to multimodal analysis which is associated originally with the work of Kress and van Leeuwen (Kress and van Leeuwan 1996a, b/2006/2021, 2001; van Leeuwen 2005), multimodal discourse analysis (MDA) which is with Halliday's systemic functional grammar (Halliday and Matthiessen 2014) as the foundation which is associated with the work of O'Toole (1994/2011), Baldry (2004), O'Halloran (2004a, b), as well as multimodal interactional analysis which is associated initially with the work of Scollon and Scollon (2003) and Norris (2004). The semiotic system is the primary problem and focus for O'Halloran's *Multimodal Discourse Analysis*. The rules, regularities and patterns that lie in modal systems of representation and communication in use are the key for Kress and van Leeuwen's *Social Semiotic Approaches*, while the rules and regularities which come about when social actors use the systems of representaiton are the focus of Norris' *Multimodal Internation Analysis*.

Each of these three perspectives emphasizes on a different aspect of an event, so as to provide different analytical routes for the studies which allow researchers to ask different sorts of questions for the same event or to select different kinds of events to study even. Though these three perspectives are distinct from each other with the aforementioned qualities, Halliday's Systemic Functional Linguistics is the theoretical basis for all of them to describe different semiotic resources, such as visual images (Kress and van Leeuwan 1996a, b/2006/2021), mathermatic signs (O'Halloran 2004a), gestures (Martinec and Salway 2005), music (van Leeuwen 1999) and to build up analytical frameworks through studying differnet modes (Bateman 2014; Liu and O'Halloran 2009; Martinec and Salway 2005).

As mentioned before, (Kress and van Leeuwan 1996a, b/2006/2021) apply Halliday's (1994, 2004, 2014) three meta-functions as the basic requirements for visual modes to function as a communicative system (Ledin and Machin 2020; Machin 2007). With the *ideational function*, visual resources are able to represent aspects of the World as it is experienced by humans. With the *interpersonal function*, visual resources are able to reflect a particular social relation between the producers and the viewers of the object represented and the object itself. With the *textual function*, visual resources also have the capacity to form texts, complexes of signs which cohere both internally with each other and externally with the context in and for which they were produced.

With Kress and van Leeuwen's terminology, these three meta-functions are termed *representation, interaction* and *composition,* respectively (Kress and van Leeuwan 1996a, b/2006/2021). *Representation* is realized with two types of *processes*: *narrative processes* and *conceptual processes*. The former depicts what participants are doing or what action or actions participants are performing, while the latter depicts participants in terms of their class, structure or meaning which are their generalized, stable and timeless essence. Under narrative processes, there are *action processes* which are similar to Halliday's *material processes*, the *mental processes* which refer to a "thought bubble" or a similar conventional device in connecting two participants, and the *verbal processes* formed by the arrow-like protrusion of a "dialogue balloon" or similar device connecting two participants (Kress and van Leeuwan 1996a, b/2006/2021, 59–63). While representation can be *narrative* as presenting unfolding actions and events, processes of change and transitory spatial arrangements, representation can be *conceptual* as representing the World in terms of permanent states of affairs and general truths, which includes the following three types: *classification processes, analytical processes* and *symbolic processes. Classification processes* relate participants to each other in terms of taxonomy to present hierarchical structures with participants who will play the role of *subordinates* with respect to (the) other participant(s) as the *superordinate*; *analytical processes* relate participants in terms of a part-whole structure involving *carriers* as the whole and some *possessive attributes* as the parts; and *symbolic processes* represent visually what a participant means or is, with a *carrier* whose meaning or identity is established in the relation (Kress and van Leeuwan 1996a, b/2006/2021, 80–109) (See Table 2.2). All these three types of processes correlate with Halliday's *relational processes* and *existential processes*. With all these processes, the *representation* dimension concerns the relationships between things in the World and in the semiotic modes. In Visual Grammar, the people, places and things (including abstract things) which are represented in semiotic systems are termed *represented participants (RP)* (Kress and van Leeuwan 1996a, b/2006/2021, 47). The represented participants with humanized qualities in visual communication are termed *social actors*, the visual realization of which functions in positioning the viewers, encouraging the viewers to relate to them and assessing them in certain ways (Machin 2007, 109).

Evolved from the lexico-grammar in Halliday's Systemic Functional Linguistics, Kress and van Leeuwan 1996a, b/2006/2021) visual grammar offers various parameters for systematically analyzing how visual resources contribute to the meta-functions of discourse. What follows is the elaboration of some of these resources which are under investigation in this study.

*Color*

Scholars working on Multimodality belives that color can be considered one of the visual resources with its qualties to be used meta-functionally (Kress and van Leeuwen 2002; van Leeuwen 2013, 2011; Painter et al. 2013). With ideational meaning, color can denote particular people, places and things as well as classes of all theses. For instance, green represents plants and nature, and flags denote nations. In its interpersonal role, it is about the attempt to act on the viewers. For example, a

**Table 2.2** Representation in visual grammar (based on Kress and van Leeuwan 1996a, b/2006/2021)

| Function | Representation | | |
|---|---|---|---|
| Ideational function | Narrative | *Process* | *Participant* |
| | | Action | Actor, Goal |
| | | Reaction | Reactor, Goal |
| | | Mental | Sensor, Phenomenon |
| | | Verbal | Sayer, Utterance |
| | Conceptual | Classification | Superordinate, Subordinate, Inter-ordinate |
| | | Analytical | Carrier, Possessive Attribute |
| | | Symbolizing | Carrier, Symbolic Attribute, Symbolic Suggestive |

text which is printed in black and white and a text which is printed in colors will definitely have distinct emotional effects on the audience. With textual meaning, different color schemes distinguish different parts of a unit and create coherence within the related units; meanwhile, the use of colors can provide effects on highlighting or foregrounding particular items. For instance, same colors are used for headings with the same status to offer coherence in between and meanwhile, very likely, highlight the headings and distinguish them from the content.

Kress and van Leeuwen (2002, 355) argue that "signifiers, and therefore also colors, carry a set of affordances from which sign-makers and interpreters select according to their communicative needs and interests in a given context". The affordance carried by colors is realized by their distinctive features including brightness, saturation, purity, modulation, differentiation, luminosity and hue.

Brightness is with the range from maximally light to maximally dark, the meaning potential of which rests on human experiences with light and darkness. Saturation ranges from the most intensely saturated (toward the dull and dark) to the most diluted versions of the same color (toward pale and pastel). It's associated with the meaning potential of expressing emotion 'temperature', as exuberance to tenderness and subtlety. Purity is from maximum purity to maximum hybridity. It's meaning potential is based on the style of modernist paintings and postmodernism. Modulation ranges from fully modulated color to flat color, the meaning potential of which rests on the experience of the play of light and texture. Differentiation is to see whether there is a full range of colors or monochrome. With full color range, the meaning potential of being energetic is represented while the opposite metaphorically represents restraint. In addition, monochrome can somehow relate to seriousness. Luminosity refers to whether the color is opaque or the light shines through it. It's meaning potential is based on the human experience of light. Usually, in many movie ads in particular, luminour color represents the supernatural while the opposite represents reality. Hue is from the warmth of red to the coldness of blue, the meaning potential of which is, more reasonably, provided by the configuration of combination of all mentioned above (Kress and van Leeuwan 1996a, b/2006, 2002; Machin 2007; Ledin and Machin 2020).

Table 2.3 summarizes the realization and meaning potential of the mentioned distinct features of colors. All the scales should be used together in the analysis of the meaning potential. Painter et al. (2013, 36) later suggested that, to interpret inter-personal meaning conveyed by the use of color in particular, the distinctive features of colors can be categorized as vibrancy, warmth and familiarity for analyzing the ambience. The system of vibrancy concerns the value and the saturation of color used. The system of warmth is realized by hue and the amount of color differentiation realizes the syste familiarity.

## *Typography*

In addition to colors, typography is considered as a visual resource that can be used meta-functionally as well. Typography is the art and technique of arranging type to make language visible in printed texts. Written language is presented by a particular *font*, which is a complete character set of a particular style of typeface to materialize language for sighted readers. Typography was not initially considered as a semiotic mode in its own right. "Most research on typography has concerned itself only with legibility" (van Leeuwen 2006, 141). In *Thams and Hudson Manual of Typography*

**Table 2.3** Color dimensions and meaning potentials

| Color dimension | Realisation | Meaning potential |
|---|---|---|
| Hue | Red <--> blue | Warm <--> cold<br>The warmth: energy, salience, etc |
| Brightness | Light(white) <--> grey | Experiences with light and darkness<br>*Clairty versus obscurity<br>*Truth versus lies<br>*Good versus evil<br>*Happy versus depression |
| Saturation | Toward pale and pastel<br><--> toward the dull and dark | Tenderness and subtety versus exuberance |
| Purity | Purity <--> hybridity | Experience of style of modernist paintings and postmodernism<br>Certainty versus Modernism |
| Modulation | Fully modulated (e.g.,the use many different shades of red)<br><--> plain/flat | Experience of the play of light and texture<br>Natural versus Simple, bold or basic, generic colors (low modality) |
| Differetiation | Full color <--> monochrome | *Energy to restraint<br>*Energetic, not classy, lack of restraint<br>*Monochrome (seriousness) |
| Luminosity | Luminour color <--> its opposite | Experience of light<br>(light shining through it)<br>Supernatural versus reality |

(McLean 1980/2000), McLean indicates that to a very limited extent, lettering may help to express a feeling or a mood this is in harmony with the meaning of the words, but for the most part lettering and calligarphy are abstract arts what moves us in something formal, and in the last resort, inexplicable (McLean 1980/2000, 54–56).

As the Internet becomes more oriented toward the written word and 'page media', such as books and magazines become more visual, typography is no longer a humber craft in serving written words but as means of communication in its own right (van Leeuwen 2006, 142). In 1980s to 1990s, scholars, such as McLean (1980/2000) and Neuenschwander (1993) suggested that typography plays a role in meaning construction in written work. As Neuenschwander (1993, 13, 31) put, typography can be "a fully developed medium of expression", possessing "complex grammar by which communication is possible". Afterwards, more linguists, such as Myers (1994), Goodman and Graddol (1996), Walker (2000) and Cook (2001), start having interest in exploring how semiotic resources in written texts function in the construction of discourse semantics.

As visual images do, van Leeuwen (2006) believes that typography can also be used ideationally to represent actions and qualities, can enact interactions and express attitudes to what is being represented, can demarcate the elements, the 'units', of a text and express their degree of similarity or difference as textual elements and foreground key elements of a text and background less important elements. The similar interpretation has already been suggested by the academic field of Typography. Sarah Hyndman, a graphic designer with a Master's degree in Typography, founded Type Tasting Studio to encourage participants to communicate with fonts. In her newly published book (Hyndman 2016), she explains with experience and experimental results of how fonts influence the meaning delivered by advertising materials to potential customers. With the particular strands of linguistics as the theoretical foundation, typography can actually be analyzed as a semiotic mode with is able to function ideationally, interpersonally and textually. With the theoretical foundation of visual grammar, van Leeuwen (2006) elaborates the analysis of typography systematically with a network of the distinctive features of letter forms, as presented in Fig. 2.4.

### *Page layout*

The relationship of all the multimodal elements when they are positioned on the same page contributes to the meaning construction as part of the multimodal configuration of discourse, which is presented in the layout of the multimodal text (Kress 2010; Kress and van Leeuwan 1996a, b/2006/2021; Ledin and Machin 2020; Machin 2007). Layout refers to the arrangement of entities in two and three-dimensional spaces. It is the design decisions in compositions that brings coherence and order, and creates hierarchies of the importance of different elements. This is termed as "visual syntax" (Kress and van Leeuwan 1996a, b/2006/2021; van Leeuwen and Jewitt 2001) to present how the elements are related to each other on a page in meaninful ways.

Kress and van Leeuwen suggest three interrelated systems that can be used to characterize the representational and interactive meanings of spatial composition, namely *Salience, Information Value* and *Framing*. The first system, *salience*, refers

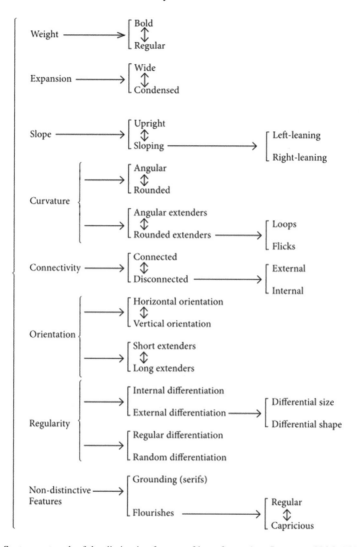

**Fig. 2.4** System network of the distinctive feature of letterforms (van Leeuwen 2006, 151)

to how certain elements might be made to stand out, that is, to have the viewer's attention drawn to them. Salience can be achieved through some basic principles, such as size, color, tone, focus, foregrounding, and overlapping. Table 2.4 elaborates how these principles achieve salience in their presentations. However, it is not necessary to consider each of them as a single salient feature because they will provide salience in different ways and different degrees (Ledin and Machin 2020, 170). Some standards of salience may be more or less significant than others in a particular composition.

The second system, *information value*, is to characterise how elements are placed that make them relate to each other and the audience. The *information value* can be

**Table 2.4** Presentation of basic principles of *salience*

| Principles | Presentation for salience |
| --- | --- |
| Size | Larger space |
| Color | Saturated<br>Striking<br>Bold<br>Rich<br>Red (Verus Green)<br>Bright |
| Tone | Brightness (e.g., surrounded by a glow, highlighted) |
| Focus | Making others out of focus |
| Foregrounding | Placed in front of other elements |
| Overlapping | Invading the space of other elements |

achieved by different kinds of composition. The main kinds of composition will be elaborated in the following (Table 2.5).

In the left and right composition, with the association to the way we write, "left" represents the past while "right" represents the present or future, as a timeline does (van Leeuwen 2005, 201). It is associated with how language builds on information as the left for the given information or the information taken for granted, and the right for the new information or the possible information (Halliday and Matthiessen 2004, 201; van Leeuwen 2005, 201). When the left and right composition is like to present a change as mentioned, the top and bottom composition are more about ranking and order, in other words, hierarchy, presenting a sense of contrast (Machin 2007, 147). With the top position, it is related to power and fantasy. In contrast, with the bottom position, it is down to earth, meanwhile, it is given extra weight, making it more forceful and with a sense of facts. This contrasting metaphorical value of high being loftier and down being more grounded is termed as "ideal" and "real" by Kress and van Leeuwan 1996a, b/2006/2021, 190).

In addition to the previous two kinds of composition, the center and margin are the other types. The central element provides meaning as well as a coherence to marginal materials. In this type of composition, the central material is the central focus or mediating role to other materials around it (Machin 2007, 147–149). All these compositional structures frequently happen in combination. Each one can combine with the other styles of composition to construct meaning.

The third system, *framing*, is the use of framing devices to connect, to relate, to group or to separate elements in the page. As presented in Table 2.6, Van Leeuwen (2005) lists six categories of semiotic resources for creating framing effects and connectivity, namely *segregation*, *separation*, *integration*, *overlap*, *rhyme* and *contrast*. With *segregation*, it means the use of a physical frame to create differences, while *separation* is the use of space to differentiate materials. In contrast to these two, *integration* is where elements occupy the same space. Rather than characterized by frames and spaces, *overlap* refers to the means in which the elements are not constrained by frames and spaces and their meaning can bleed into other spaces.

**Table 2.5**  Kinds of composition for creating *information value*

| Kinds of composition | Meaning | |
|---|---|---|
| Left and right | Left:<br>Past, given, taken for granted | Right:<br>Present/future, new, possible |
| Top and bottom | Top:<br>Power, fantasy | Bottom:<br>Down to earth, given extra weight, more forceful |
| Centre and margin | Centre:<br>Central focus | Margin:<br>Related to the central one |

While *rhyme* means the use of resources, such as color, posture, and size to create links between elements, *contrast* refers to the use of similar resources to indicate difference among elements. The above three systems, as mentioned, are interrelated, and we have to understand their meaning potential with the analysis of a combination of other compositional structures.

As mentioned before, within page layout, there is the involvement of particular types of elements and visual qualities, such as color and letterform which contribute to not only the compositional meaning but also the ideational meaning and the interpersonal meaning as well.

### *Representation of social actors in the image*

Semiotic resources are available for positioning the viewers regarding the participants in the image, how the audience is encouraged to relate to the represented participants, and how the audience is encouraged to assess the represented participants (Machin 2007, 109). Aligning the viewers with the experiences of the participants, categorizing participants visually and presenting what the represented participants are doing can be realized by different semiotic resources in an image.

For aligning the audience with the experiences of the participants, this function of semiotic resources is realized by the aspects including *gaze*, *angle of interaction* and *distance*. In images, as in real life, the represented participants can maintain symbolic contact or interaction with the audience by looking at them. By not looking at the audience, this kind of contact and interaction between the RPs and the audience is

**Table 2.6**  Framing and connectivity devices

| Devices | Realization |
|---|---|
| *Segregation* | Use of physical frames to create a difference |
| *Separation* | Separation by space rather than by frames |
| *Inegration* | Where elements occupy the same space |
| *Overlap* | Meaning of the elements can also bleed into other spaces |
| *Rhyme* | Use of color, posture, size, etc. to create links between elements |
| *Contrast* | Use of color, poster, size, etc. to indicate a difference |

absent. With Kress and Van Leeuwen (1996a, b/2006, 127–128)'s terms, this is a visual act that is based on Halliday (1994, 1985), Halliday and Matthiessen 2004, 2014)'s speech act in language. Instead of four types of acts as language realizes, Kress and van Leeuwan (1996a, b/2006, 129) suggest two *image acts*: *offer* and *demand*. With the engagement of the *gaze*, the audience is encouraged to be involved, to empathize or to provide a response, which can be recognized as different particular kinds of demand and termed as the visual act of *demand*. Without being engaged by the *gaze*, the audience looks at the RPs as observers instead of being demanded to respond. They are offered the images as information available for scrutiny, which is termed the visual act as *offer*. However, there is meaning potential in terms of where the RPs look in the images. The simple metaphorical association suggests positive meaning by looking up and negative by looking down. One more case without the engagement of *gaze* is showing the back of RPs, which can suggest anonymity or create the effect as if the audience stands with the RPs and view the World as they do (Machin 2007, 110–113).

Similar to the visual acts of *offer* and *demand*, the different angles from which the audience looks at the RPs suggest distinct relations in between. The metaphorical association is with our physical association of being removed from a scene, a moment in time, as well as the associations of height and power. With the associations of height and power, it is realized by the vertical angle. By moving with the vertical angle, the audience can be addressed by looking up at the RPs or looking down at the RPs. The former one is with the meaning potential as the RPs have higher status or stronger position than the audience, while the latter one provides the audience a sense of power and the RPs a sense of vulnerability. With the same physical association in real life, if the RPs are presented at the same level as the audience, the equality of power in between is suggested (Machin 2007, 114–115). Correspondingly, by moving with the horizontal angles, the audience's involvement is changed. Similar to the use of the engagement of gaze, different effects will be created by viewing the RPs from the front or from the side, with the latter one to reduce audience's involvement and create detachment in between. The meaning potential is with the real-World association of being involved in situations where we are asked to react or where we are the observers of the people who have business with others. These *angles of interaction* create differences in the meaning of elements in images (Machin 2007, 113–114).

Withal, in daily interaction, social relations determine the distance (literally and figuratively). We keep our distance from some people we are not familiar with and get close to people we see as intimates. In pictures, distance is translated as the size of the frame, namely close shot, medium shot, long shot, etc. (Kress and van Leeuwan 1996a, b/2006, 124). The use of close shots allows the audience to identify the RPs as individuals to reveal their reactions and emotions. While the decrease in distance between RPs and the audience suggests intimacy, the increase in distance creates anonymity (Machin 2007, 116). However, close shots can also suggest negative meaning potential as a threat if the participant depicted is actually not welcome in the context. These changes in the audience's viewing position of the RPs via the above visual realization create distinct status relationships in between.

For considering how visually participants are categorized, this function is realized by *individualization or collectivization*, as well as *categorisation*. Individualization is realized linguistically by singularity and collectivisation is realized linguistically by plurality. In language, we can draw to specific people and humanize them by single form while referring to a group of people in plural form. Visually, individualization is realized by shots showing one person only while collectivisation is realized by shots showing a crowd. Meanwhile, the members of a crowd can be 'homogenised' with other semiotic resources, such as the same clothing, the same poses. Thus, individualization and collectivisation can occur in RPs at the same time. Visual individualization is a matter of degree. It can be reduced by the increase of distance and the decrease of the distinctiveness of individual features (Machin 2007; Ledin and Machin 2020). The linguistic and visual representation of participants can also categorize them, regardless of whether they are also with *individualisation* or *collectivisation* (Machin and van Leeuwen 2005, 134). *Categorisation* of RPs is the resource for informing the audience what kinds of participants they are involved with. Visual categorisation is either 'cultural' or 'biological' (the two may also be combined). Cultural categorisation is realised through standard attributes of dress, hair style, body adornment etc., while biological categorisation is achieved through stereotyped physical characteristics (Machin 2007, 119–121). Biological categorisation can invoke both positive and negative connotations, such as racist stereotypes or focusing on the positive qualities of a stereotype (Machin and van Leeuwen 2005, 134). While it is significant to examine the participants represented in images, it is also crucial if some particular participants are not represented in an image. As mentioned in the elaboration of the linguistic resource *nominalisation*, the absence of actors or agents contribute to the meaning construction of discourse. Likewise, a certain category of participants might not be represented in a picture with the context where they should have been present. In this kind of case, the absence of a certain group of participants, presumably, contributes to the meaning potential of the image as well.

For analyzing what RPs are doing, this is realized by the *visual processes* in the images. As elaborated in the sections above, this is realized by processes linguistically. In multimodal analysis, this is realized by visual processes. As mentioned, Kress and van Leeuwen's *narrative representation* consists of Halliday's processes with actions as *material*, *behavioural*, *mental* and *verbal processes*, while *conceptual representation* consist of Halliday's *relational* and *existential processes*. By examining what the participants do in the images with *processes*, the level of agency and power or the lack of it can be revealed (Machin 2007, 124). When investigating the agency of the processes, the agents can be represented as being very busy but actually achieving very little by being involved in the processes producing no outcome on the World, such as *existential processes* or *mental processes*. In this case, the agents are not depicted as having power over the World. In *conceptual representation*, the RPs act as the carriers rather than actors and goals in the narrative representation, and what the carriers carry, which is termed *attributes* (Halliday and Matthiessen 2014, 2004; Halliday 1994, 1985; Kress and van Leeuwan 1996a, b/2006), creates the meaning.

With the definition of multimodality, the majority of printed texts can be considered multimodal texts as well due to the functions of layout, letterform and color in discourse semantics as mentioned. All mentioned above are the potential multimodal resources that contribute to the meaning construction of printed discourse. Similar to the meaning potential of lexical items work in distinctive contexts,as mentioned, all semiotic modes function together and provide meaning potential depending on the combination with each other.

## 2.3   Translation Shifts

As *Systemic Functional Linguistics* suggests, language is regarded as interrelated sets of options for meaning making (Halliday and Matthiessen 2014, 2004; Halliday 1994, 1985). A specific semiotic configuration choice in the meaning construction process is determined by the context. As Eggins (1994/2004, 53) puts, "a text must relate in relatively stable, coherent ways to the contexts in which it is functioning to mean". One dimension of coherence is the functional-semantic relationship between a text and its situational context, which is realized by the concept of register. Meanwhile, the context of the situation is manipulated by the text's generic purpose in the particular culture, which reveals the other dimension of coherence as the relationship between a text and its cultural context. In other words, with Halliday's top-down model of language (Halliday and Matthiessen 2014, 2004; Halliday 1994, 1985), a particular lexical choice in the meaning construction process is determined by the situational context, which is further shaped by the conventional practice in the cultural context. This is also elaborated in Eggins' (1994/2004) model of context as summarized in Fig. 2.5. Due to the distinctive cultural backgrounds of different languages, changes will happen in translation processes to conform with the generic purpose of the text in the target language and with the target culture as a whole. In Translation Studies, the change that happens in translation processes is termed *translation shifts*.

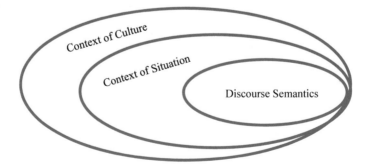

**Fig. 2.5**  Relationship between texts and contexts (based on Eggins (1994/2004)'s model)

Since 1950s, there has been a variety of linguistic approaches toward translation analysis, which propose taxonomies to categorize translation processes. Vinay and Darbelnet's (1958a, b/2000) taxonomy acts as the earliest model referring the phenomenon as involving "shifts" in translation process. In Vinay and Darbelnet's (1958a, b/1995) book, they conducted a comparative study toward French and English to identify the different translation strategies and methods. Vinay and Darbelnet's model proposes two general strategies as **direct (or literal) translation** and **oblique translation.**

With direct translation, Vinay and Darbelnet refer to transposing the source language message element by element into the target language with "(i) parallel categories, in which case we can speak of structural parallelism, or (ii) parallel concepts, which are the result of metalinguistic parallelisms", to attain same overall impression of the two messages (Vinay and Darbelnets (1958a, b/2000, 84). However, other methods should be implemented when certain stylistic effects can only be transposed into the target language with a change of the syntactic order or even the lexis. All these procedures are defined as oblique translation in Vinay and Darbelnets (1958a, b/2000)'s.

These two general strategies cover seven different translation procedures: *borrowing, calque, literal translation, transposition, modulation, equivalence* and *adaptation.* Within all these procedures, Vinay and Darbelnets (1958a, b/2000, 85) rate *borrowing* as "the simplest of all translation methods" in which the SL words are transferred directly to the TL. Together with *calque* and *literal translation*, these three are the procedures under *direct translation*. A *calque* is where SL expression or structure is transferred in a *literal translation* while *literal translation* refers to word-for-word translation which Vinay and Darbelnet describe as being most common within languages of the same family and culture.

Rather than the translation procedures referring to *direct translation*, there are four other procedures identified in Vinay and Darbelnet's model, namely *transposition, modulation, equivalence* and *adaptation. Transposition* refers to a change of part of speech (without changing the meaning) in the translation process, while *modulation* indicates a change of semantics and point of view of the ST. *Equivalence* denotes cases where languages describe the same situation by different stylistic or structural means and *adaptation* means the involvement of changing cultural references when the situation in the source culture is unknown in the target culture (Munday 2016, 85–92; Vinay and Darbelnet (1958a, b/2000, 82–92). All these procedures are generalized as *oblique translation* in Vinay and Darbenet's model.

Vinay and Darbenet's comparative stylistic analysis "is the classic model and […] has had a very wide impact" (Munday 2016, 87) in the investigation of translation products and procesess. Moreover, in the same year as Vinay and Darbenet proposed their comparative model toward translation procedures, Loh Dian-yang (1958a, b) published a two-volume translation textbook in English to propose his taxonomy of linguistic changes in translation process (Zhang and Li 2009).

Though Loh (1958a, b)'s taxonomy has different terminology, it refers to more or less the same phenomenon as Vinay and Darbenet (1958/2000)'s model. Similar to Vinay and Darbenet (1958/2000)'s model, two general translation ways are proposed in Loh (1958a, b)'s taxonomy: *literal translation* and *free translation*. There are four parts in Loh (1958a, b)'s taxonomy.

In part one, Loh proposes six ways of translating nouns that denote things of foreign origin into Chinese, namely *transliteration, semantic translation, combination of transliteration and semantic translation, transliteration plus semantic translation, symbolic translation with a semantic explanation* and *coinage of new characters*.

In part two, Loh presents a grammatical framework to summarize the change of parts of speech in the translation process, which includes relative, demonstratives, indefinite, interrogatives, articles, verbs, modifiers, numerals and connectives. In part three, Loh identifies the significant differences between Chinese and English as word formation, morphology, and syntax.

In the last part, Loh suggests six translation "principles" or "techniques": *omission, amplification, repetition, conversion, inversion* and *negation. Omission*, according to Loh, can be used to solve the 'apparent paradox' in which 'what is considered necessary, indispensable and even a characteristic feature in one language may be deemed useless, superfluous, and even a stumbling block in another" (1958a, 96). He defines *amplification* as the process of providing necessary words "to make the target text correct and clear" (Loh 1958a, 122). *Repetition* is described in Loh's taxonomy as a device for achieving stylistic effect. By *conversion*, Loh means substituting SL words with TL words that are "identical in meaning but different in terms of part of speech" (1958b, 186). He refers *inversion* to the method by which "the constituent elements of a sentence are arranged in a way that is different from the general rules of word-order of the language in question" (1958a, 229); and *negation* to translating a negative sentence with an affirmative one, or vice versa.

These concepts are widely accepted in the Chinese context and have been widely used in translation textbooks in China. Correspondently, both Loh (1958a, b)'s taxonomy and Vinay and Darbenet (1958/2000)'s model investigate the "change" in the translation process via comparative study (Zhang and Li 2009).

While both Loh and Vinay and Darbelnet's models study the occurrence of linguistic changes when translating, Catford (1965) introduces the term "translation shift" to label this sort of the change in the translation process. Catford originated two concepts, *formal correspondence* and *textual equivalence*.

Catford refers to a *textual equivalent* as "any TL form (text or portion of text) which is observed to be equivalent of a given SL form (text or portion of text)" (1965, 27). For instance, the English question "What time is it?" is translated into "而家幾點?" in Cantonese. In terms of grammatical structure, it is different in ST and TT with complement followed by verb and subject in the ST, and subject followed by complement in TT. In terms of lexis, the English "what time" is translated into "幾點" in Cantonese, which cannot be considered as a word-for-word translation. However, the Cantonese translation is viewed as the equivalent of the English question as a text/portion of a text.

With *formal correspondence*, Catford refers the correspondent to "any TL category which may be said to occupy, as nearly as possible, the 'same' place in the economy of the TL as the given SL category occupies in the SL" (1965, 32). For instance, an English statement "His name is John" is translated into "他的名字是約翰". With Catford's definitions, *formal equivalence* is "a more general system-based concept between a pair of languages" while textual equivalence is "tied to a particular ST-TT pair" (Munday et al. 2001/2016/2022, 81).

It is not easy to attain a *formal correspondent* when doing translation between languages which are not with exactly the same linguistic systems. When changes occur, "shift" happens. With *translation shift*, Catford defines it as "departures from formal correspondence in the process of going from the SL to the TL" (Catford 1965, 73). Catford summarizes two significant types of shifts occur in the translation process: *level shifts* and *category shifts.*

With *level shifts*, Catford refers to SL items at one linguistic level have TL translation equivalents at a different linguistic level. For example, the English statement *We are having class* is translated as 我們正在上課 (BT: We, at the moment, have class) in Chinese. The grammatical units, tense and aspect, used in English to express time are replaced by Chinese with lexis 正在 (BT: at the moment) in TT. This sort of *shifts* from grammatical units to lexical units is expected in the translation process (Catford 1965, 73).

Most of Catford's analysis is for another type of *shift— category shift* (Catford 1965, 75–82), which consists of four sub-types: *structural shifts, class shifts, unit/rank shifts* and *intra-system shifts. Structural shift* is considered as "the most frequent category shifts at all ranks in translation" (Catford 1965, 77) and mostly involves shifts in grammatical structure. For instance, the English sentence *I go to school happily every day* is translated as我每天高興地上學 (BT: I, every day, happily go to school.) in Chinese. The structure of ST, Subject-Verb-Complement-Adjunct (manner)-Adjunct (time), is replaced by the structure, subject-adjunct (time)-adjunct (manner)-verb, in Chinese.

In accordance with Catford, *class shifts* occur when the translation equivalent is a member of a different word class from the one in the ST. For instance, the English sentence: *The taxation of Fantan started in 1949.* is translated into Chinese as *1849 年, 番攤開始 被徵稅*。(BT: 1849, Fantan started *to be taxed*). In this example, the underlined **noun phrase** in English is replaced by the underlined **verb phrase** in Chinese.

By *unit shifts,* Catford refers to the situation where the translation equivalent in TL is at a different grammatical rank (the hierarchical linguistic units of sentence, clause, group, word and morpheme) to the SL. By *intra-system shifts,* Catford refers to the cases where SL and TL possess systems that are approximately corresponding but invovle selecting non-corresponding term in translation process (Catford 1965, 80).

Catford's *translation shift* is a significant move to systematically application of the linguistics research finding into Translation Studies. However, it is criticized by scholars as a purely linguistic analysis with unauthentic examples that are idealized and decontextualized (Munday et al. 2001/2016/2022, 82).

After Catford's definition, some scholars define *shift* again in the later work to respond to its criticism. Popovic (1970)'s *shift* involves more elements than those at linguistic level only. It is described as not only the linguistic phenomena, but also the replacements arising from textual, literary or cultural considerations. Popovic considers *translation shift* as not only the unavoidable linguistic differences, but also the fact that the translator is working within the constraints of NORMS which will influence the decisions made during the translation process. He defines *shift* as the translator's attempt "to reproduce [the work] as faithfully as possible and to grasp it in its totality, as an organic whole" (Popovič 1970, 80).

Van Leuven-Zwart (1990, 1989)'s shifts provided a detailed analysis of this concept (Munday 2002, 543). Her model comprises two complementary models: *a comparative modal* and *a descriptive model*. The *comparative model* involves a detailed manual classification of microstructural *shifts* between ST and TT, which consists of semantic, stylistic and pragmatic, modulation, modification and mutation. The *descriptive model* investigates the effects of the microstructural *shifts* on the macrostructural level with the three language meta-functions from SFL (*interpersonal*, *ideational* and *textual functions*).

As discussed here, "translation" is typically thought of as involving written or spoken languages. However, non-verbal resources involve in translation processes as Jakobson defines the three ways of translations. According to Jakobson (1956/1966/2004, 232) there are basically three types of translation, namely *interlingual*, *intralingual* and *intersemiotic*. *Interlingual translation* refers to an interpretation of verbal signs by means of some other languages. *Intralingual translation* refers to an interpretation of verbal signs employing other signs of the same language. *Intersemiotic translation* is defined as an interpretation of verbal signs employing signs of nonverbal sign systems.

Among these three types of translation, intersemiotic translation is quite different from the other two types, and information loss is at its highest (Gorlée 1994, 168). While both intralingual and interlingual translations are at least potentially reversible, intersemiotic translation is a one-way prcoess (Sturrock 1991, 310). With these distinctive features, intersemiotic translation is also an area that is less explored in the field of translation studies compared with the other two types. As O'Sullivan (2013, 5–6) mentioned, translation studies has 'stuggled at times with the concept of multimodality'. Though some progress has been made in developing methodologies for analysis on translations of multimodal texts, challenges on technical and logistic issues remain and there are difficulties in developing a critical and analytical toolbox which is enabled to theorise and model the shifts of meaning that occur in the process of intersemiotic translation (O'Sullivan 2013, 6).

As mentioned, with the ideas of Multimodality, non-verbal resources, along with linguistic resources, function in structuring experience and creating logical connections in the World, as well as depicting social relations and conceiving a stance about the World. Thus, the selection of semiotic choices in the process of intersemiotic translation may result in new meaning potential. As mentioned before, Halliday's *Systemic Functional Grammar* provides the necessary theoretical tools for analyzing the meaning signified in the selection of semiotic resources. O'Halloran et al.'s (2016) model demonstrates that Halliday's meta-functions of language can be applied to the investigation of the selection of resources in inter-semiotic translation process which shows that the selection of resources from one mode reinforces meta-functionally aligned choices made from the other mode of resources which results in semantic expansions as complementary and compounding meaning (O'Halloran et al. 2016, 213). In other words, translation shifts also happen in inter-semiotic translation process, which falls into the differences in meta-functional meaning potential constructed across the configurations of different resources which are fundamentally different in nature (O'Halloran et al. 2016, 229).

## 2.4 Summary

In this chapter, with the review of the relevant theoretical concepts, the theoretical basis of the present study is built. With Critical Discourse Analysis as the macro theoretical foundation of the study, the chapter started with a review of the definition of an umbrella term, Discourse Analysis, which is followed by an elaboration of the development of Critical Discourse Analysis. Within the models of Critical Discourse Analysis, Fairclough's three-dimensional framework is selected to be elaborated due to the present research aims. Given that Halliday's Systemic Functional Linguistics provides a systemic scheme for Critical Discourse Analysis and acts as the significant theoretical foundation of the analytical framework of the study, Halliday's Systemic Functional Grammar is reviewed with the more detailed revisions of the potential semiotic constituents under investigation in the present study. In addition to verbal resources, non-verbal resources play a role in discourse semantics. The concept of Multimodality is, hence, reviewed, which is followed by the detailed elaboration of the potential non-verbal resources for analysis in the present study. Positioning itself as in the research field of discourse analysis in translation studies, the concept of translation shifts is then reviewed, contributing to the analytical framework for the translation-oriented analysis in the present study. With all these relevant theoretical concepts, an analytical framework is built, which is presented in Chap. 3.

## References

Althusser, L. 1971. *Lenin and philosophy and other essays.* London: New Left Book.
Baker, Mona. 1992/2011/2018. *In other words*, 3rd ed. London and New York: Routledge.
Baker, Paul. 2004. Querying keywords. *Journal of English Linguistics* 32 (4): 346–359. https://doi.org/10.1177/0075424204269894.
Baker, Mona. 2006. *Using Corpora in discourse analysis.* London: Continuum.
Baker, Paul, and Sibonile Ellege. 2011. *Key terms in discourse analysis.* London and New York: Continuum.
Bakhtin, Mikhail. 1986. *Speech genres and other late essays.* Trans. by Vern W. McGee, ed. by Caryl Emerson and Michael Holquist. Austin, TX: Texas University Press.
Baldry, Anthony. 2004. Phase and transition, type and instance: patterns in media texts as seen through a multimodal concordance. In *Multimodal discourse analysis*, ed. by Kay L. O'Halloran, 83–108. London and New York: Continuum.

Bateman, John A. 2014. *Text and image: A critical introduction to the visual/verbal divide*. New York: Routledge.

Biling, Michael. 2008. The language of critical discourse analysis: The case of nominalization. *Discourse and Society* 19 (6): 811–819.

Blommaert, Jan. 2005. *Discourse: A critical introduction*. Cambridge: Cambridge Unviersity Press.

Brown, R., and A. Gilman. 1960. The pronouns of power and solidarity. In *Style in language*, ed. by T.A. Sebeok, 253–276. MIT Press.

Catford, J.C. 1965. *A linguistic theory of translation*. London: Oxford University Press.

Cook, Guy. 2001. *The discourse of advertising*, 2nd ed. London: Routledge.

Dayrell, Carmen. 2007. A quantitative approach to compare collocational patterns in translated and non-translated texts. *International Journal of Corpus Linguistics* 12 (3): 375–414.

Dijk, Teun A. van. 1993. Editor's foreword to critical discourse analysis. *Discourse & Society* 4(2), 131–132

Dijk, Teun A. van. 2008. Critical discourse analysis and nominalization: problem or pseudo-problem?*Discourse and Society* 19(6): 821–828.

Eggins, Suzanne. 1994/2004. *An introduction to systemic functional linguistics*, 2nd ed. New York and London: Continuum.

Fairclough. 1989/2001. *Language and power*, ed. by Christopher N. Candlin.*Language in social life series*. London & New York: Routledge.

Fairclough, Norman. 1989. *Language and power*. London: Longman Inc.

Fairclough, Norman. 1992. *Discourse and social change*. Cambridge, England: Polity.

Fairclough, Norman. 1995a. Critical discourse analysis: The critical study of language. edited by 1st. London and New York: Longman.

Fairclough, Norman. 1995b. *Media discourse*. London and New York: Edward Arnold.

Fairclough, Norman. 1996. A reply to Henry Widdowson's discourse analysis: A critical view'. *Language and Literature* 5 (1): 49–56.

Fairclough. 2001. The discourse of new labour: Critical discourse analysis. In *Discourse as data: A guide for analysis*, ed. by Margaret Wetherell, Stephante Taylor and Simeon J. Yates. London: The Open University.

Fairclough, Norman. 2006. *Language and globalisation*. London: Routledge.

Fairclough, Norman. 2008a. The language of critical discoruse analysis: Reply to Michael Biling. *Discourse and Society* 19 (6): 811–819.

Fairclough, Norman. 2008b. The language of critical discourse analysis: Reply to Michael Biling. *Discourse and Society* 19 (6): 811–819.

Fairclough, Norman. 2009. A dialectical-relational approach to critical discourse analysis in social research. In *Methods of critical discourse analysis*, ed. Ruth Wodak and Michael Meyer, 162–186. Los Angeies, London, New Delhi, Singapore, Washington DC: SAGE.

Fairclough, Norman, and Ruth Wodak. 1997. Critical discourse analysis. In *Discourse as social interaction*, ed. by Teun A. van Dijk, In Discourse Studies: A Multidisciplinary Introduction, 258–284. London: Sage.

Forceville, Charles J. 1996. *Pictorial Metaphor in advertising*. London: Routledge.

Forceville, Charles J., and Eduardo Urios-Aparisi. 2009. Multimodal Metaphor, ed. by Gitte Kristiansen, Michel Achard, Rene´ Dirven and Francisco J. Ruiz de Mendoza Iba´n˜ez.Applications of Cognitive Linguistics. Berlin.

Forgacs, D., ed. 1988. *A Gramsci reader*. London: Lawrence and Wishart.

Foucault, Michel. 1988. *Power and knowledge: Selected interviews and other writing*, ed. by Colin Gordon. New York: Pantheon Books.

Foucault, Michel. 1991. *Discipline and Punish: The birth of a prison*. London: Penguin.

Fowler, Roger, Gunther Kress, Bob Hodge, and Tony Trew. 1979. *Language and control*. London and Boston: Routledge & K. Paul.

Fowler, Roger, Bob Hodge, Gunther Kress, and Tony Trew. 1991. Language and control. 2nd ed. In *Routledge library editions: Sociolinguistics*. London and New York: Routledge.

Goodman, Sharon, and David Graddol. 1996. *Redesigning English: New texts, new identities.* London: Routledge.

Gorlée, Dinda L. 1994. *Semiotics and the problem of translation: With special reference tot eh semiotics of Charles S. Perice.* Amsterdam: Rodopi.

Gramsci, Antonio. 1971. *Selection from the prison notebooks of Antonio Gramsci.* Translated by Quintin Hoare and Geoffrey Nowell, ed. by Quintin Hoare and Geoffrey Nowell. London: Lawrence & Wishart.

Habermas, Jürgen. 1971. *Knowledge and Huan interests.* Boston, MA: Beacon Press.

Halliday, Michael. 1973. *Explorations in the functions of language.* London: Edward Arnold.

Halliday, Michael. 1985. *An introduction to functional grammar,* 1st ed. London: Edward Arnold.

Halliday, Michael. 1994. *An introduction to functional grammar,* 2nd ed. London: Edward Arnold.

Halliday, Michael, and Ruqaiya Hasan. 1976. *Cohesion in English.* London: Longman.

Halliday, Michael, and Christian Matthiessen. 2004. *An introduction to functional grammar,* 3rd ed. Great Britain: Hodder Arnold.

Halliday, Michael, and Christian Matthiessen. 2014. *Hallidays introduction to functional grammar,* 4th ed. London and New York: Routledge.

Hodge, Robert, and Gunther Kress. 1988. *Social semiotics.* Cambridge: Polity.

Hu, Kaibao, Tao Li, and Ningzi Meng. 2018. *Introducing Corpus-based critical translation studies.* Beijing: Higher Education Press.

Hyndman, Sarah. 2016. *Why fonts matter.* UK: Penguin Random House.

Jakobson, Roman. 1956/1966/2004. On linguisitcs aspects of translation. In *The translation studies reader,* ed. by L. Venuti. London and New York: Routledge.

Jaworski, Adam, and Nikolas Coupland. 1999. Introduction: Perspectives on discourse analysis. In *The discourse reader,* ed. Jaworsk Adam and Coupland Nikolas, 1–44. London: Routledge.

Jewitt, Carey. 2009/2017. *The Routledge handbook of multimodal analysis,* 2nd ed., ed. by Carey Jewitt. London: Routledge.

Jones, Rodney H. 2012. *Discourse analysis: A resource book for students. Routledge English language introductions.* USA & Cannda: Routledge.

Kempannen, H. 2004. Keywords and ideology in translated history texts: A Corpus-based analysis. *Across Languages and Cultures* 5 (1): 89–106.

Kenny, Dorathy. 2001. *Lexis and creativity in translation: A corpus-based study.* Manchester: St. Jerome.

Kim, Kyung Hye. 2013. Mediating American and South Korean news discourses about North Korea through translation: A Corpus-based critical discourse analysis. PhD, School of Arts, Languages and Cultures.

Kress, Gunther. 2010. *Multimodality: A social semiotic approach to contemporary commnication.* London and New York: Routledge.

Kress, Gunther, and Robert Ian Vere. Hodge. 1979. *Language as ideology.* London: Routledge.

Kress, Gunther, and Theo van Leeuwen. 1996a/2006/2021. *Reading images: The grammar of visual design.* Third ed.

Kress, Gunther, and Theo van Leeuwen. 1996b/2006. *Reading images: The grammar of visual design,* 2nd ed. New York and London: Routledge.

Kress, Gunther, and Theo van Leeuwen. 2001. *Multimodal discourse: The modes and media of contemporary communication.* UK: Arnold.

Kress, Gunther, and Theo van Leeuwen. 2002. Colour as a semiotic mode: Notes for a grammar of colour. *Visual Communication* 1 (3): 343–369.

Kristeva, Julia. 1986. *The Kristeva Reader,* ed. by Toril Moi. New York: Columbia University Press.

Lakoff, Robin Tolmach. 1990.*Talking power: The politics of language in our lives.* New York: Basic Book.

Laviossa, Sara. 2000. TEC: A resource for studying what is "in" and "of" translation English. *Across Languages and Cultures* 1 (2): 159–178.

Ledin, Per, and David Machin. 2020. *Introduction to multimodal analysis,* 2nd ed. London and New York: Bloomsbury Academic.

van Leeuwen, Theo. 1999. *Speech, music, sound*. London: Macmillan.

van Leeuwen, Theo. 2005. *Introducing social semiotics*. London: Routledge.

van Leeuwen, Theo. 2011. *The language of colour: An introduction*. Abingdon, Oxon: Routledge.

van Leeuwen, Theo. 2006. Towards a semiotics of typography. *Information Design Journal* 14 (2): 139–155.

van Leeuwen, Theo. 2013. Colour schemes. In *Multimodality and social semiosis: Communication, meaning making, and learning in the work of Gunther Kress*, ed. Margit Bock and Norbert Pachler, 62–70. New York and London: Routledge.

van Leeuwen, Theo, and Carey Jewitt. 2001. Visual meaning: A social semiotic approach. In *Handbook of visual analysis*, ed. Theo Van Leeuwen and Carey Jewitt, 134–156. London: Sage.

Lim, F. V. 2004. Developing an integrative multi-semiotic model. In Multimodal discourse analysis: Systemic-functional perspectives, ed. by Kay L. O'Halloran, 220–244. London and New York: Continuum.

Liu, Yu, and Kay L. O'Halloran. 2009. Intersemiotic texture: analyzing cohesive devices between language and images.*Social Semiotics* 19(4): 367–388. https://doi.org/10.1080/103503309033 61059

Locke, Terry. 2004. *Critical discourse analysis*. London and New York: Continuum.

Loh, Dian-yang. 1958a. 英漢翻譯理論與技巧2 *[Translation: Its principles and techniques. Book Two]*. Beijing: Times Publishing.

Loh, Dian-yang. 1958b. 英漢翻譯的理論與技巧 *[Translation: Its principles and techniques]*. Beijing: Times Publishing.

Louw, B. 1993. Irony in the text or insincerity in the writer? The diagnostic potential of semantic prosodies. In *Text and technology: In honour of John Sinclair*, ed. G. Francis M. Baker and E. Tognini-Bonelli, 157–176. Amsterdam and Philadelphia: John Benjamins.

Lu, Xiaojun. 2016. *National image and Chinese-English translation strategies for China's global communication*. Shanghai: Foreign Language Teaching and Research Press.

Machin, David. 2007. *Introduction to multimodal analysis*, 1st ed. London and New York: Bloomsbury Academic.

Machin, David, and Theo van Leeuwen. 2005. Computer games as political discourse. *Journal of Language and Politics* 4 (1): 119–141.

Martin, J.R. 2008. Incongruent and proud: De-vilifying "nominalization." *Discourse & Society* 19 (6): 801–810.

Martinec, R., and A. Salway. 2005. A system for image-text relations in new 9and Old) media. *Visual Communication* 4 (3): 337–371.

Marx, Karl, and Friedrich Engels. 1964/1978. The German Ideology. In *The Marx Engels Reader*, ed. by Robert C. Tucker. New York, London: W. W. Norton & Company.

McLean, R. 1980/2000. *The thames and Hudson manual of typography*. London: Thames and Hudson.

Munday, Jeremy. 2002. A Computer-assisted approach to the analysis of translation shifts. *Meta* 43 (4): 542–556. https://doi.org/10.7202/003680ar.

Munday, Jeremy. 2016. *Introducing translation studies: Theories and applications*, 4th ed. London and New York: Routledge.

Munday, Jeremy, Sara Ramos Pinto, and Jacob Blakesley. 2001/2016/2022. *Introducing translation studies: Theories and applications.*, 5th ed. London and New York: Routledge.

Myers, G. 1994. *Words in ads*. London: Edward Arnold.

Neuenschwander, B. 1993. *Letterwork—Creative letterforms in graphic design*. London: Phaidon.

Norris, S. 2004. *Analysing multimodality interaction: A methodological framework*. London: Routledge.

Oakes, M. 1998. *Statistics for corpus linguistics*. Edinburgh: Edinburgh University Press.

O'Halloran, Kay L. 2004a. Mathematical discourse: Language, symbolism and visual image. In *Multimodal discourse analysis: Systemic functional perspectives*, ed. by Kay L. O'Halloran, 109–130. London and New York: Continuum.

O'Halloran, Kay L. 2004b. *Multimodal discourse analysis: Systemic-functional perspectives.* London and New York: Continuum.

O'Halloran, Kay L., Sabine Tan, and Peter Wignell. 2016. Intersemiotic translation as resemiotisation: A multimodal perspective. *Signata* 7: 199–229. https://doi.org/10.4000/signata.1223.

O'Sullivan, Carol. 2013. Introduction: Multimodality as challenge and resource for translation. *The Journal of Specialized Translation* 20: 2–14.

O'Toole, M. 1994/2011. The language of displayed art. London: Leicester University Press.

Painter, Clare, J.R. Martin, and Len Unsworth. 2013. *Reading visual narratives: Image analysis of children's pictures books.* London: Equinox.

Paltridge, Brian. 2012. *Discourse analysis,* 2nd ed. London: Bloomsbury.

Popovič, Anton. 1970. The Concept "Shift of Expression" in translation analysis. In *The nature of translation,* ed. J.S. Holmes, F. De Haan, and A. Popovič, 78–87. The Hague: Mouton.

Rabinow, Paul. 1991. *The Foulcault reader: An introduction to Foulcault's thought.* London: Penguin.

Schiffrin, Deborah. 1994. *Approaches to discourse.* Oxford: Blackwell.

Schiffrin, Deborah, Deborah Tannen, and Heidi E. Hamilton. 2003/2015. Introduction to the First Edicction. In *The handbook of discourse analysis,* ed. by Deborah Tannen, Heidi E. Hamilton and Deborah Schiffrin, 1–7. UK: Wiley Blackwell.

Scollon, Ron, and Suzie Wong Scollon. 2003. *Discourse in place: Language in the material world.* New York: Routledge.

Scollon, Ron. 2001. Action and text: Toward an integrated understanding of the place of text in social (inter)action, mediated discourse analysis and the problem of social action. In *Methods of critical discourse analysis,* ed. by Ruth Wodak and Michael Meyer, 139–183. London: Sage.

Scott, M. 1999. *Word Smith tools help manual. Version 3.0* Oxford: Oxford University Press.

Simpson, Paul. 1993. *Language, ideology and point of view interface.* USA and Canada: Routledge.

Sinclair, John. 1991. *Corpus, concordance, collocation.* Oxford: Oxford University Press.

Stubbs, Michael. 1996. *Text and corpus analysis.* London: Blackwell.

Stubbs, Michael. 2001. *Words and phrases: Corpus studies of lexical semantics.* London: Blackwell Publishing.

Sturrock, John. 1991. On Jakobson on translation. In *On Jakobsona and Translation,* ed. by Thomas A. Sebeok and Jean Umiker-Sebeok. Berlin and New York: Mouton de Gruyter.

Teo, Peter. 2000. Racism in the news: A critical discourse analysis of news reporting in two Australian newspapers. *Discourse & Society* 11 (1): 7–49.

Tian, Hailong, and Yi Zhao. 2012.*Critical discourse analysis: Essential Readings.* Tianjing: Nankai University Press.

Thompson, Geoff. 1996/2004/2014. *Introducing functional grammar,* ed. by 3rd ed. London and New York: Routledge.

Van Leuven-Zwart, Kitty M. 1990. Translation and original: Similarities and dissimilarities, II.*Target* 2(1): 69–95.

Van Leuven-Zwart, Kitty M. 1989. Translation and original: Similarities and dissimmilarities, I.*Target* 1 (2): 151–181.

Vinay, Jean-Paul, and Jean Darbelnet. 1958a/1995. *Comparative stylistics of Rench and English: A methodology for translation.* Trans. by J. C. Sager and M.-J. Hamel. Amsterdam and Philadelphia, PA: John Benjamins.

Vinay, Jean-Paul, and Jean Darbelnet. 1958b/2000. A methodology for translation. In *The translation studies reader,* ed. by Lawrence Venuti, 84–93. London & New York: Routledge.

Walker, S. 2000. *Typography and language in everyday Life.* London: Longman.

Wang, Chenghua. 2016. *Systemic functional linguistics: A course book.* East China Normal University Press.

Widdowson, H.G. 1995. Discoruse analysis: A critical view. *Language and Literature* 4 (3): 158–172.

Williams, Raymond. 1976/1983. *Keywords: A vocabulary of culture and society*. Revised ed. New York: Oxford University Press.

Wodak, Ruth. 1999. CDA at the end of 20th century. *Research on Language and Social Interaction* 32 (1&2): 185–193.

Wodak, Ruth. 2001. What CDA is about–A summery of its History, important concepts and its developments. In *Methods of critical discourse analysis*, ed. Ruth Wodak and Michael Meyer, 1–13. London: Sage.

Wodak, Ruth. 2006. Dilemmas of discoruse. *Language in Society* 35: 595–611.

Xin, Bin. 2005. *Critical linguistics: Theory and application*. Shanghai: Shanghai Foreign Language Education Press.

Zhang, Meifang, and Pan Li. 2009. Introducing a Chinese perspective on translation shifts. *The Translator* 15 (2): 351–374. https://doi.org/10.1080/13556509.2009.10799285.

Zhu, Xiaomin. 2011. A corpus-based critical discourse analysis of the English translation of report on the work of the government: First person plural pronouns. *Foreign Languages Research* (3): 73–78+112. https://doi.org/10.13978/j.cnki.

# Chapter 3
# Methodology

This chapter introduces the data and methodology of the study. The data and the research tools used in the study are first introduced and followed by the presentation of the overall theoretical framework of the study which is built based on the theories reviewed in the previous chapter. Last but not least, the chapter outlines the analytical procedures of the study.

## 3.1 Data and Tools

With the aim of investigating the change of ideologies in the first two decades of the Macao Special Administrative Region Government, this study selects the Policy Addresses (PAs) released from 2000 to 2018, which are the Policy Address 2000 to 2019 (PA2000 to PA2019). As mentioned before, in Macao SAR, a Policy Address is the government work report presented by the Chief Executive annually in the role of the leading figure on behalf of the whole administration of the Government to all relevant social agents.

There are Macao's Policy Addresses in printed texts and infographics released to the Public. The Policy Addresses in printed texts released by the Government consist of Chinese, Portuguese and English versions, with the mark "translated copy" printed only on the English versions. Since the second term of Dr. Chui's office, there have been infographics of the Policy Addresses with simple texts in both Chinese and Portuguese released to the public to supplement the verbal versions, which is released online after the verbal versions. With all this evidence, the printed verbal version of Macao's Policy Addresses in English is considered as the interlingual translations of the verbal Policy Addresses in Chinese, while the infographics of the Policy Addresses are the inter-semiotic translations of the verbal versions.

With the theoretical belief about all semiotic modes playing a role in the constitutive and constructive contribution of discourse and the aim of examining the role of the translation in this discourse constructive and constitutive contribution, as well as the research limitation in languages, the verbal version of the Policy Addresses in Chinese and English of the first four terms of Macao SAR Government with Ho's offices and Chui's offices, as well as the infographics of the Policy Addresses with simple Chinese texts offered by Chui's second office are selected to form the core corpus of research data for this study.

In addition to the core corpus with different versions of Macao's Policy Addresses, another corpus with the texts in the same discourse type in native English is built. It is a corpus formed with the State of the Union Addresses. As a corpus with the texts in the discourse type of important government work reports as Macao's Policy Addresses but in native English, this is a corpus to serve as the authentic linguistic context to help to analyze the linguistic configuration of the English translations of Macao's Policy Addresses. Table 3.1 presents the details of the selected data of the present study.

The corpora included in the whole corpus of the data are named in accordance with the names of the two Chief Executives of these four terms of office in the first two decades of the Macao SAR Government, as well as the abbreviation of the State of Union Addresses (SOTU). In the corpus with Macao's Policy Addresses, all the Policy Addresses from Ho's offices, which are Policy Address 2000 to Policy Address 2009, form a corpus named CHPA; while all the Policy Addresses from Chui's offices, which are Policy Address 2010 to Policy Address 2019, form the corpus named CCPA.

**Table 3.1** Data of the study

| | | CHPA | | CCPA | | CSOTU |
|---|---|---|---|---|---|---|
| Verbal version in Chinese | PAs | CHPAC | PA2000c–PA2009c | CCPAC | PA2010c–PA2019c | ——— |
| | Type | | 6120 | | 4968 | ——— |
| | Token | | 84,521 | | 68,922 | ——— |
| Infographics | PAs | | ——— | CCPAP | PA2015p–PA2019p | ——— |
| Verbal version in English | PAs | CHPAE | PA2000e–PA2009e | CCPAE | PA2010e–PA2019e | The State of the Union Addresses 2002 to 2008 |
| | Type | | 5866 | | 4614 | 7080 |
| | Token | | 98,652 | | 88,034 | 100,165 |

In CHPA, there are verbal Policy Addresses in Chinese (PA2000c−PA2009c) which form the corpus named CHPAC, as well as verbal Policy Addresses in English (PA2000e−PA2009e) which form the corpus named CHPAE. In CCPA, similarly, there are verbal Policy Addresses in Chinese (PA2010c−PA2019c) and English (PA2010e−PA2019e) which form the corpora named CCPAC and CCPAE respectively. In addition, there are infographics of the Policy Addresses included in CCPA. They are PA2010p−PA2019p which form a corpus named CCPAP. All the mentioned Macao Policy Addresses are downloaded from the official website of the Macao SAR Government,[1] which are accessible to the public. In addition to the corpus with Macao's Policy Addresses, the State of the Union Address from 2002 to 2018 form a corpus named CSOTU. It is a corpus with similar capacity in terms of types and tokens with CHPAE and CCPAE.

With the corpora built as the research data, presented in Table 3.1, the study conducts a corpus-assisted investigation with software. A few sorts of software are used in this study, namely AntConc, version 3.5.7 (Anthony 2018), Nvivo 12 Plus and Corpus Word Parser, version 3.0.0.0 (Xiao 2014). Since Chinese texts are included in the selected data, Corpus Word Parser is the software used in the study to deal with Chinese verbal resources. It offers the tools for researchers to identify and mark the semantic chunks of Chinese texts. In this study, with Corpus Word Parser, the Chinese texts in the selected data are divided into semantic chunks before being analyzed with the other corpus software, AntConc.

AntConc is a corpus software that is used for quantitative analysis of the whole corpus with the corpus tools of *Keyword List*, *Collocate*, and *Concordance*. *Keyword List* is the corpus tool that shows which words are unusually frequent or infrequent in the corpus compared to the words in a reference corpus. It allows the researchers to identify the characteristic words in a corpus, even in a large corpus.

*Collocates* is the other corpus tool that offers the researcher to search for the words that collocate with the node word (the word used for searching). They are termed as *Collocates* of the node words. The Collocates can be ordered by the value of a statistical measure between the node word and the collocate, which consists of T-score and mutual information (MI). T-score is a measure not of the strength of the association but of the confidence with which we can assert that there is an association. MI is more likely to give high scores to fixed phrases, wherea T-score will work out significant collocates that occur relatively frequently.

*Concordance* is the tool that works out the linguistic contexts of the node word. It allows researchers to see how words and phrases are commonly used in a corpus of texts. Figure 3.1 presents the interface of this corpus software with the three tools used in this study circled.

Different from AntConc, Nvivo is another corpus software that allows researchers to conduct qualitative research. It offers functions for quantitative analysis to support qualitative analysis as well. With Nvivo, nodes can be created in accordance with the semiotic features to be analyzed. The function of coding can be used to code the imported texts with the nodes created, enabling reserachers to analyze semiotic

---

[1] Www.policyaddress.gov.mo.

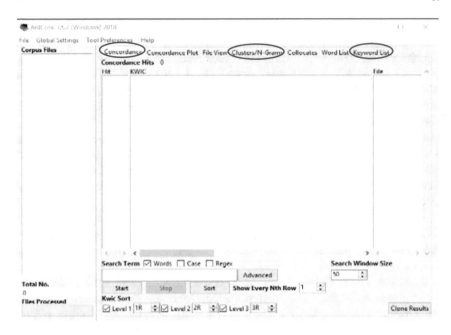

**Fig. 3.1**   AntConc 3.5.7 (Anthony 2018)

features and translation shifts both qualitatively and quantitatively. Figure 3.2 shows the interface of Nvivo when analyzing for this study with some nodes created for the text coding.

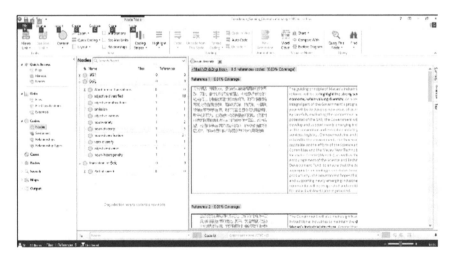

**Fig. 3.2**   Nvivo 12 plus

## 3.2  Analytical Framework

With the relevant theoretical concepts reviewed in the previous chapter, the theoretical basis of this study is constructed. This study basically follows the three procedures depicted in Fairclough's three-dimensional model of *Critical Discourse Analysis* (1992). This model is implemented in the study to investigate Macao's Policy Addresses to describe their semiotic configuration, to interpret the function of Macao's Policy Addresses as a discourse type in the constitutive and constructive contribution to the change in the ideologies of Macao, and to explain the relationship between Macao's Policy Addresses as a discourse type and the socio-cultural contexts of the city.

In terms of theoretical framework, this three-dimensional model from Fairclough is used as the macro framework, and Halliday's *Systemic Functional Grammar* (Halliday and Matthiessen 2014) and Kress and van Leeuwen's *Visual Grammar* (1996/2006) are employed as the framework to offer a system of parameters for the detailed textual analysis. To examine how translation also functions in the ideological effect of discourse, the categories of *Translation Shifts* are used for analyzing the translation procedures.

To respond to the first research question, a detailed textual analysis is conducted to describe the specific features of the semiotic configurations of the selected data, which is positioned as "text" at this stage. With the objective to investigate the change in ideologies of the city in the two decades, twenty Policy Addresses, their English translations and infographics are selected to build the corpus for examination as mentioned. The corpus-assisted approach is implemented in the study with a large set of data to deal with the whole set of selected data. The textual analysis starts with the *Keyword* search, with a one-million-word balanced corpus of recent Chinese, ToRCH 2009 (Text of Recent Chinese)[2] as the reference corpus to look for the *Keyword list* of the corpora consisted in the data set with the assistance of the corpus software AntConc. With the intention to probe into the semantic prosody identified in the textual analysis for interpreting the semiotic realization as the potential ideologies represented in the next stage, other corpus tools, *Collocate* and *Concordance,* are used to examine the collocation of the key words of the selected data attained in the *Keyword* search. To analyze the ideational meaning in the *Concordance* lines, types of Transitivity in Halliday's systemic functional grammar is used as the node for examination. As mentioned, in addition to the ideational effect, semantic prosodies reveal the attitudes of the users of languages. With Halliday's Systemic Functional Grammar, this is to do with the interpersonal role of discourse. To probe into this aspect, Simpson's (Simpson 1993) four modal systems of language are specifically applied in the analysis of speakers' attitudes toward the propositions mentioned in the

---

[2] ToRCH 2009 (available from http://www.bfsu-corpus.org/content/conll-2013) is a Chinese corpus containing 1,087,619 words (1,703,635 characters) with 671 texts from 15 text types, namely Press: Reportage, Press: Editorial, Press: Reviews, Religion, Skill and hobbies, Popular lore, Belles-lettres, Miscellaneous: Government and house organs, Learned, Fiction: General, Fiction: Mystery, Fiction: Science, Fiction: Adventure, Fiction: Romance, and Humour.

selected Policy Addresses. With the aim to investigate the role of translation in constitutive and constructive effects of discourse, the interlingual translation process of the
key words from Chinese-to-English are analyzed with the categories of translation
shifts with the software NVivo 12 Plus. In addition to the verbal resources, the verbal
Policy Addresses' visual resources and their infographics are analyzed with Kress
and van Leeuwen's (Kress and van Leeuwen 1996/2006) visual grammar in terms of
the ideational, interpersonal and textual role of non-verbal resources. The discourse
prosodies of the infographics and the verbal versions of the Policy Addresses are
compared to analyze the shifts in the inter-semiotic translation process from the
verbal versions to the infographics of the Policy Addresses (Fig. 3.3).

The semiotic configurations and translation shifts identified in the textual analysis are interpreted within a communicative event of distributing the discourse to
its consumers, which is to respond to the second research question about how the
semiotic realization functions in the ideological effects of discourse. At this stage,

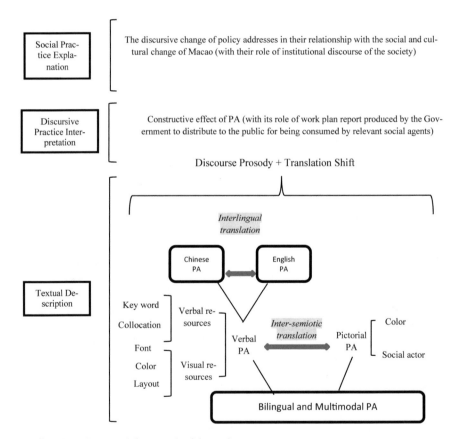

**Fig. 3.3**  Overall research framework of the study

the selected data is positioned as "discourse" in the role of the governmental report with government's work plan set for the coming year announced to the public and the relevant social agents.

The interpretation will then be moved forward to the explanation of the functions of the discourse in constructing the ideologies within the relevant socio-cultural contexts. At this stage, the selected data is positioned as a social practice, which is in a role of institutional discourse that contributes to the social realities that directly and/or indirectly shape and constrain it. Figure 3.3 presents the analytical framework of the study.

## 3.3  Summary

This chapter presents the methodological framework with the integration of the *Critical Discourse Analysis* model with the corpus-assisted approach to be implemented in this study. After the description of the data and relevant tools of the study, the detailed analytical procedure is introduced to present the analytical framework with the theoretical structure, which acts as the framework of the detailed analysis to be presented in the following chapters.

## References

Anthony, L. 2018. AntConc (Version 3.5.7). [Computer Software]. Tokyo, Japan: Waseda University. Retrieved from http://www.laurenceanthony.net/software

Fairclough, Norman. 1992. *Discourse and social change*. Cambridge, England: Polity

Halliday, Michael., and Christian Matthiessen. 2014. *Hallidays introduction to functional grammar*. 4th ed. London & New York: Routledge

Kress, Gunther., and Theo van Leeuwen. 1996/2006. *Reading images: The grammar of visual design*, 2nd ed. New York & London: Routledge

Simpson, Paul. 1993. *Language, ideology and point of view.interface*. USA and Canada: Routledge

Xiao, H. 2014. CorpusWordParser (Version 3.0.0.0). [Computer Software]. Beijing, China: Institute of Applied Linguistics Ministry of Education. Available from www.cncorpus.org

# Chapter 4
# Case Analysis

This chapter presents the case analysis of the study. Adhering to the analytical framework outlined in Chap. 3, an analysis of the texts with the verbal and non-verbal resources is performed in detail, to present their semiotic configuration which contributes to the meaning construction of the discourse. The chapter is presented in four main sections, with the first three sections devoted to the examination of the verbal texts and the fourth section devoted to the investigation of other para-texts and visual elements which contributes to the meaning construction. The examination of the verbal texts is carried out in three steps and presented in the three sections, first, identifying the keywords; second, contextualizing the keywords; and third, translating the keywords. The analysis results provide evidence to explore the function of discourse in the socio-cultural context in the following chapter.

## 4.1 Identifying Key Words

This section is to start examining the particular linguistic configuration which contributes to the ideology construction of the Macao Special Administrative Region by identifying the words with conspicuous salience in the verbal texts of the selected Policy Addresses. To fulfil this objective, a corpus-assisted analysis is made with the software *AntConc*, version 3.5.7 (Anthony 2018).

To start with, the analysis is first operated with the corpus tool provided by the software, *Keyword* search, with the selected verbal resources in Chinese. The *Keyword* search compares the selected Policy Addresses in Chinese texts with the selected reference corpus, which is a two-million-word Chinese corpus combined

M. Lam Sut I, *A Corpus-assisted Multimodal Analysis to Policy Addresses of Macao SAR Government*, Corpora and Intercultural Studies 11, https://doi.org/10.1007/978-981-99-1195-0_4

**Table 4.1** Top ten *Keywords* of CCPAC and CHPAC

| CHPAC | | | CCPAC | | |
|---|---|---|---|---|---|
| Frequency | Keyness | Keywords | Frequency | Keyness | Keywords |
| 980 | 3404.80 | 政府<br>(government) | 665 | 3922.52 | 澳門<br>(Macau) |
| 600 | 3261.29 | 澳門<br>(Macau) | 434 | 2972.74 | 特區政府<br>(SAR government) |
| 566 | 2922.56 | 市民<br>(citizens) | 394 | 2476.07 | 澳<br>(Macau) |
| 383 | 2449.55 | 施政<br>(governance) | 355 | 2408.27 | 施政<br>(governance) |
| 236 | 1517.63 | 特區政府<br>(SAR government) | 437 | 2034.35 | 居民<br>(residents) |
| 260 | 1478.31 | 澳<br>(Macau) | 836 | 1514.18 | 發展<br>(to<br>develop/development) |
| 2018 | 1403.61 | 和<br>(and/with) | 491 | 1389.91 | 政府<br>(government) |
| 874 | 1356.11 | 發展<br>(to<br>develop/development) | 206 | 1303.11 | 特區<br>(SAR) |
| 760 | 1309.21 | 社會<br>(society) | 436 | 1066.40 | 及<br>(and) |
| 186 | 1095.56 | 特區<br>(SAR) | 332 | 1041.99 | 合作<br>(to collaborate /<br>collaboration) |

with ToRCH2009[1] and ToRCH2014.[2] With this *Keyword* search, a *Keyword* list of CHPAC and a *Keyword* list of CCPAC are attained to study the words with apparent significance in the selected texts. Table 4.1 shows the beginning of the two *Keyword* lists with the top ten *Keywords*.

The *Keywords* presented in Table 4.1 show that there are function words and repetition in the list, such as 澳門 (Macao) and 澳 (Macao). In order to obtain a

---

[1] ToRCH 2009 (available from http://www.bfsu-corpus.org/content/conll-2013) is a Chinese corpus containing 1,087,619 words (1,703,635 characters) with texts mainly published in 2009 from 15 text types, namely Press: Reportage, Press: Editorial, Press: Reviews, General Prose: Religion, General Prose: Skill and hobbies, General Prose: Popular lore, General Prose: Belles-lettres, General Prose: Miscellaneous; Learned: Science, Fiction: General, Fiction: Mystery, Fiction: Science, Fiction: Adventure, Fiction: Romance, and Humour.

[2] ToRCH 2014 (available from http://www.bfsu-corpus.org/content/conll-2013) is a Chinese corpus containing 1,029,385words (1,632,882characters) with texts mainly published in 2014 from 15 text types, namely Press: Reportage, Press: Editorial, Press: Reviews, General Prose: Religion, General Prose: Skill and hobbies, General Prose: Popular lore, General Prose: Belles-lettres, General Prose: Miscellaneous; Learned:Science; Fiction: General, Fiction: Mystery, Fiction: Science, Fiction: Adventure, Fiction: Romance, and Humour.

manageable list of salient words to study the ideology construction of Macao, the words to be identified in this section, are not all the words provided by the *Keyword* list yet are those attained after the manual modifications toward the top 30 ones as 1) omitting the function words, such as 和 (LT: with/and) and 的 (a function word used at the end of a word to form an adjective); 2) excluding the words commonly used in policy addresses, such as 年 (LT: year), 元 (LT: dollars). 3) combining the repetition as 澳門 (Macao) and 澳 (Macao). The words obtained via the *Keyword* search and the technical adjustment, are termed as **key words** in the following.

Within all the key words, there is only one proper noun with the referent of the region, which is the name of the context of the present study, 澳門 (Macao). It is a standard key word in both CHPAC and CCPAC. It is easy to understand that the topics discussed in the policy addresses have little or no reference to other cities or countries but the city itself as the word 澳門 (Macao) is frequently used in the policy addresses in both corpora. All other key words obtained via the *Keyword* search with technical adjustment are classified into different categories in accordance with their denotation as **social groups/institutes**, **policy foci**, and **actions**. They are presented in categories in Table 4.2.

**Table 4.2**   Key words identified in CHPAC and CCPAC

| Category | | CHPAC | CCPAC |
|---|---|---|---|
| Social groups/institutes | | 政府 **(government)**, 市民 (citizens), 特區政府 **(SAR government)**, 特區 **(SAR)**, 我們 **(we, us, our, ours)**, 立法會 (legislative assembly) | 特區政府 **(SAR government)**, 居民(residents), 政府 **(government)**, 特區 **(SAR)**, 立法會(legislative assembly) |
| Policy foci | | – | 民生 (people's lives), 多元 (diversification), 博彩 **(gambling)** |
| Action | Process of growth and change | 發展(to develop/development), 繼續 (to continue) | 發展 (to develop/development),, 繼續 (to continue) |
| | Process of improving and refining | 提升(to increase/increase), 優化 (to optimise), 促進 (to reinforce), 加強 (to enhance) | 提升(to increase/increase), 優化 (to optimise), 促進 (to reinforce), 加強 (to enhance), 完善 (to refine) |
| | Process of promising the occurrence of goals | 確保 (to ensure) | |
| | Process of introducing new goals | – | 建設 (to build/construction), 落實 (to implement) and 發放 (to grant/to offer/to provide) |

### 4.1.1  Key Words with Reference to Policy Foci

As presented in Table 4.2, there are distinctive key words in CCPAC with reference to the Government's policy foci, as 民生 (LT: people's lives), 多元 (LT: diversification) and 博彩 (LT: gambling). The former two key words reflect different aspects of government's attention. 民生 (LT: people's lives) denotes the experience, activities and the ways of living of the public while 博彩 (LT: gambling) is with reference to the pillar industry of the city, which has started creating huge impacts on the economy of the city since sixteenth century. The other one 多元 (LT: diversification), hence, is not with referent to the concrete fields of policy. Instead, it denotes the state of having varieties. The detailed distribution of these three key words is examined respectively in the following.

*Distribution of 民生 (LT: people's life)*

民生, with the literal translation as people's life, in a broad sense, means the way people live. As a distinctive key word in CCPAC, 民生 (LT: people's life) is with the *Keyness* nearly 6 times higher than it does in CHPAC. The frequency of the key word 民生 (LT: people's life) throughout the investigated period is presented in Fig. 4.1. The statistics show that the *Keyness* of 民生 (LT: people's life) rockets in Chui's terms, with the highest in Chui's first term as 16.46 times higher than it does in Ho's first term and 4.11 times higher in Ho's second term. The *Keyness* of 民生 (LT: people's lives) falls in Chui's second term but is still 8.18 times higher than it does in Ho's first term and 2.04 times in Ho's second.

*Distribution of 博彩 (LT: gambling)*

When examining the frequency of the key word 博彩 (LT: gambling), it is found that there is an apparent upward trend in the application of this key word throughout the period under investigation. However, there is a significant cluster of 博彩 (LT: gambling) in CCPAC as 非博彩 (non-gambling). With a negative modifier 非 (LT: non-), the denotation of this word group turns into the opposite. In order to investigate the actual distribution of the key noun 博彩 (LT: gambling), a phrase 非博彩

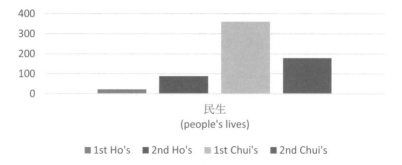

**Fig. 4.1**  Keyness of 民生 (LT: people's lives) in the investigated period

(non-gambling) is formed in the corpora to be studied. Figures 4.2 and 4.3 present the *Keyness* of 博彩 (LT: gambling) and 非博彩 (non-gambling) in the whole investigated period. The statistics present a relatively apparent raise in the *Keyness* of not only 博彩 (LT: gambling) throughout the four terms but also 非博彩 (non-gambling) in Chui's second term, which reflects the attention of the government of Chui's second term on both 博彩 (LT: gambling) and 非博彩 (non-gambling) related elements.

*Distribution of 多元 (LT: diversification)*

The only one left from this particular group, 多元 (LT: diversification), does not refer to any particular aspect of the governmental policies in terms of its denotation. Figure 4.4 presents the *Keyness* of this key word in the texts of each term. The statistics show that its *Keyness* rocketed in Ho's second term, was four times higher than the previous, and maintained a considerable increase in Chui's first term, two times higher than the previous. It then leveled off in Chui's second term.

With the examination of the distribution of this group of key words throughout the investigated period, the noticeable increase in the significance of 民生 (LT: people's lives) and 多元 (LT: diversification) is found from Ho's first term to Chui's first

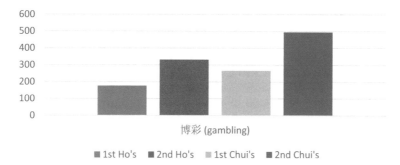

**Fig. 4.2** *Keyness* of 博彩 (LT: gambling) in the investigated period

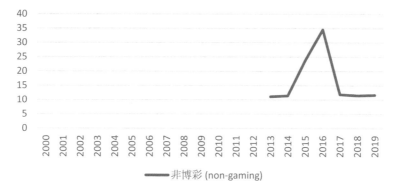

**Fig. 4.3** *Keyness* of 非博彩 (non-gambling) in the investigated period

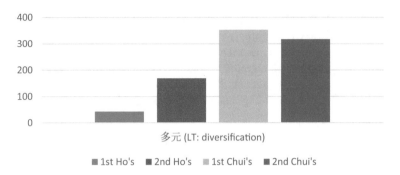

**Fig. 4.4** *Keyness* of 多元 (LT: diversification) in the investigated period

term. In contrast, the significance of the key word 博彩 (LT: gambling) presents an upward trend generally throughout the investigated period, with the increase of the significance of the word group denoting it is opposite rocketing in Chui's terms.

### 4.1.2   Key Words with Reference to Actions

The identified key words denoting different sorts of the Government's actions are similar in both CHPAC and CCPAC. The most significant key words with reference to the Government's actions identified in each corpus are the same as 發展 (LT: to develop/development), which denotes **the process of growth and change**. Aside from the most salient one in the group, there is another group of common key words which are with positive references to **actions of improving and refining** as 提升 (LT: to increase/increase), 優化 (LT: to optimise), 促進 (LT: to reinforce), 加強 (LT: to enhance) in both corpora, and 完善 (LT: to refine) in CCPAC.

In addition to the key words with common references, there are distinctive key words identified in each corpus. 確保 (LT: to ensure), which denotes making certain that something will happen, is the distinctive one identified in CHPAC. It is used to **promise the occurrence of the goals**, which conveys a positive attitude toward the goals. In CCPAC, 建設 (LT: to build/construction), 落實 (LT: to implement), and 發放 (LT: to grant/to offer/to provide) are the distinctive ones identified. 建設 (LT: to build/construction) signifies the process of building something. It is used when **introducing new goals**. 落實 (LT: to implement) signifies the process of putting something into effect, and 發放 (LT: to grant/to offer/to provide) signifies the process of giving.

With the common key words conveying actions for growth and achievement, the distinctive one in CHPAC conveys the mental processes of promising. In contrast, the distinctive ones in CCPAC convey the material processes of introducing new goals, putting goals into effect, and giving.

**Table 4.3** Frequency of apparent keywords denoting participants in CHPAC and CCPAC

| Keyword | Frequency | Frequency |
|---|---|---|
| | CHPA | CCPA |
| 我們 (we/us/our) | 858 (38%) | 253 (18.35%) |
| 政府 (government)/特區政府 (SAR government)/特區 (SAR) | 1400 (62%) | 1126 (81.65%) |

### 4.1.3  Key Words with Reference to Social Groups and Institutes

The identified key words with the reference to social groups and institutes in both CHPAC and CCPAC are primarily in common as the nouns denoting the name of the speaker of Policy Addresses as 特區 (LT: SAR), 特區政府 (LT: SAR) and 政府 (LT: the government),[3] the audience of the Policy Addresses as 立法會 *(legislative assembly)*, and other participants of the Policy Addresses as 市民 (LT: *citizens*) and 公務人員 *(LT: civil/public servants)*. However, in CHPAC, there is a distinctive one identified in the same group. It is a first person-plural pronoun, 我們 *(LT: we, us, our, ours)*. Personal pronouns and all these names of the groups of people and institutes are alike, the references of which are typically unique.

For the only key pronoun which is attained in CHPAC, with the theoretical foundation built in Chap. 2, it is believed that the investigation the use of this pronoun in the two selected corpora of this study would be a useful way of revealing discourse prosodies due to the nature of personal pronouns (Baker 2006, 143) As one of the key words of the CHPAC but not in the other corpus, the first-person plural pronoun, 我們 (LT: *we/us/our/ours*), is with the *Keyness* of 912.807 in CHPAC, which is 40 times higher than its *Keyness* in the CCPAC (as 22.649 in CCPAC). The key pronoun 我們 (LT: we, us, our, ours) is with inclusive or exclusive usage as representing the speaker's own voice on behalf of the Government in the Policy Addresses or the Government as well as the audience (legislative assembly and/or Macao citizens). The former usage is with the same references as the other two key words 政府 (LT: government) and 特區 (LT: Special Administrative Region, SAR). With the common reference, it is worth investigating the only key pronoun 我們 (LT: we, us, our) with 特區 (SAR) and 政府 (LT: government). Table 4.3 summarizes their application in the selected Policy Addresses with their frequency and Fig. 4.5 presents the proportion of the application of the two groups within all the key words with references to the speaker in the two selected corpora.

As shown in Fig. 4.5, when labeling the Government, though the names of the Government are the common diction in both corpora, in CHPAC, the first-person plural pronoun accounts for more than one-third (38%) in the application yet only

---

[3] The Cluster search of 政府 (government) indicates that there are different representation representing other parties as 中央政府 (Central Government), 中葡兩國政府 (LT: the Governments of China and Portugal), 粵澳兩地政府 (LT: The Governments of Guangdong and Macao) etc. In the following of analysis, the words with other representations are excluded, yet only 政府 (government) with the reference to Macao SAR government counts.

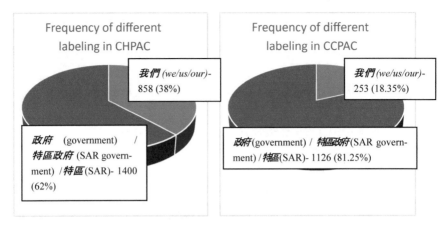

**Fig. 4.5** Different naming of the speaker

less than one-fifth (18.35%) in CCPAC, which responds to the significance of 我們 (*we, us, our, ours*) in CHPAC as one of the top key words but not in CCPAC. When probing into the contexts of the key words with reference to the naming of the Government, the differences in labeling the Government per se throughout the investigated period are presented, which, as mentioned, contributes to the language modality. (Halliday and Matthiessen 2004, 84) These would be further elaborated on in the following sections.

*Summary of distribution of key words*

With the corpus tool *Keyword* search, the key words of the two corpora are identified. It is found that the denotation of the key words identified can be categorized into three primary types, namely policy foci, the Government's actions, as well as social groups and institutes. In the examination of the distribution of the key words, some diachronic changes are discovered. While there is no key word referring to the policy foci occurring in the *Keyword* search of CHPAC, there are three attained in CCPAC, generally with an upward trend of their *Keyness* throughout the investigated period. However, while two of them distribute very differently in the two corpora, with their *Keyness* rocketing in Chui's first term, the other one, 博彩 (LT: gambling), has its *Keyness* started rocketing in Ho's second term and is with identical *Keyness* in Ho's second and Chui's first term. Throughout the period under investigation, the *Keyness* of 博彩 (LT: gambling) presents a general upward trend. In the examination of this key word, it is found that there is an increase in the involvement of the opposite, "non-gaming". Regarding the key verbs attained from the *Keyword* search, there is a key verb for making a promise in CHPAC while there are key verbs for putting plans into practice in CCPAC. While there are key verbs for improving and refining in both corpora, there is a key verb for introducing new goals in CCPAC. For the key words for labeling the speaker of the Policy Addresses, the first-person plural pronouns are far more frequently applied in CHPAC, while the Government is labeled with the name of the Government per se more often in CCPAC.

## 4.2 Contextualizing Key Words

Lexical items are with open representation in different collocations, or more broadly, in different linguistic contexts. More specific meanings can be interpreted in the lexical items with particular collocations. This section implements other corpus tools, *Collocates* and *Concordance*, to examine the linguistic contexts of the key words identified in the previous section to investigate their representation with more detail.

The collocation analysis in this section is first done with the corpus tool *Concordance* to examine the colligation of the key words, which is followed by the examination with another corpus tool, *Collocates*. The *Collocates* search provided by corpus software can be done with various measures. As Galasova et al. (2017) say, despite the existence of different *Collocates* measures, T-score and MI-score are holding the dominant positions in most recent studies, such as Bestgen and Granger (2014), Durrant & Schmitt (2009), Ellis et al. (2008), Granger and Betgen (2014), Siyanova-Chanturia (2015). To get the more apparent and convincing results, the *Collocates* search in the present study is done with both measures. Taking reference from Sinclair (1991), the range for the *Collocates* search is set as 4L to 4R, which means four words on the left and four words on the right. To attain a manageable range of apparent collocations of the key words, the *Collocates* search focuses on the results with meanwhile MI higher than three and a T-score higher than three.

After obtaining the *Collocates* with the mentioned setting, the corpus tool *Concordance* will be implemented again to attain the frequent clusters in particular structures in accordance with the apparent trend of the colligation of the nodes if any.

### 4.2.1 Key Words with Reference to Policy Foci

As mentioned, the key words with the referent of policy foci are only identified in CCPAC. Two of them refer to the two different aspects of the Government's attention and the other one refers to the state of some particular aspects. The following, three key words are used as the node words to examine their linguistic contexts.

*Collocations of 博彩 (LT: gambling)*

博彩 (LT: gaming/gambling) presents an upward trend in the frequency and *Keyness* throughout the whole investigated period. With the detailed examination of its *Concordance* lines, it is found that the colligation of this key word is mainly Noun (key word)+Noun, in both corpora. To further investigate the linguistic context of this key word, a *Collocate* search is conducted with the mentioned setting. Table 4.4 summarizes the apparent *Collocates* attained from the search.

**Table 4.4**  Collocates of 博彩 (LT: gambling) in CHPAC and CCPAC

| CHPAC | | | CCPAC | | |
|---|---|---|---|---|---|
| Collocate | T-score | MI | Collocate | T-score | MI |
| 業 | 6.70094 | 9.85107 | 業 | 7.2609 | 8.56611 |
| 發展 | 3.83231 | 4.57611 | 發展 | 4.99111 | 4.66347 |
| 旅遊 | 3.1384 | 7.04888 | 企業 | 4.55729 | 7.50181 |
| 管理 | 3.13788 | 7.01818 | 推動 | 3.39029 | 5.55244 |
| | | | 監管 | 3.30096 | 7.72647 |
| | | | 加強 | 3.20058 | 4.83694 |

With the *Collocates*, in CHPAC, this key word most frequently acts as part of the noun group 博彩業 (LT: gaming industry) as 65.6% of all the *Concordance* lines of this key word in the corpus. This word group denotes the name of the pillar industry of the city. This noun group also acts as part of another noun group that refers to the industry in a broader sense as 旅遊博彩業 (LT: tourism and gaming industry) in 12.5% of all the *Concordance* lines of the key word in the corpus. The salient word group 博彩業 (LT: gaming industry) also collocates with the word 管理 (LT: management) in 11.9% of its Concordance lines to form the noun groups denoting the process of managing the industry, such as 博彩業管理 (LT: management of gaming industry). In addition to the mentioned neutral noun groups, the key word also collocates with a positive word 發展 (LT: to develop/development) to form word groups denoting the process of the growth and change of the gaming industry,, such as 發展旅遊博彩業 (LT: to develop tourist and gaming industry) and 博彩業發展 (LT: gaming industry's development).

In CCPAC, there are more neutral and positive *Collocates* with certain significance. Similar to CHPAC, with the most significant *Collocate*, this key word forms the neutral noun group 博彩業 (LT: gaming industry). In addition to the one denoting the general economic activity related to the gaming elements, with the apparent *Collocates*, there is another neutral noun group formed to denote the specific companies involved in the gaming industry as 博彩企業 (LT: gaming enterprises). The salient word group which is the name of the industry 博彩業 (LT: gaming industry) also frequently co-occurs with the positive Collocate 發展 (LT: to develop / development) to form the groups with reference to the healthy and long-term growth of the industry as 博彩業健康發展 (LT: healthy development of gaming industry), 博彩業有序發展 (LT: development of gaming industry in an orderly manner) and 博彩業的長遠發展 (LT: long-term development of gaming industry).

It is worth noticing that one of the distinct Collocates in CCPAC, 推動 (LT: to promote), co-occurs not only with the noun groups 博彩業 (LT: gaming industry) and 博彩企業 (LT: gaming enterprises), but also, more significantly and more frequently, with the noun group 負責任博彩 (LT: responsible gaming), in which, the modifier 負責任 (LT: responsible) acts as a positive modal lexical for the root of the noun group 博彩 (LT: gambling). 負責任博彩 (LT: responsible gaming) is a noun group that first appears in Chui's first Policy Address (PA 2010), with the precise definition given by the Institute for the Study of Commercial Gaming, which is an institute of the University of Macau, "Responsible Gambling occurs in a properly regulated environment where one's involvement in gambling activities brings no harm to the gamblers, family members, friends, other gamblers, or casino staff; nor would it lead to negative consequences for the local community and residents. In other words, the objective of Responsible Gambling is a practice that confines the gambling related damage to a socially acceptable level." From the definition above, this noun group conveys the meaning of the control on the gaming industry.

The other distinctive positive *Collocate* in CCPAC, 加強 (LT: strengthen), co-occurs with not only the name of 博彩業 (LT: gaming industry), but also, meanwhile, the words with reference to the supervision and control over the gaming industry as 監管 (LT: monitor) and 調控 (LT: facilitate and control). Compared with the relatively more neutral *Collocate* as 管理 (LT: management) in CHPAC, the apparent word groups with 監管 (LT: monitor) and 調控 (LT: facilitate and control) in CCPAC are with reference to having more control and making changes to the industry.

**Example 1** Linguistic Context of 博彩 (LT: gambling) in CHPAC and CCPAC

| Corpus | Text |
|---|---|
| CHPAC | 博彩業的發展, 是社會關注的焦點。<br>LT: The development of the gaming industry is the focus of the public attention |
| CCPAC | 推動博彩企業承擔負責任博彩的社會責任, 共同促進 旅遊博彩業健康發展。<br>We will also urge gaming operators to act with social responsibility to promote "responsible gaming", and join efforts to facilitate the healthy development of tourism and the gaming industry |
| CHPAC | 如何審視和處理博彩業發展, 亦是落實經濟適度多元化方針 的重要一環。<br>As we implement adequate diversification of the economy, it is important to determine how to review and manage the gaming industry's development |
| CCPAC | 維持博彩業健康發展, 培育新興行業成長<br>Maintain healthy growth of the gaming industry and develop other emerging industries<br>積極建設世界旅遊休閒中心, 堅定推進經濟適度多元, 務實調控博彩業 的發展速度, 促進博彩業有序發展。<br>With the aim of establishing Macao as a World tourism and leisure centre, the Government promoted optimum diversification of the economy, and controlled the pace of growth of the gaming industry to achieve progress in an orderly manner<br>適時對貴賓廳營運進 行分析, 研究加強監管, 以有利博彩業的長遠發展。<br>The Government will also examine the operations of VIP rooms when appropriate, and consider strengthening regulations to facilitate long-term development of the gaming industry |
| CHPAC | 由於澳門博彩業過去長期維持獨家經營的環境, 故此, 開放模式之下的 博彩業管理經驗還有待進一步積累。<br>[S]ince Macao's gaming business was long operated as a monopoly, we need more time to accumulate management experience in the new era of liberalization |
| CCPAC | 加強對博彩業的監管和調控, 努力降低相關社會成本。<br>We shall also impose stronger supervision and regulation of the gaming industry, to minimise related social costs |

(continued)

(continued)

| Corpus | Text |
|--------|------|
| CCPAC | 加大力度防治病態賭博和問題賭博, 致力推動負責任博彩。<br>[T]he Government will make more effort to prevent and regulate pathological gambling and problem gambling |

*Collocations of 民生 (LT: people's lives)*

The key word 民生 (LT: people's lives) denotes the public's experience, activities, and ways of living. As mentioned in the section about the distribution of the key words, the *Keyness* of this key word rockets in Chui's terms, with the highest in Chui's first term. Though it falls in Chui's second term, the *Keyness* of 民生 (LT: people's lives) in this term is still 12.62 times higher than it does in Ho's first term and 3.15 times higher than it does in Ho's second. With the setting mentioned before, the significant *Collocates* of this key word are summarized in Table 4.5.

Though the key word 民生 (LT: people's lives) is with far higher *Keyness* in CCPAC than it does in CHPAC, the linguistic context of this key word presents similarly in both corpora as having 改善 (LT: refine) as the most significant *Collocate*. With this most salient Collocate, 民生 (LT: people's lives) forms the word groups which denote removing unwanted elements and making minor changes to improve the people's lives in the city,, such as 改善民生素質 (LT: improve the quality of life) and 民生的改善 (LT: the improvement of people's lives).

There is another significant *Collocate* in CHPAC, which forms a noun group with the key word denoting the general public system of the Government in terms of the people's lives, as 民生服務 (LT: services with respect to people's wellbeing).

In CCPAC, the *Collocate* which is ranked second on the list following 改善 (LT: refine) is with reference to the governmental policy foci as 經濟 (LT: economy). The key word's co-occurrence with the other policy focus reflects that these two policy

**Table 4.5** Collocates of 民生 (LT: people's lives) in CHPAC and CCPAC

| CHPAC | | | CCPAC | | |
|-------|---------|---------|-------|---------|---------|
| Collocate | T-score | MI | Collocate | T-score | MI |
| 改善 | 3.58175 | 7.24331 | 改善 | 5.88505 | 7.5748 |
| 服務 | 3.393 | 5.60641 | 經濟 | 4.44073 | 5.01376 |
| 發展 | 3.00982 | 4.37448 | 措施 | 4.40386 | 6.03343 |
| | | | 發展 | 4.13704 | 3.7383 |
| | | | 持續 | 3.65955 | 5.51003 |
| | | | 各項 | 3.26184 | 5.91975 |
| | | | 完善 | 3.18389 | 4.64315 |
| | | | 綜合 | 3.0906 | 5.4633 |
| | | | 機制 | 3.06394 | 5.00712 |

foci, 民生 (LT: people's lives) and 經濟 (LT: economy) are frequently discussed together by the Government.

While there is a salient Collocate in CHPAC 服務 (LT: service) forms a word group with the key word 民生 (LT: people's lives) denoting the general public system of the government in terms of the people's lives, there are other significant *Collocates* in CCPAC to form word groups with the key word to similarly refer to the name of the system of people's livelihood. They are 措施 (LT: initiative or measures) and 機制 (LT: mechanism). The latter one, similarly, denotes the general public system in terms of people's wellbeing; the former one, as the more significant one, denotes, more specifically, the Government's plan or course of action for the lives of the people in the city as 民生措施 (LT: initiatives concerning people's well-being) or 民生政策措施 (LT: livelihood-related policy measures).

As presented in Table 4.5, there is another significant Collocate, 完善 (LT: to perfect), which is with a similar denotation to the most salient Collocate of both corpora, 改善 (refine). 完善 (to perfect) co-occurs with the key word 民生 (LT: people's lives) to form word groups denoting to perfect the governmental measures related to people's lives,, such as 完善民生措施 (LT: perfect livelihood measures).

持續 (LT: continue, continuously) is another significant Collocate of the key word 民生 (LT: people's lives) in CCPAC. It acts as a modal lexical to modify the other *Collocates* 改善 (LT: refine) and 完善 (LT: perfect) as well as other words with similar reference as making positive progress as 提升 (LT: improve), 提高 (LT: improve/increase) and 優化 (LT: optimise) to form word groups with reference to making positive process toward people's livelihood and well-being in a non-stopping manner.

The other distinctive *Collocate* from CCPAC, 各項 (LT: various), co-occurs with the key word 民生 (LT: people's livelihood) to form word groups denoting different sorts of livelihood-related policies and measures, such as 各項民生政策措施 (LT: various livelihood-related policy measures) and 民生領域的各項工作 (LT: policies affecting many aspects of people's well-being).

**Example 2** Linguistic Context of 民生 (LT: people's lives) in CHPAC and CCPAC

| Corpus | Text |
| --- | --- |
| CHPAC | 發展經濟的根本目的, 就在於改善民生<br>The basic objective of economic development is to improve people's livelihoods<br>從明年開始, 政府的民生服務, 將更加明確地指向提升市民綜合生活素質的目標。<br>Beginning next year, Government services related to people's livelihoods will specifically aim to enhance the holistic quality of life for Macao's citizens |
| CCPAC | 整體來看, 經濟保持增長, 財政金融穩健, 民生持續完善<br>As a whole, our economy has maintained growth, our fiscal and financial conditions have been sound and stable, and our people's standard of living has steadily improved<br>力求更科學、更客觀地完善各項民生政策措施<br>Through studying population policy, the Government will employ more scientific and objective methods to improve every policy and initiative for enhancing people's livelihoods |

**Table 4.6** Collocates of 多元 (LT: diversification) in CHPAC and CCPAC

| CHPAC | | | CCPAC | | |
|---|---|---|---|---|---|
| Collocate | T-score | MI | Collocate | T-score | MI |
| 適度 | 4.79253 | 7.504 | 經濟 | 8.24071 | 3.978 |
| 經濟 | 3.56053 | 3.324 | 適度 | 7.53604 | 6.096 |
| | | | 促進 | 4.72576 | 3.097 |

*Collocations of 多元 (LT: diversification)*

As mentioned in Sect. 4.3.1, the frequency of 多元 (LT: diversification) presents an upward trend throughout the investigated period and there is a noticeable increase in 2007 as well. With the mentioned setting of *Collocate* search, the significant *Collocates* of 多元 *(LT: diversification)* are attained. They are summarized in Table 4.6.

The results of the *Collocates* search reveal that 適度 (LT: adequate) and 經濟 (LT: economy) are the common *Collocates* in both corpora and both act as the most frequent ones in both CHPAC and CCPAC. With these two common significant *Collocates*, the key word 多元 (LT: diversification) forms noun groups with reference to the adequate diversification of the economic system of the city, such as 經濟多元 (LT: diversified economy), 經濟適度多元 (LT: adequate economic diversification). The word groups with this reference first appeared in PA2007c as 經濟適度多元化 (LT: adequate diversification of the economy), which are in use in the verbal version of each Policy Address in Chinese in the rest of the investigated period and account for 69.2% of all the Concordance lines of the key word 多元 (LT: diversification) in the corpus with all the verbal version of the Policy Addresses in Chinese.

In CCPAC, the other salient *Collocates* of 多元 (LT: diversification) in CCPAC show that those apparent noun groups of the key word 多元 (LT: diversification) coexist alongside the verb 促進 (LT: to reinforce) to convey meaning of making the diversification happen earlier and faster, for example 促進經濟適度多元 (LT: to facilitate adequate economic diversification).

**Example 3** Linguistic Context of 多元 (LT: diversification) in CHPAC and CCPAC

| Corpus | Text |
|---|---|
| CHPAC | 經濟適度多元化, 有助於優化產業結構、促進經濟安全, 也有利於增加 就業選擇 和機會<br>Adequate diversification of the economy facilitates the streamlining of industry structure, enhances economic security, and increases employment choices and opportunities |
| CCPAC | 促進彼此互補共贏, 並藉此突破自身發展的瓶頸, 拓展特區發展空間, 促進經濟適度多元。<br>We will also foster complementary and win–win relationships, overcome bottlenecks in our present development, identify new areas for development, and promote adequate economic diversification |

The *Collocate* and *Concordance* search display linguistic contexts of these three key words referring to policy foci and their similarity and differences in CHPAC and CCPAC. In the observation of their linguistic contexts, it is found that the most apparent word groups of the key words are with similar denotations in both CHPAC and CCPAC. However, the apparent *Collocates* in CCPAC present more specific or various governmental work relevant to the general foci.

## *4.2.2 Key Words with Reference to Actions*

As mentioned above, there are key words that are with reference to the Government's actions identified in both CHPAC and CPPAC. The key words in this group are with common denotation as improving and refining the goals, and meanwhile, some of them are with distinctive references respectively in both corpora. While there are distinctive key words which convey the mental processes for reflecting positive attitude toward the participants in CHPAC, there are distinctive ones in CCPAC that conveys the material processes for introducing new goals, putting the goals in effect, as well as giving and supplying. In examining the *Concordance* lines of these key words, it is found that they mainly serve the role as verbs in the texts. With the objective of investigating the significant actions taken by the Government, the following sections aim at identifying the significant processes introduced by this group of key words in the verbal version of the selected Policy Addresses in Chinese. The collocation analysis in the following, hence, focuses on the key words act as verbs which are named as key verbs in the rest of the following.

*Collocations of common key verbs (improving and/or refining)*

The common key verbs in CHPAC and CCPAC are with reference to improving or refining the goals as 提升 (LT: to increase), 優化 (LT: to optimize), 促進 (LT: to reinforce) and 完善 (LT: to refine). Through examining the Concordance lines of the common key verbs, it is found that the colligation of this group of key verbs is mainly Verb+Noun/noun group, with Halliday's terms, vector (introducing material processes) and goal(s). To further examine the nouns or noun groups that collocate with this particular group of key words, the *Collocate* search is firstly done with the mentioned setting but with the range set as from 0 to 4R, which means to examine the four words on the right of the key verbs. Table 4.7 presents the top 15 significant nouns attained and Tables 4.8 and 4.9 summarize their application.

The nouns attained from the *Collocate* search are categorized in accordance with their references (Table 4.8). There are nouns referring to the goals about governmental operations, people's livelihood, different areas of political concerns, and a goal related to the economic environment. While the salient *Collocates* with the first three references are attained in both corpora, the significant *Collocate* with the last reference is attained from CHPAC only.

**Table 4.7** Significant nouns co-occurring with the common key verbs

| CHPAC | | | CCPAC | | |
|---|---|---|---|---|---|
| Collocate | T-score | MI | Collocate | T-score | MI |
| 社會 | 7.06888 | 4.71608 | 發展 | 7.18918 | 4.66914 |
| 素質 | 6.49316 | 6.67261 | 服務 | 7.10122 | 6.03616 |
| 服務 | 6.45566 | 5.22308 | 建設 | 6.62615 | 5.44049 |
| 政府 | 6.24356 | 4.08931 | 居民 | 6.52897 | 5.22601 |
| 經濟 | 5.76131 | 5.25648 | 經濟 | 6.48932 | 5.52628 |
| 市民 | 5.75295 | 4.60211 | 社會 | 5.96803 | 4.97221 |
| 發展 | 5.52633 | 3.92403 | 區域 | 5.76253 | 6.4132 |
| 教育 | 5.45546 | 5.63159 | 合作 | 5.76168 | 5.25989 |
| 水平 | 5.4283 | 6.80668 | 公共 | 5.65596 | 6.01866 |
| 生活 | 5.00814 | 5.81015 | 教育 | 5.62866 | 5.63117 |
| 就業 | 4.72831 | 6.15033 | 素質 | 5.6194 | 7.23886 |
| 環境 | 4.72133 | 6.00831 | 政府 | 5.59927 | 4.65353 |
| 合作 | 4.6346 | 8.02886 | 機制 | 5.57612 | 6.1306 |
| 管理 | 4.41284 | 6.43982 | 管理 | 5.51637 | 6.7594 |
| 市場 | 4.39973 | 5.9487 | 醫療 | 5.41343 | 6.42385 |

**Table 4.8** Categories of the significant nouns co-occurring with the common key verbs (improving/refining)

| | CHPAC | CCPAC |
|---|---|---|
| Governmental operation | 服務 (service), 政府 (government), 管理 (management) | 服務 (service), 政府 (government), 機制 (mechanism), 管理 (management) |
| People's livelihood | 社會 (society), 市民 (citizen), 生活 (living), 就業 (employment) | 居民 (residents), 社會 (society) |
| Areas of policy | 經濟 (economy), 教育 (education) | 經濟 (economy), 教育 (education), 醫療 (medical care) |
| Economic environment of the society | 市場 (market) | – |
| Other policy foci | 合作 (cooperation) | 區域(regions), 合作(cooperation) |
| Other general references | 素質 (quality), 發展 (development), 水平 (level), 環境 (environment) | 發展 (development), 建設 (construction), 公共 (public), 素質 (quality) |

**Table 4.9** Significant goals being improved/refined in CHPAC and CCPAC

| Corpus | CHPAC | | CCPAC | |
|---|---|---|---|---|
| Goals (being improved/refined) | Economy | 34.8% | Economy | 32.8% |
| | People's livelihood | 21.7% | People's livelihood | 22.7% |
| | Public administration | 15.2% | Regional cooperation | 16.4% |
| | Regional cooperation | 9.8% | Public administration | 14.8% |
| | Population quality | 8.7% | Population quality | 5.5% |
| | Social development | 6.5% | Legal environment | 4.7% |

When conducting the *Collocate* search with each of the five common key verbs, it is found that the most significant *Collocate* (the Collocate with the highest T-score and MI) of each of the five common key verbs remain the same in CHPAC and CCPAC. They co-occur as 提升 (LT: to enhance) with 素質 (LT: quality), 優化 (LT: to optimise) with 環境 (LT: environment), 促進 (LT: to promote) with 經濟 (LT: economy), 加強 (LT: strengthen) with 合作 (LT: cooperation), as well as 完善 (LT: improve) with 機制 (LT: mechanisms). To further examine the linguistic contexts of the common key verbs, a *Concordance* search is done with these five pairs of significant collocations. In CHPAC, it is found that 34.8% of the *Concordance* under investigation are with reference to the **economy**, 21.7% to **people's livelihood**, 15.2% to **public administration**, 9.8% to **regional cooperation**, 8.7% to **quality of the population** and 6.5% to **social development** (Table 4.9).

Correspondingly, in CCPAC, there are 32.8% of the lines with reference to the **economy**, 22.7% to **people's livelihood**, 16.4% to **regional cooperation**, 14.8% to **public administration** and 5.5% to **population quality** (Table 4.9). Hence, different from CHPAC, the *Concordance* lines with regional cooperation as the goals are more frequent than those with public administration in CCPAC. Instead of the goals referring to social development, 4.7% of the *Concordance* lines in CCPAC are with reference to the **legal environment** of the society as 法治環境 (LT: legal environment), 立法籌機制 (LT: the legal coordination mechanism), which do not exist in CHPAC. These references of the Concordance directly reflect the categories of goals of the five common key verbs.

Though the goals with general reference to the **economy** are similar in proportion and ranked as the top in both corpora, they are differences in their more specific references. In CHPAC, the word groups used to represent this type of goals mainly refer to **recovery of economic system of the society** as 經濟復甦 (LT: recovery of economy) with 25% of the goals with general reference as economy, and **coordinated economic development** as 經濟的協調發展 (LT: the coordinated development of economy) with 9% of the same group. Differently, in CCPAC, 53% of the goals with the same general reference are represented by the word groups, which denote the **adequate diversification of the economic system of the society** as, such as 經濟適度多元 (LT: adequate economic diversification), which only exist in one of the *Concordance* lines attained from the search in CHPAC. This most apparent one is followed by the goals with similar proportion represented by the word groups which denote **coordinated economic development**, such as 經濟社會協調發展 (LT: orderly development of economy and society) in 18% of all the goals with the same general reference to economy in the corpus, **the economic environment of the society**, such as 營商環境 (LT: business environment) with 13% and **the continuation of socioeconomic development**, such as 經濟社會可持續發展 (LT: sustainable socio-economic development) with 11%.

**People's livelihood**, as a common goal of the process of improving and refining in both corpora, different from economy, is represented by the word groups with similar specific references in CHPAC and CCPAC. 65% of the goals with this general reference in CHPAC denotes the living quality of the residents, such as 提升居民生活素質 (LT: enhance residents' living quality) and 優化居民生活環境 (LT: improve the living environment), which are followed by the ones referring to education with 25%, such as 提升教學質素 (LT: enhance the teaching quality) and 提升師資的素質 (LT: improve teachers' quality). Likewise, in CCPAC, within the goals of the processes of improving or refining which are referring to people's livelihood, residents' living quality and education are also ranked as the most frequent two references. In CCPAC, 63% of the goals of the processes of improving and refining are represented by the word groups which are specifically denoting residents' living quality, such as 改善人居環境 (LT: improve overall quality of life) and 優化居民的出行環境 (LT: improve commuting conditions), and 21% denoting education, such as 優化持續教育 (LT: optimize continuous education) and 加強校園愛國愛澳教育 (LT: enhance patriotic education). The examples above show that, in CCPAC, the distribution of the categories of the goals presents similarly to how they do in CHPAC, yet, the goals themselves in CCPAC are relatively more specific when compared to the similar ones in CHPAC.

Another apparent distinctive feature identified in this investigation is related to one of the top four goals, **public administration**. In CHPAC, the goals with this general reference are represented by the word groups denoting **the quality of governing**, such as 施政素質 (LT: administration quality), **the quality of the civil servants**, such as 公務人員素質 (LT: quality of civil servants), **the cooperation among governmental departments**, such as 部門合作 (LT: departmental cooperation), and **the governmental mechanism for the communication between the public and the Government as consultation and complaining**, such as 投訴機制 (LT: mechanism for dealing with complaints) and 諮詢機制 (LT: enquiry system). In CCPAC, the goals with the same general reference are represented by the word groups denoting, similarly, **the quality of civil servants**, such as 公務人員素質 (LT: quality of civil servants) and **the quality of governmental services**, such as 公共服務評估機制 (LT: the mechanism for evaluating public services quality). In CCPAC, there are also goals represented by the word groups with distinctive denotation as the response mechanism to emergency, such as 應急機制 (LT: emergency response mechanism) and 氣候通報機制 (LT: weather forecast system), which do not exist in the whole data set of CHPAC.

**Example 4** Linguistic Context of common key verbs in CHPAC and CCPAC

| Corpus | Text |
|---|---|
| CCPAC | 特區政府將致力通過加強區域法律交流, 以及與其他國家或地區的法務聯繫, 優化法治環境, 以更好地保障澳門居民的切身利益。<br>The Government is dedicated to improving the legal environment through enhancing regional exchange and connections with other countries and regions on legal matters, to best safeguard the vital interests of Macao people<br>特區政府繼續完善立法統籌機制, 推進重大立法計劃的落實。<br>The Government will also continue to perfect the legal coordination mechanism, and step up the implementation of major legislative plans |
| CHPAC | 未來一年, 為了應對經濟環境和客源狀況波動, 促進本地區經濟的協調發展, 澳門特區將在強化原有產業優勢的同時, 加大經濟適度多元化的力度。In the coming year, to tackle the fluctuations in the economic environment and the tourist market, and to facilitate the coordinated development of the local economy, the MSAR Government will reinforce adequate economic diversification while consolidating the advantages of existing industries |
| CCPAC | 面向居民, 聆聽民意, 廉安守法, 促進經濟適度多元發展, 構建社會包容與和諧的氛圍, 使特區邁向一個發展新階段。<br>We will put people first, heed public opinion, and maintain clean administration as well as the rule of law, to promote adequate diversification of the economy and build an inclusive and harmonious society<br>特區政府加強對外交流, 積極參與區域合作, 發展澳台關係, 努力輔助中小企業, 不斷優化營商環境<br>The Government has continued to strengthen overseas exchanges, participate in regional cooperation, develop Macao-Taiwan relations, support small and medium-sized enterprises, and improve the business environment<br>加速建設"一個中心, 一個平台", 促進澳門經濟社會可持續發展<br>Expedite the establishment of "One Centre, One Platform", to promote sustainable socio-economic development of Macao |
| CHPAC | 切實推進交通問題的解決, 是特區政府當務之急, 這既是發展經濟的要求, 更是提升居民生活素質的需要。<br>Practical steps to solve traffic problems are currently a pressing issue for the MSAR Government. These are also essential for both Macao's economic development and the enhancement of the quality of life of our citizens<br>電信、科技、能源、港務發展與時並進, 環保宣傳加大力度, 持續優化居民生活環境, 提高城市現代化水平。<br>Telecommunications, technology, energy and maritime services developed with the times. The Government also doubled its efforts in promoting environmental protection, improving the living environment and facilitating urban modernisation<br>高等院校致力提升教學素質, 培育具有國際視野、創新思維及具備人文素養的高素質人才。<br>Tertiary education institutions strived to improve the quality of education, cultivating talented individuals with global vision, creative minds and cultural knowledge |

(continued)

(continued)

| Corpus | Text |
|--------|------|
| CCPAC | 優化居民的出行環境, 構建無障礙步行空間<br>The Government will improve commuting conditions for the public by developing accessible walkways<br>加強師資培訓及優化持續教育<br>The Government will also strengthen teacher training and optimise continuous education<br>官民合作加強校園愛國愛澳教育, 增強學生的國家意識和民族認同。<br>Cooperation between the Government and the public will be promoted in schools, to enhance patriotic education and students' national awareness and belonging |
| CHPAC | 我們要求各級官員面對特區發展新階段的考驗, 提高施政素質<br>Government officials at every level must face up to the challenges that have arisen in this new stage in our development, and raise the quality of their administration<br>肅貪倡廉是保持和提升公務人員素質的重要一環。<br>Fighting corruption and advocating honesty and integrity constitutes a vital link in maintaining and improving the quality of public servants<br>政府將繼續積極聽取市民的意見, 故將檢討並完善投訴機制, 以達促進溝通、加強監督、改進工作的目的;<br>The Government will continue to listen to opinions from citizens, review and improve the mechanisms for administrative complaints so as to enhance communication, strengthen public supervision and improve administrative work<br>擴大、完善政府的諮詢機制, 使之成為支持政府施政, 優化政府決策的重要民意中介<br>We will expand and enhance the consultation system, transforming it into a key intermediary between the Government and the public that supports policy-making and optimises the decision-making process |
| CCPAC | 優化培訓工作的質量, 提升公務人員素質, 更好地為特區建設服務。<br>We will also improve training to enhance quality of civil servants, so they can provide better services for Macao and its people<br>穩步推進政府績效管理, 完善公共服務評估機制。<br>We will steadily implement government performance management, improve the mechanism for evaluating public services quality<br>完善應急機制, 強化公共安全<br>Optimise the emergency response mechanism and enhance public safety<br>完善氣候預報機制, 增強各區渠網的排放能力, 重視颱風和水浸問題對城市的影響。<br>improve the weather forecast system; enhance the discharge capability of drainage networks in different districts, and pay special attention to the impacts of typhoons and flooding |

*Collocations of distinctive key verbs in CHPAC*

確保 (LT: ensure) is the distinctive key verb identified in CHPAC, which is used to make a promise that the goal(s) introduced will occur or be the case. With the *Concordance* search of this key verb, it is found that the colligation of it is mainly Verb+Noun/Noun group. To further investigate the nouns or noun groups which collocate with this key verb, in a like manner, the *Collocate* search is done with the mentioned setting but with the range set as from 0 to 4R, which means to examine the four words on the right of the key word. As a word with far lower *Keyness* in

**Table 4.10** Significant lexical collocates of 確保 (ensure) in CHPAC

| Collocate | T-score | MI |
|-----------|---------|---------|
| 社會 | 4.07824 | 3.95705 |
| 市民 | 3.64509 | 4.08701 |

CCPAC than in CHPAC, there is no Collocate with a T-score higher than 3 attained in CCPAC with the *Collocate* search in the mentioned setting. The *Collocate* search in this section, hence, focuses on CHPAC only to examine the goals of this distinctive key verb in CHPAC (Table 4.10).

With the apparent *Collocates*, it is found that the stability and harmony of the society, as well as the living quality of the citizens, are the most important phenomenon of the apparent mental process, promising, in CHPAC, which is to bring the idea into hypothetical existence. With the most apparent Collocate 社會 (LT: society), the key verb 確保 (ensure) acts as the root in the verb groups for promising the stability and harmony of the society, such as 確保社會穩定 (LT: guarantee social stability) and 確保社會和階 (LT: ensure social harmony). With the second apparent *Collocate* 市民 (LT: citizen), the key verb forms some significant verb groups refer to ensuring the living quality of citizens, such as 確保市民安居樂業 (LT: ensure the quality of life of the citizens).

**Example 5** Linguistic context of distinctive key verbs in CHPAC and CCPAC

| Corpus | Text |
|--------|------|
| CHPAC | 這就說明, 提高市民的生活質量, 是"以民為本"理念的體現, 是澳門社會 對人的關懷的回應, 亦是確保社會穩定和發展的客觀要求。<br>Raising our citizens' quality of life is an example of the principle of "Putting the people's interests first", and of the entire community caring for the wellbeing of its individual members; it is also a prerequisite for ensuring stability and development<br>改善生活質素, 確保社會和諧<br>Improving living standards and ensuring social<br>這對確保市民安居樂業、建設更具吸引力的 市場環境, 産生積極的作用。<br>These agencies are helping to ensure that Macao residents are adequately protected and appreciated by society. These are necessary conditions for building an attractive market environment |

(continued)

(continued)

| Corpus | Text |
|---|---|
| CCPAC | 建設世界旅遊休閒中心, 推動經濟適度多元發展<br>Establish Macao as a World tourism and leisure centre and promote adequate diversification of the economy<br>全力落實教育興澳, 人才建澳的發展戰略。<br>The Government will next year fully implement the development strategy of "Letting Macao thrive through education" and "Building Macao with talent"<br>繼續對就讀大專和研究生課程的本澳學生, 發放學習用品津貼3,000元。<br>We will continue providing a Stationery Allowance of 3,000 patacas to each Macao student pursuing tertiary education or postgraduate studies<br>延續發放 "書簿津貼", 維持幼兒教育學生每學年 2,000 元, 小學生每 學年 2,600 元, 中學生每學年 3,000 元。<br>The Government will continue to disburse the Textbook Allowance. The allowances per academic year for each kindergarten pupil, primary school student and secondary school student will remain at 2,000 patacas, 2,600 patacas and 3,000 patacas, respectively<br>建議繼續向受益家庭多發放一份全數經濟援助金; 向三類弱勢家庭發放特別補助; 透過"社會融和計劃"發放特別生活津貼。<br>The Government suggests continuing to disburse an extra one month's financial assistance to families registered with the Social Welfare Bureau, a special subsidy for three categories of disadvantaged families, and a special living allowance through the Social Inclusion Scheme |

*Collocations of distinctive key verbs in CCPAC*

In CCPAC, the distinctive key verbs identified are 建設 (LT: to build/construction), 落實 (LT: to implement) and 發放 (LT: to grant/to offer/to provide). With the denotation of these key verbs, they are the vector for introducing material processes. Following the mentioned setting for *Collocate* search, the *Collocate* search of these three distinctive key verbs is done to examine the goals of these vectors in the material processes. Table 4.11 summarizes the significant lexical *Collocates* of each of these distinctive key verbs in CCPAC.

With the apparent *Collocates*, the most salient distinctive key verb attained in CCPAC, 建設 (to build/construction), forms some significant verb groups with reference to the construction of the World Centre of Tourism and Leisure, such as 建設世界旅遊休閒中心 (LT: building a World travel and leisure hub). "World Centre of Tourism and Leisure" is a new concept that first appeared in Policy Address 2010 (the start of Chui's two terms), which is a phrase created for the recent revolution of the development of Macao's economic pillar, the gaming industry.

The second salient distinctive key verb attained in CCPAC, 落實 (LT: to implement), with its apparent *Collocates*, acts as the vector in the verb groups that refer to putting the goals about people's livelihood, public administration, regional cooperation, legal environment of the city, the economy as well as tourism into effect. Most of the goals in the verb groups relate to people's livelihood, which account for 27% of all and is followed by the goals relate to public administration and regional

**Table 4.11** Significant lexical *Collocates* of distinctive key verbs in CCPAC

| Identified key verb | *Collocate* | T-score | MI |
|---|---|---|---|
| 建設 (LT: to build/construction) | 中心 (LT: centre) | 4.55236 | 5.08635 |
| | 城市 (LT: city) | 4.50226 | 4.63974 |
| | 休閒 (LT: leisure) | 4.15484 | 5.59465 |
| | 世界 (LT: World) | 4.14944 | 5.50849 |
| | 旅遊 (LT: travel) | 3.93964 | 4.49016 |
| | 宜 (LT: suitable) | 3.24751 | 5.58460 |
| 落實 (LT: to implement) | 澳 (LT: Macau) | 3.76835 | 4.10998 |
| | 澳門 (LT: Macau) | 3.46918 | 3.26171 |
| | 粵 (LT: Guangdong) | 3.26344 | 5.96264 |
| | 施政 (LT: to govern) | 3.02767 | 4.55411 |
| 發放 (LT: to grant/to offer/to provide) | 津貼 (LT: allowance) | 4.87718 | 7.81181 |
| | 金額 (LT: amount) | 3.98425 | 7.98868 |
| | 特別 (LT: special) | 3.98220 | 7.81181 |
| | 學習 (LT: study) | 3.29763 | 7.44812 |
| | 用品 (LT: tools) | 3.15492 | 8.74671 |

cooperation (both with 22% of all). In the goals which are related to people's livelihood, 40% of their Concordance lines refer to education, such as 落實教育興澳 (LT: letting Macao thrive through education).

With the apparent Collocates, the other distinctive key verb in CCPAC, 發放 (LT: to grant/to offer/to provide), serves as a vector in the material process of providing financial support to the public with the word groups, such as 發放學習用品津貼 (LT: offer stationery allowance), 發放「書簿津貼」 (LT: offer textbook allowance), 膳食津貼 (LT: meal allowance) and 發放特別生活津貼 (LT: offer special living allowance). The Stationery allowance is the subsidy that is offered to all undergraduate students, graduates, and postgraduates students starting in 2011. With the policy of 15-year free education, the textbook allowance and the meal allowance are the subsidies which are offered to the primary and secondary school students from low-income families. The Special living allowance is the living subsidy which are provided for families with different types of difficulties. The salient word groups serve as the goals co-occurring with the key verb 發放 (to grant/to offer/to provide) are all related to the financial support to different aspects for vulnerable communities, as the families with financial problems as well as for supporting education.

### 4.2.3  Key Words with Reference to Social Groups and Institutes

As mentioned before, the identified key words with the reference to social groups and institute are mostly in common in both CHPAC and CCPAC as the nouns which denote the name of the speaker, the audience and other participants of the Policy Addresses but with a most distinctive one in CHPAC, the only personal pronoun obtained from the Keyword search, 我們 *(we, us, our, ours)*. This key pronoun is with similar reference to other key words in the same group as 政府 (LT: government), 特區政府 (LT: SAR government) or 特區 (LT: SAR), all of which are different labeling of the Government of the city under investigation in the present study. The following presents a detailed examination of the linguistic contexts of these different labeling of the Government.

*Collocation of* 我們 *(we/us/our/ours)*

The colligation of the key pronoun 我們 (*we/us/our/ours*) is mostly as collocating with an adverb and/or a verb instead of other linguistic constituents as Pronoun+(Adv.)+Verb in both CHPAC and CCPAC, which is with the similar grammatical role as the first-person plural subject pronoun *We* in English. In order to examine the adverbs and verbs collocated with this key pronoun, in particular, a *Collocate* search with the same setting as analyzing the key verbs is done with the key pronoun 我們 (*we/us/our/ours*). As set in this study, the collocation analysis will always focus on lexical words only.

As shown in Table 4.12, the apparent *Collocates* of 我們 (*we*) with both T-score and MI higher than 3 co-occurring on its right-hand side consisting of auxiliary verbs, prepositions, articles etc. **In CHPAC, there are lexical verbs with reference to the actions of pursuing progress with effort** as 加強 (LT: strengthen/enhance) and 鼓勵 (LT: encourage) **to indicate the positive attitude of the speaker**. There is also **a modal lexical verb with high epistemic modality representing high confidence of the speaker** as 相信 (LT: believe), which is with the denotation as to be sure that something is actual or possible. However, with the setting defined for this study, there is no significant *Collocate* identified in CCPAC.

*Collocates search of* 政府 *(LT: the Government) and* 特區政府 *(LT: SAR Government)*

The colligation of 政府 (LT: the Government) and 特區政府 (LT: SAR Government) are more diversified than 我們 (we/us/our)'s. Similarly, *Concordance* lines with them as the agents of the processes are the majority while there are also *Concordance* lines in which 政府 (the government), 特區政府 (SAR Government) and 特區 (SAR) serve as the modifiers of noun phrases and as the objects of verbs. With the similar setting as mentioned before, a *Collocate* search of the key words 政府 (the government), 特區 *(SAR)* and 特區政府 (SAR Government) is conducted. Because of the more diversified colligation, the range of the *Collocate* search is set as from 4L to 4R, which means 4 words from the left and 4 words from the right.

**Table 4.12** Apparent Collocates of 我們 (*we*) in CHPAC and CCPAC

| CHPAC | | | CCPAC | | |
|---|---|---|---|---|---|
| Collocate | T-score | MI | Collocate | T-score | MI |
| 繼續 | 4.93823 | 3.34509 | | | |
| 加強 | 4.04839 | 3.10075 | | | |
| 充份 | 3.78988 | 4.25069 | | | |
| 相信 | 3.26594 | 6.03205 | | | |
| 各種 | 3.25589 | 3.36617 | Nil | Nil | Nil |
| 鼓勵 | 3.16991 | 3.55767 | | | |
| 廣大 | 3.13049 | 3.37623 | | | |
| 人文 | 3.12023 | 4.07786 | | | |
| 信心 | *3.06925* | *5.08720* | | | |

It is found that, similarly, in both corpora, the names of the Government, 政府 (LT: the Government), 特區政府 (LT: SAR Government) and 特區 (LT: SAR) frequently collocate with the neutral lexical words, such as 施政 (LT: to govern), 繼續 (LT: to continue), 社會 (LT: society), 工作 (LT: work), 服務 (LT: to serve) etc. Modal lexical verbs can also be attained via the *Collocate* search of these two key words. They are, similar to the result of 我們 (we/us/our/ours), the lexical verbs that indicate the speaker's positive attitude toward the propositions, such as 發展 (LT: to develop) and 加強 (LT: to strengthen). This group of Collocates accounts for similar proportion over all *Collocates* in both corpora as 5.24% in CHPAC and 6.74% in CCPAC.

In addition to the contexts in common, there is a *Collocate*, 陽光 (LT: sunshine), in CCPAC with a T-score as 4.45 but not existing in the whole data set in CHPAC. This *Collocate* first exists in the first Policy Address of Chui's two terms, PA2010c, and is with the only collocation as 陽光政府 (LT: sunshine government) in the entire corpus, which is to label the Government with the naming as a clean and open administration for a new age.

From the above analysis, it is found that the key words with reference to social groups and institutes are with similarities and differences in their linguistic contexts in CHPAC and CCPAC. Regarding the only key pronoun in the present study, when labeling the Government, it is more frequently used in CHPAC than CCPAC. The *Collocate* search shows that it is with salient Collocates in CHPAC but not in CCPAC. With the salient Collocates, this key pronoun, in CHPAC, is apparently followed by the positive lexical verbs which refer to actions pursuing progress with effort to indicate the positive attitude of the speaker as well as modal lexical words with high epistemic to indicate the speaker's confidence and certainty toward the propositions, hence, this distinctive key pronoun is considerably applied in the linguistic contexts with lexical words which represent the positive attitude toward the propositions mentioned.

In terms of denotation of the pronoun, 我們 *(we, us, our, ours)*, it is mainly with exclusive use denoting the Government, which is with the same reference to the other two key words in the same category as 政府 (LT: the Government) and 特區政府 (LT: SAR Government). The analysis presents the statistics to show that these two key words are more frequently used in CCPAC when labeling the Government. In both corpora, they are similarly surrounded by neutral lexical verbs as well as modal lexical verbs indicating positive attitude, but with their frequency% higher in CCPAC. In addition, there is a word group with the key word 政府 (LT: the Government) in distinctive collocation in CCPAC as 陽光政府 (sunshine government). It is a word group to label the Government with the positive naming as an open government for the new age, which does not exist in CHPAC.

**Example 6** Linguistic Context of key words with reference to social groups and institutes in CHPAC and CCPAC

| Corpus | Text |
|--------|------|
| CHPAC | 我們亦加強對有發展潛力的新興產業、環保產業、高增值技術產業的扶持,力爭形成新的經濟增長點。 |
|       | We will support new industries with good growth potential,, such as the environmental protection industry and high value-added technological industries, creating new focuses for economic growth |
|       | 在弘揚公僕精神,培養優質服務文化方面,我們繼續鼓勵和要求全體公務人員將服務市民的意識常記於心 |
|       | To foster a spirit of public service and to nurture a culture of service quality, we will continue to encourage civil servants to pursue the principle of "Putting the people's interests first" |
|       | 我們相信,廣大的社工和義工朋友,一定能以其愛心和服務,鼓勵被援助者以積極的態度面對和克服困難,與我們一起建設進步而祥和的社會。 |
|       | We are confident that our social worker-friends and our volunteer-friends will, with their loving care and devotion, inspire those being helped to adopt a positive attitude and overcome their difficulties so that they will join hands with us and build up a progressive, harmonious and prosperous Macau together |
| CCPAC | 充分聽取社情民意, 致力建立陽光政府 |
|       | Heeding Public Opinion and Building an Open Administration |

*Summary of the investigation to contexts of key words*

In the investigation of the linguistic contexts of the key words, there are similarities and differences identified in the two different corpora. For the key words with reference to policy foci, three of them present similarly in their contexts as involving more elements to their meaning with their Collocates. For 博彩 (LT: gam-bling), three diachronic changes are identified: (1) there is an upward trend in the involvement of gaming enterprises rather than the industry in general; (2) modifiers which indicate healthy and long-term development of the gaming industry are with certain salience in CCPAC; (3) while there are salient word groups which denote the management of the gaming industry in CHPAC, there are salient word groups with reference to the control of the gaming industry in CCPAC.

For 多元 (LT: diversification), while its application in the texts primarily refers to the diversification of the economic system in CHPAC, it works with its linguistic contexts in CCPAC to introduce the reinforcement in the implementation of diversifying the economic system. It frequently acts as the goal for the action of growth and change in CCPAC.

For 民生 (LT: people's lives), it collocates with the verb which denotes the action of improving in CHPAC but verbs which denote the actions of improving as well as perfecting in CCPAC. Salience is also put to the related word groups with the modifier to construct the meaning of making positive progress toward people's livelihood and well-being in a non-stopping manner. It also forms salient word groups for generally naming the public system for people's lives in CHPAC but more specifically, the Government's plans or course of actions for people's lives in CCPAC.

For the key words with reference to the Government's actions, contrasts in the goals of the key verbs are discovered. In the inves-tigation into the common key verbs in CHPAC and CCPAC, it is found that economy, people's livelihood and public administration are the first three goals of the key verbs for improving and refining with particular salience in both corpora.

In terms of people's livelihood, the denotation of the goals is with similar references in both corpora as residential quality and education. However, the goals identified in CCPAC are specified into more specific aspects to these two fields.

In terms of public administration, the goal referring to the quality of the governance in general is with special salience in both corpora. However, the mechanism for public consultation and complaining is the salient one in CHPAC while the mechanism for the response to the emergency is salient in CCPAC, which does not even exist in CHPAC.

In terms of economy, the goals with particular salience in the two corpora refer to different aspects of the economic system. In CHPAC, they refer to the recovery of the economic system and coordination of economic development. In contrast, in CCPAC, while there is no particular salience put to the recovery of the economic system, the goals referring to the coordination of the economic development, the improvement of the economic environment as well as the continuation of the socioeconomic development are with certain salience in the texts.

For the key words with reference to social groups and institutes, while the first-person pronoun significantly collocates with neutral action verbs in both corpora, it also apparently collocates with positive action verbs and a modal lexical verb with high epistemic warranty in CHPAC. When examining the contexts of the names of the Government, it is found that, in both corpora, they collocate significantly with the neutral action verbs as the first-person pronoun does but meanwhile with the positive action verbs as well. In addition, in CCPAC, there is a special apparent Collocate as the positive modifier to the name of the Government, which does not even exist in the whole set of data in CHPAC.

## 4.3  Translating Key Words

After investigating the distribution and the contexts of the identified key words, their translations in the verbal version of the Policy Addresses in English are traced and analyzed with the concepts of Translation Shifts. As mentioned in Chapter three, to investigate the English translations of the key words with their authentic linguistic contexts in the same discourse type, the corpus named CSOTU is built with the State of the Union Addresses. To draw a comparison among the three corpora (namely CHPAE, CCPAE, and CSOTU), CSOTU is formed with 17 of the State of the Union Address from 2002 to 2018, with similar capacity of types and tokens with CHPAE and CCPAE. This part of analysis narrows down to focusing only on the key words with more apparent significance in representing the change of ideology construction after comparing key words attained from CHPAC and CCPAC. They consist of (1) the key words with reference to government's policy foci identified in both corpora; (2) the common key verbs in both corpora, which serve as the majority of the key verbs identified in the present study; (3) and the only personal pronoun identified in the key word search.

### 4.3.1  Key Words with Reference to Policy Foci

The translations of the three key words identified in this category, 博彩 (LT: gambling), 民生 (LT: people's lives) and 多元 (LT: diversification), are traced in the verbal version of the Policy Addresses in English to examine English translations of the key words.

*Translation of 博彩 (LT: gambling)*

A shift in the translation process is identified when tracing the key word 博彩 (LT: gambling) in the verbal version of the Policy Addresses in English. Table 4.13 summarizes the variations of the English translations of this key word throughout the investigated period. There are three translation shifts: substitution, omission and diction. In some instances, the key word 博彩 (LT: gambling) is omitted in the English version as shown in Example 7.1. In some other instances, the key word 博彩 (LT: gambling) is replaced by pronouns in the English version, as shown in Example 7.2. In conjunction with the shifts as substitution and omission with very few instances, three different words used as the English translations of the key word 博彩 (LT: gambling), namely *gambling*, *gaming* and *casino*. As evident in the statistics, the most frequent translation is *gaming* throughout the whole investigated period, which accounts for 93.8% of its English translations in CHPAC and 88% in CCPAE. The following elaborates the translation shift, diction, with contexts and examples.

In CHPAE, the key word is first translated as *gambling*, which does not act as the translation of 博彩 (LT: gambling) in any texts in CCPAE. The other translation, *gaming* first appeared as the English translation of the key word 博彩 (LT: gambling)

**Table 4.13** Translations of key word 博彩 (LT: gambling)

| Year/freq.% | 2000 | 2001 | 2002 | 2003 | 2004 | 2005 | 2006 | 2007 | 2008 | 2009 | CHPAE |
|---|---|---|---|---|---|---|---|---|---|---|---|
| Gambling | 100% | 67% | – | – | – | – | – | – | – | – | 6.3% |
| Gaming | – | 33% | 100% | 100% | 100% | 100% | 100% | 100% | 100% | 100% | 93.8% |
| Casino | – | – | – | – | – | – | – | – | – | – | 0 |
| Pronoun | – | – | – | – | – | – | – | – | – | – | 0 |
| Omission | – | – | – | – | – | – | – | – | – | – | 0 |

| Year/freq.% | 2010 | 2011 | 2012 | 2013 | 2014 | 2015 | 2016 | 2017 | 2018 | 2019 | CCPAE |
|---|---|---|---|---|---|---|---|---|---|---|---|
| Gambling | – | – | – | – | – | – | – | – | – | – | 0 |
| Gaming | 81.8% | 75% | 66.7% | 100% | 66.7% | 86.7% | 88.9% | 100% | 100% | 100% | 88% |
| Casino | – | – | – | – | – | 6.7% | 5.6% | – | – | – | 2.2% |
| Pronoun | 18.2% | 12.5% | – | – | 16.7% | – | – | – | – | – | 4.3% |
| Omission | – | 12.5% | 33.3% | – | 16.7% | 6.7% | 5.6% | – | – | – | 5.4% |

in PA2001e, which accounts for 33% of all of its translations in the same year. Thereupon, *gaming* becomes the only English translation of this key word in the rest of the texts in CHPAE. In 5.4% of the cases in CCPAC, the key word 博彩 (LT: gambling) is omitted in the English version; it is replaced by a pronoun in the English version in 4.3% of the cases. Instead of *gambling*, *casino* is the translation of this key word in 2.2% of the cases in CCPAE. Example 7 presents some instances of each of these three types of translation shifts in translating the key word 博彩 (LT: gambling). When probing into the translations, the three words *gambling*, *gaming* and *casino*, are with similarities and differences in their denotation and connotation. The word *gambling* is the gerund form of the verb "gamble" which means to risk money or possessions on the result of something uncertain, while the word *gaming* is the gerund form of the verb "game" which means to play and to amuse oneself.

Comparing the denotation of the two translations, *gaming* and *gambling*, the former one is with more general meaning as any activities for fun and amusement, while the latter one denotes more specific activities of risking money or possessions for uncertain results. Meanwhile, the idea of "risking" is emphasized in the meaning of *gambling* which offers the word negative connotation when compared to the translation *gaming* which is with a more general reference without mentioning harmful elements. In addition to *gambling* and *gaming*, the other translation, *casino*, means the public room or building where gambling activities happen, hence, it is with a negative connotation as the translation *gambling* does. As shown in Example 7.3, the translation *casino* is applied in translating the word group 博彩企業穿梭巴士 (LT: gaming enterprises shuttle buses) into *casino shuttle buses*. When using these three translations, *gambling*, *gaming* and *casino*, as the node words to search in CSOTU with the selected State of Union Addresses, it is found that these three words don't even exist in the selected State of the Union Addresses, which indicates that this group of words convey the specific significance in Macao context.

**Example 7**  Translations of the key word 博彩 (LT: gambling)

|     | Year | English text | Chinese text | Translation shift |
|-----|------|--------------|--------------|-------------------|
| 7.1 | 2014 | The government promoted optimum diversification of the economy, and controlled the pace of growth of the gaming industry *to achieve progress in an order manner* | 堅定推進經濟適度多元, 務實調控博彩業的發展速度, 促進博彩業有序發展。 | Omission |
|     | 2016 | This year, we conducted an interim review of the gaming industry, which examined the implementation of *casino operators'* concession agreements; | 政府今年進行博彩業的中期檢討, 檢視娛樂場幸運博彩經營批給執行情況, … | |

(continued)

(continued)

|  | Year | English text | Chinese text | Translation shift |
|---|---|---|---|---|
| 7.2 | 2010 | The committee will soon help to formulate policies for the development of the gaming industry, supervise *its* development and operation, enact the related provisions and regulations, and publish the guidelines | 委員會將就博彩業的發展制定有關政策, 監管博彩業的發展和運作, 訂定規範並發出指引。 | Substitution |
|  | 2014 | We will further step up our efforts in monitoring and regulating the gaming industry to ensure *its* healthy development | 持續加強對博彩業的監管, 確保博彩業健康發展。 |  |
| 7.3 | 2015 | We will optimize the operating model of bus services, and adjust and control the number and routes of *casino shuttle buses*, to ease traffic pressure on roads | 優化巴士營運模式, 調控博彩企業穿梭巴士的數量和行車路線, 減輕道路交通壓力。 | Diction |

To further probe into the linguistic contexts, the three English translations of the key word 博彩 (LT: gambling) are used as the node word to conduct *Collocate* search respectively. With the mentioned setting, the significant *Collocates* of the translations are obtained and listed in Table 4.14. The *Collocate* search shows that the translation, *gambling*, very different from the key 博彩 (LT: gambling) does in the Chinese texts, co-occurs with the negative words to form word groups denoting disadvantages of the risking activities and getting away from the related bad influences, such as *problem gambling*, *pathological gambling*, which act as the targets of *prevention* in both CHPAE and CCPAE.

The translation, *gaming*, in CHPAE, co-occurs with the neutral words to form word groups denoting the names of the industry, such as *tourism gaming industry*, which act as part of the word groups with the positive word *development* referring to the change and growth of the industry, such as *local gaming industry's development*. Correspondingly, the salient *Collocates* of *gaming* in CCPAE are with neutral and positive words. With the neutral *Collocates*, *gaming* forms word groups denoting the names of the industry as the gaming industry, and more specifically, word groups

**Table 4.14** *Collocates* of *gambling*, *gaming* and *casino*

|  | CHPAE | CCPAE |
|---|---|---|
| Gambling | Problem, prevention | Problem, pathological, prevent |
| Gaming | Industry, tourism, development | Industry, development, operators, responsible, enterprises |
| *Casino(s) | Gambling, entertainment | Shuttle, controls |

denoting the names of the corporations involved in the industry as *gaming operator* and *gaming enterprises*. With positive *Collocates*, *gaming* acts as part of the noun group with reference to the growth and change of the industry,, such as *gaming industry's development*, as well as the root of the noun group *responsible gaming*. As mentioned, it is a word group coined by the Macao SAR government to promote the practice of confining gambling-related damage to a socially acceptable level, with the connotation of social control over the gaming industry.

The other translation, *casino*, appears in the selected texts with shallow frequency as only two in CHPAE and four in CCPAE. It appears in the translations to form word group representing the negative references to gambling activities as *gambling and casino business*. In CCPAE, it forms the word group with reference to circumstances for particular activities, such as *smoking controls in casinos* and *casino shuttle buses* (the buses regularly travel between important spots of Macao and the casinos).

The *Collocate* search further reflects that the negative reference is offered to the word *gambling*, and the more specific reference is offered to *casino*. In contrast, the word *gaming* carries general and neutral references.

It is found that the key word is prominently translated with the shift *diction*, which is supplemented by *substitution* and *omission*. The cases of substitution are those in which the key word is replaced with pronouns. This group of cases is with neutral reference. For the prominent translation shift, *diction*, there are word choices with neutral and negative reference. However, the application of the word choice with negative reference decreased diachronically, with 6.3% in CHPAC down to 2.2% in CCPAC. And the word choice with negative reference used in some of the cases in CHPAC, starting from 2004, is used in different context in the rest of the investigated period. With its significance *Collocates*, this particular translation forms word groups denoting the disadvantages of the risky activities and getting away from the related bad influences rather than attaching negative meaning to the English version of the key word 博彩 (LT: gambling) in the translation process. Given the primary trend of translating 博彩 (LT: gambling) into *gaming* rather than the other two, the diction in the translated texts reveals that the key word 博彩 (LT: gambling) is reframed as the more general and neutral concept for entertainment.

*Translation of 多元 (LT: diversification)*

The other key word with reference to policy foci, 多元 (LT: diversification), is translated dynamically in both corpora. In CHPAE, the key word 多元 (LT: diversification) is translated into nouns as *variety, diversity, diversification* and *heterogeneity*; adjectives as *diversified, various, diverse* and the adjectives with the prefix *multi-*; a verb *diversify* and by omission. In CCPAE, the key word 多元 (LT: diversification) is translated into nouns as *diversity* and *diversification*; verbs as *expand, enrich* and *diversify*; adjectives as *broad, pluralistic, various, different, wide, multiple, diversified, diverse* and the adjective with the prefix *multi-*; a determiner *all* and by omission. Their distribution is presented in Table 4.15. The statistics show that the translations of the key word are primarily in noun form and secondly in adjective form, which is similar in both corpora. Thus, nominalization is widely used in the English translations of this particular key word.

**Table 4.15** Translations of key word 多元 (LT: diversification)

| Freq.%     | CHPAE (%) | CCPAE (%) |
|------------|-----------|-----------|
| Noun       | 55.8      | 58.6      |
| Verb       | 1.9       | 4.5       |
| Adjective  | 40.4      | 34.3      |
| Determiner | 0         | 1.8       |
| Omission   | 1.9       | 0.8       |

With the *Concordance* search of all these translations, it is found that the linguistic contexts of them can be categorized in accordance with their different references, namely **economic reference** (e.g.,, *diversity of Macao's industrial structure* and *diversification of economy*), **cultural reference** (e.g.,, *pluralistic cultural heritage* and *cultural diversity*), **governmental measures for people's livelihood** (e.g.,, *various sports activities, diversified communication channels*) and **other social references** (e.g.,, *a high degree of diversification, diversity and tolerance*). In CHPAE, 79.3% of the translations in **noun** form are with **economic reference**, and 13.8% of the translations in **noun** form are with **general social references depicting "a diversified city"**, such as *a high degree of diversification*. In CCPAE, likewise, 95.3% of the translations in **noun** form are with **economic reference**. The *Concordance* search of the translations proclaims that nominalization is widely applied in the translations of the key word 多元 (LT: diversification) and in the translations with economic reference in particular, which is identical in both CHPAE (79.3%) and CCPAE (95.3%). When probing into all the *Concordance* lines of the key word with economic reference in the English texts, a change from CHPAE to CCPAE is identified. In CHPAE, when the key word is with economic reference, its translations are varied as nouns, such as *diversity* and *diversification*, and as adjectives, such as *diversified*. On the contrary, in CCPAE, when it is with economic reference, the key word is translated, more consistently, into a noun and the only noun *diversification*.

To explore whether the nominalisation in the English version is the direct translation from Chinese or the result of the conversion in translating process, a comparison of this group of translations and their original Chinese texts is drawn. It is found that the nominalized translations are generally the direct translations of the Chinese texts (as presented in Example 8.1. In all the lines with nominalized translations of 多元 (LT: diversification), 37% of them are those added to the English version via the translation shift of *conversion*, with 26.7% added to CHPAE (Example 8.1) and 10.3% added to CCPAE (Example 8.1).

**Example 8**  Translations of the key word 多元 (LT: diversification)

|     | Year | English Text | Chinese Text | Translation Shift |
| --- | --- | --- | --- | --- |
| 8.1 | CHPA 2003 | The Government will also make significant investments in traditional industries to maintain **the diversity of Macao's industrial structure** | 為了保持產業結構的多元化, 政府亦將投放一定資源於傳統產業的優化。 | Diction |
|     | CCPA 2010 | We shall continue to drive **diversification of the economy** | 推進經濟適度多元 |  |
| 8.2 | CCPA 2017 | Safeguarding **cultural diversity** and promoting ethnic harmony<br>LT: Safeguarding developing the **diverse culture**, actively promoting ethnic harmony | 保護發展多元文化, 積極促進族群和諧[。] | Conversion |
|     | CCPA 2018 | Foster **cultural diversity** to enhance cultural soft power<br>LT: Foster **diverse culture** and enhance cultural soft power | 發展多元文化, 加強文化軟實力[。] |  |
|     | CCPA 2015 | By promoting **optimum diversification of the economy**, the Government will nurture the emergence of various industries[.]<br>LT: Actively promote **the economic adequately diverse development**. Nurture the growth of various industries | 積極推進經濟適度多元發展, 培育多元產業成長[。] |  |
| 8.3 | CHPA 2006 | We have **a variety of social traditions** that can stand the test of time[.]<br>LT: We have **diversified social traditions** that can stand the test of time | 我們擁有經得起漫長歷史考驗的多元社會傳統[。] | Conversion |

When searching in the CSOTU, the corpus of the State of the Union Addresses, it is found that the translations of this key word are all with rare applications in the same discourse type in native English. There is no existence of the most frequent translation *diversification*, as well as other translations in the same root as *diverse* and *diversified*. Only the verb form diversify exists in the corpus but with the minimal frequency as twice only in a corpus with 100,165 tokens. This linguistic presentation suggests the peculiar significance of the translation *diversification* in the Macao context.

The analysis of the translation of this key word shows that its English versions are dynamic with the translation shifts as *diction, substitution, omission* and *conversion*, and prominently with *diction* and *conversion*. Nominalization is widely applied in the presentation of this key word in both Chinese and English texts, and noticeably frequently in the word groups with reference of the economy. With the translation shifts of *diction* and *conversion* (translating a word in other word forms into a noun), the application of nominalization is even enhanced in English translation.

*Translation of 民生 (LT: people's lives)*

When tracing the English translations of the key word 民生 (LT: people's lives), it is found that this key word is translated inconsistently in the selected data with the translation shift of *diction* in the word choice as *livelihood, well-being, living, life, lives, sphere, relief, welfare, benefits* and *needs*, together with *people* or *social* to form word groups. In both CHPAE and CCPAE, the word group *people's livelihood* is used in around 50% of the translations of the key word 民生 (LT: people's lives). The other word choice, *people's well-being*, acts as the second frequent one, with around 20% of all the translations of this key word, in both CHPAE and CCPAE. This translation is followed by *lives* and *needs* (9.5%) in CHPAE and *living* (8.2%) in CCPAE. Table 4.16 summarizes the proportion of the application of all different translations of the key word 民生 (LT: people's lives) and Example 9 presents instances of the use of the most frequent two. With the explanation provided by *Oxford English Dictionary*, the word *livelihood* denotes a means of securing the necessities of life, while *wellbeing* means the state of being comfortable, healthy or happy. The word *wellbeing* was first used in the English translations of PA2006 (PA2006e) and then appeared as the translation of the key word 民生 (LT: people's lives) occasionally in nearly every Policy Address in the following years, except the English translations of PA2012, PA2017, and PA2019 (PA2012e, PA2017e, and PA2019e). When probing into the collocation of the two top frequent translations, *livelihood* and *wellbeing,* with the mentioned setting of the *Collocate* search, it is found that only the function words act as the significant *Collocates* in both CHPAE and CCPAE.

**Example 9** Translations of the key word 民生 (LT: people's livelihood)

|     | Year | English text | Chinese text | Translation shift |
|-----|------|--------------|--------------|-------------------|
| 9.1 | CHPA 2002 | Promote various projects concerning **people's livelihood** | 推動各種社會民生工作 | Diction |
|     | CCPA 2015 | The Government will strive to strengthen its legal system, and expedite promulgation of fundamental laws, especially laws that are related to **people's livelihoods** | 政府將全力加強法制建設, 抓緊完善基礎性法律, 尤其是民生事務法律的立法工作。 | |

**Table 4.16** Word choices in translating 民生 (LT: people's lives)

| English translation | CHPAE (%) | CCPAE (%) |
|---|---|---|
| *Livelihood* | 50.0 | 56.8 |
| *Well-being* | 16.7 | 20.7 |
| *Living* | 2.4 | 8.1 |
| *Life* | 2.4 | 5.4 |
| *Lives* | 9.5 | 0 |
| *Sphere* | 0 | 1.8 |
| *Relief* | 0 | 0.9 |
| *Welfare* | 0 | 1.8 |
| *Benefits* | 0 | 0.9 |
| *Needs* | 9.5 | 0 |
| *Omission* | 4.8 | 1.8 |
| *Public* | 2.4 | 0 |
| *Community* | 2.4 | 0.9 |
| *Bread and butter issue* | 0 | 0.9 |

The analysis of the translation of the key word 民生 (LT: people's lives) shows that it is translated inconsistently throughout the investigated period with the shifts of diction and specification. With the most frequent word choice, which occupies more than half of the translations, the key word 民生 (LT: people's lives) is specified into materials lives rather than the abstract well-being in the English translations, throughout the investigated period.

When using the more frequent translations as the node words to search in CSOTU (the corpus with the selected State of the Union Addresses), it is found that the most frequent word choices of the English translations of the key word 民生 (LT: people's lives), *livelihood* and *wellbeing*, exist very rarely in the same discourse type in native English, with only once in the whole set of selected State of the Union Addresses for each of the two. Instead, the less frequent translations, such as *lives*, *benefits* and *needs*, which are relatively with more concrete denotations regarding people's lives, are far more frequent in CSOTU. The mentioned linguistic presentation of the word choices in translating the key word 民生 (LT: people's lives) indicates that the group of translations (*livelihood* and *wellbeing*) with the abstract denotation generalizing different aspects of people's lives are not commonly used in the same discourse type in native English. This linguistic presentation, meanwhile, specifies the significance of these translations in Macao context.

For **the key words with reference to the policy foci**, it is found that the translations take a role in constructing the shift in meaning in the English version. Specifically, the three key words representing three significant political fields are with the different linguistic presentation in the English translation.

For the key word 博彩 (LT: gambling), with the translation shifts of diction, substitution and omission, there is the primary trend in translating the key word by the word choice without negative reference, and the word choice with negative reference has been used in other relevant contexts after 2004, which are with the representation of disadvantages of the risking activities and getting away from the related bad influences. Given the primary trend of translating 博彩 (LT: gambling) into *gaming*, the translations re-frame the key word 博彩 (LT: gambling) as a more general and neutral concept for entertainment.

For the key word 多元 (LT: diversification), it is found that the key word is translated dynamically with the shifts as *diction, substitution, omission* and *conversion*, and prominently with *diction* and *conversion*. Nominalization is widely applied in the presentation of this key word in both Chinese and English version and noticeably frequently in the word groups with reference to economy. With the translation shifts of *diction* and *conversion* (translating a word in other word forms into a noun), the application of nominalization is even enhanced in English translation.

For the key word 民生 (LT: people's lives), it is translated inconsistently and mainly with shifts in *diction* and *specification*. The most frequent word choice in its English version, which occupies more than half of the translations of the key word, specifies the signified of the key word into materials lives rather than the abstract well-being.

After the analysis of the translations of the key words with reference to the policy foci, the analysis of the translations moves forward to the key verbs of the study.

## 4.3.2 Key Words with Reference to Actions

Three groups of key verbs attained at the stage of identifying key words. The first group is the common key verbs in both CHPAC and CCPAC, with denotation as improving and refining the goals. The second group is the distinctive key verbs in CHPAC, which convey mental processes for reflecting positive attitude toward the participants. The third group is the distinctive ones in CCPAC, which convey material processes for introducing new goals and putting the goals in effect. With the objective of investigating how this group of key words are presented in the English translation, in the following, the English translations of these key verbs are traced in CHPAE and CCPAE, and the linguistic presentation of the translations is compared with those in CSOTU, to study their linguistic contexts in the translated texts with their authentic linguistic contexts in the same discourse type in native English.

*Translating the common key verbs*

The key words with common denotation as conveying the process of improving and refining in both corpora are translated dynamically in the English versions.

In CHPAE, this group of key words are translated with 18 different words, such as *improve, raise, enhance, promote* and with *improve* as the most frequent one (26.9% of all the translations). This particular translation is presented in different parts of speech throughout the whole set of selected data. It is presented in the word forms as nouns (*improvement*), to-infinitives (*to improve*), bare infinitives (*improve*), gerunds (*improving*) and verbs (*improve/improves*), and with to-infinitives (55.6% of all word forms) as the most frequent form. The frequency of the application of the lemma *improve* as the English translations of this group of key verbs is followed by the application of another lemma, *raise* (14.9%), as the translations, in the word form as to infinitive (*to raise*), bare infinitive (*raise*) and gerund (*raising*). Among these word forms, to-infinitive is the most frequent one with 60% of all existing forms. The word choice, *enhance*, acts as the third frequent one in the translations of this group of key verbs in CHPAE (with 13.4% of the translations). It is presented in the word forms as to-infinitive (*to enhance*), noun (*enhancement*), verb (*enhances*) and bare infinitive (*enhance*), with to infinitive (66.7%) as the most frequent word form.

In CCPAE, withal, this group of key verbs is translated with 14 different word choices and with the lemma *improve* as the most frequent one. It is also presented in different part of speech in the translated texts, as to-infinitive (*to improve*), bare infinitive (*improve*), gerund (*improving*), verb (*improves*), noun (*improvement*) and participle acting as adjective (*improved*). Among all these forms, to-infinitive acts as the most frequent one, as it does in CHPAE. The high frequency of the use of the lemma *improve* as the translations of this group of key verbs in CHPAE is followed by the use of another word choice *enhance* (18%). This lemma is, similarly, presented in different word forms as to infinitive (*to enhance*), noun (*enhancement*), gerund (*enhancing*) and bare infinitive (*enhance*), with to infinitive (50% of all forms) as the most frequent one. The lemma *promote* (14.6% of all translations) acts as the third frequent one in the application in translating this group of key verbs in CCPAE. It is presented in the word forms as to-infinitive (*to promote*), noun (*promotion*), verb (*promotes*), gerund (*promoting*) and bare infinitive (*enhance*), with to-infinitive (53.8%) as the most frequent one. The application of these top three word choices in the translations of this particular group of key verbs is summarized in Table 4.17. Table 4.18 presents the differences in the application of these translations in CHPAE, CCPAE and CSOTU. The result of the comparison reveals that the frequent application of the mentioned translations does not appear in the texts in this particular discourse type in native English. Instead, it is the distinctive feature of the selected data in particular, as a piece of translated texts of this discourse type.

Since the bare infinitive of verb is with higher collocability (Kjellmer 1990, 172), the lemma of the above translations, *improve*, *enhance*, *raise* and *promote* are selected as the node words to investigate the prominent presentation of the key words with this particular reference in the English translations. Applying the mentioned setting, an advanced *Collocate* search is conducted with CHPAE, CCPAE and CSOTU. Table 4.19 presents the top ten lexical *Collocates* of each lemma. The results reveal the distinctiveness in the English translations under investigation which contrasts with the texts of the same discourse type in native English.

As summarized in Table 4.19, among all the salient Collocates attained from the Collocate search with the mentioned setting, *quality* and *standards* are identified as the only two common ones among CHPAE, CCPAE and CSOTU. Even these two common salient *Collocates* are with considerable divergence in the statistics as *quality* with nearly five times higher T-score in CHPAE and CCPAE than in CSOTU, and *standards* with nearly three times higher T-score in CHPAE than in CSOTU. When investigating the distinct *Collocates* in CHPAE and CCPAE, it is found that

**Table 4.17** Top three word choices in translating key verbs with referent to improving/refining

| CHPAE | | CCPAE | |
|---|---|---|---|
| Lemma | Word form | Lemma | Word form |
| Improve (26.9%) | – To-infinitive (55.6%)<br>– Gerund<br>– Bare infinitive<br>– Noun | *Improve* (24.7%) | – To-infinitive (40.9%)<br>– Gerund<br>– Bare infinitive<br>– Verb |
| Raise (14.9%) | – To-infinitive (60%)<br>– Bare infinitive<br>– Gerund | *Enhance* (18%) | – To-infinitive (50%)<br>– Bare infinitive<br>– Noun<br>– Gerund |
| Enhance (13.4%) | – To-infinitive (66.7%)<br>– Noun<br>– Verb<br>– Bare infinitive | *Promote* (14.6%) | – To-infinitive (53.8%)<br>– Bare infinitive<br>– Noun<br>– Verb<br>– Gerund |

**Table 4.18** Normalised frequency of the word choices in translating key verbs denoting improving /refining

| Normalized freq. over 100,000 words<br>Lemma | CHPAE | CCPAE | CSOTU |
|---|---|---|---|
| Improve | 193.6 | 279.4 | 21.0 |
| Enhance | 136.8 | 279.4 | 0 |
| Raise | 60.8 | 81.8 | 32.9 |
| Promote | 147.0 | 231.7 | 18.0 |

some significant *Collocates* in the English translations do not even exist in CSOTU, as *government*, *development*, *services*, *Macao*, *management* and *cooperation*. This result reveals that this group of key verbs are not only with specific frequency in the English translations under investigation but also with unique collocations which do not exist in the texts in the same discourse type in native English, which is evidence of the result of the translation process.

In the above analysis of the translation of the common key verbs, the primary translation shift identified throughout the investigated period is diction. And the word choices and the proportion of the application of the word choices are similar in both CHPAC and CCPAC. However, though the common key verbs are with very high *Keyness* in the Policy Addresses under investigation, the considerable significance of these verbs does not exist in the texts in this particular discourse type in native English. These key verbs are not only with specific frequency in the English translations of the Policy Addresses but also with unique collocations which rarely exist in the texts in the same discourse type in native English. All these serve as evidence of the distinctive features of the translated Policy Addresses in English.

**Table 4.19** Top lexical Collocates of *improve, enhance, raise* and *promote*

| CHPAE | | CCPAE | | CSOTU | |
|---|---|---|---|---|---|
| Collocate | T-score | Collocate | T-score | Collocate | T-score |
| Quality | 9.273 | Government | 9.095 | Health | 2.437 |
| Government | 8.587 | Development | 8.795 | Security | 2.436 |
| Development | 7.238 | Macao | 7.467 | Wages | 2.234 |
| Public | 6.804 | Quality | 7.431 | America | 2.189 |
| Services | 6.785 | Public | 7.419 | Minimum | 1.999 |
| Macao | 5.558 | System | 7.288 | Care | 1.988 |
| Standards | 5.538 | Services | 7.026 | Help | 1.979 |
| Service | 5.399 | People | 6.627 | Conservation | 1.732 |
| Environment | 5.052 | Cooperation | 6.280 | Quality | 1.729 |
| Management | 4.763 | Education | 5.781 | Ideas | 1.7296 |
| Education | 4.723 | Continue | 5.779 | Employees | 1.7295 |
| Citizens | 4.581 | Medical | 5.676 | Standards | 1.7289 |
| Social | 4.562 | Social | 5.318 | Deserve | 1.728 |
| Administration | 4.508 | Administration | 5.231 | Stronger | 1.727 |
| Community | 4.472 | Regional | 5.220 | Technology | 1.7266 |

### 4.3.3   Key Words with Reference to Social Groups and Institutes

This section investigates the translations of the key words with reference to social groups and institutes. As reviewed in Chap. 2, the theoretical foundation of this study believes that personal pronouns are one sort of linguistic resources that convey language modality (Hu et al. 2018; Lakoff 1990; Zhu 2011). While 我們 (LT: we, us, our, ours) acts as the only key pronoun attained from the *Keyword* search of this study, with the theoretical basis to support the significance of the application of personal pronouns in discourse, the following examines the presentation of all first-person plural pronouns in the English translations of the Policy Addresses (CHPAE and CCPAE).

The first-person plural pronouns in CHPAC and CCPAE are *we, us, our* and *ours*, and as shown in Table 4.20, with the majority as the subject pronoun, *We.* The statistics show that this first-person-plural pronoun(s) is much more frequent in the English translations (CHPAE and CCPAE) than the Chinese texts (CHPAC and CCPAC), as 3.3 times higher in CHPAE and even 6.7 times higher in CCPAE when comparing to their Chinese versions respectively, which proves that the first-person plural pronouns are very commonly added to the English texts in the translation process. Among all the selected texts in each corpus, this shift is most considerable in PA2005e in CHPAE, and PA2010e in CCPAE. In order to examine this particular translation shift, the *Concordance* lines of first-person pronouns in PA2005e and

PA2010e are traced for further investigation. The study of the parallel *Concordance* lines of the first-person plural pronouns in the English and Chinese versions of the Policy Addresses shows that the translation shift of addition and substitution happen most frequently and these two types of translation shifts happen for dealing with the following three situations: (1) **adding a modifier to a noun with the first-person pronoun *our*** as shown in Example 10.1, (2) **adding the subject *We* to the clauses starting with verbs in the Chinese texts** (Example 10.2), and the purpose of (3) **replacing the names in the STs with pronouns in TTs** (Example 10.3).

As presented in Example 10.1, "*our*" is added to the nouns relating to governing responsibilities and merits of the Government, as translating the ST 五年的施政經驗 (LT: *five years of administrative experience*) into *our five years of administrative experience* and 有關策略 (LT: *relevant strategies*) to amplifying the Government's administrative experience and their governing strategies with the exclusive use of

**Table 4.20**   Frequency of 我們 *(we, us, our, ours)* in ST and TT

| Corpus | Year | Chinese texts | English texts | | | | | Difference between CHPA and CCPA |
|---|---|---|---|---|---|---|---|---|
| | | Frequency | Frequency | | | | | |
| | | 我們 | We | Our | Ours | Us | Total | |
| CHPA | 2000 | 26 | 23 | 11 | 0 | 1 | 35 | 9 |
| | 2001 | 87 | 97 | 63 | 1 | 12 | 173 | 86 |
| | 2002 | 108 | 116 | 97 | 0 | 13 | 226 | 118 |
| | 2003 | 108 | 185 | 86 | 0 | 9 | 280 | 172 |
| | 2004 | 114 | 250 | 189 | 1 | 19 | 459 | 345 |
| | 2005 | 119 | 231 | 283 | 0 | 15 | 529 | 410 |
| | 2006 | 84 | 204 | 172 | 0 | 14 | 390 | 306 |
| | 2007 | 76 | 164 | 28 | 0 | 1 | 193 | 117 |
| | 2008 | 76 | 234 | 90 | 0 | 4 | 328 | 252 |
| | 2009 | 60 | 177 | 75 | 0 | 4 | 256 | 196 |
| | Total | 858 | 1681 | 1094 | 2 | 92 | 2869 | 2011 |
| CCPA | 2010 | 35 | 174 | 82 | 0 | 3 | 259 | 224 |
| | 2011 | 20 | 170 | 49 | 0 | 5 | 224 | 204 |
| | 2012 | 35 | 111 | 32 | 0 | 1 | 144 | 109 |
| | 2013 | 68 | 135 | 46 | 0 | 0 | 181 | 113 |
| | 2014 | 14 | 115 | 54 | 0 | 2 | 171 | 157 |
| | 2015 | 25 | 119 | 51 | 0 | 5 | 175 | 150 |
| | 2016 | 12 | 85 | 19 | 0 | 2 | 106 | 94 |
| | 2017 | 18 | 160 | 18 | 0 | 0 | 178 | 160 |
| | 2018 | 18 | 106 | 29 | 0 | 2 | 137 | 119 |
| | 2019 | 8 | 104 | 24 | 0 | 0 | 128 | 120 |
| | Total | 253 | 1279 | 404 | 0 | 20 | 1703 | 1450 |

the pronoun in the English translation. Similarly, as presented in Example 10.2, *We* is added to translate 加強對博彩業的監管和調控 (LT: *impose stronger supervision and regulation of the gaming industry*) into **We** *shall also impose stronger supervision and regulation of the gaming industry* to indicate the Government as the agent of the actions to emphasize the Government's role of offering controls over the gaming industry. By adding the pronouns as the modifiers of nouns and the subjects of the imperative sentences in ST to indicate the agents of the actions, the translations function to accentuate the governing responsibilities and merits of the Government.

In addition, the type mentioned above of translation shifts also suggests the offices' intention to create social affinity with the Government. For instance, in Example 10.1, adding "*our*" to *people* and *space* to translate 保障居民的基本權利和自由 (LT: protecting residents' basic rights and freedoms) into *protecting our people's basic rights and freedoms* and to translate 拓展發展空間 (LT: expand space for development) into *expand our space for development* shortens the distance between the Government and the recipients of the Policy Addresses, which suggests solidarity and social affinity of the Government by the inclusive use of the pronouns to involve the recipients. Example 10.3 presents examples dealing with situations in the translation process for equal representation. Different from the Chinese texts (STs) as labeling the Government by its name, the first-person plural pronoun *We* is used instead to label the Government to build up different relationships between the Government and the public. All these translation shifts suggest accentuating the responsibilities and merits of the administrations and, meanwhile building up relationships between the Government and the public.

**Example 10** Concordance lines of first-person plural pronouns in CHPA and CCPA

|  | Year | English text | Chinese text | Translation shift |
|---|---|---|---|---|
| 4.1 | CHPA 2005 | We must continue to roll out new plans based on a forward-looking approach and new methods, and based on *our 5 years of administrative experience* | 我們必須以新的思維, 新的模式, 結合過去五年的施政經驗, 繼續開展各項工作。 | Addition (adding a modifier to a noun with the first-person pronoun *our*) |
|  |  | The Government's policy approach will be to consolidate the foundations of the various business sectors in our community and adjust *our relevant strategies* [.] | 政府的施政方向, 將是進一步打好社會各項事業的根基, 並調整有關策略[。] |  |
|  | CCPA 2010 | … protecting *our people's basic rights and freedoms* … | … 保障居民的基本權利和自由 … |  |

(continued)

(continued)

| | Year | English text | Chinese text | Translation shift |
|---|---|---|---|---|
| | | … expand *our space for development* … | … 拓展發展空間 … | |
| 4.2 | CHPA 2005 | We have encouraged and monitored complaints in a proper and transparent way, and *we have arranged for them to be handled in a timely, correct and inclusive manner* | 我們讓投訴個案在應有的透明度之下獲得監督, 確保投訴得到及時、恰當和全方位的處理[。] | Addition (adding a subject *WE* to the clauses starting with verbs in the Chinese texts) |
| | | Firstly, *we will invite prominent legal experts—both local and overseas and within or outside our legal institutions* to meet and discuss legal reform | 第一, 集合區內外, 建制內外優秀的法律專家參與法律修訂 [。] | |
| | CCPA 2010 | **We** shall also impose stronger supervision and regulation of the gaming industry […] | 加強對博彩業的監管和調控 […] | |
| | | **We** have successfully held a number of large international sports events and been inscribed on the UNESCO World Heritage List | 舉辦大型國際運動競賽, 成功申報世界遺產[。] | |
| 4.3 | CHPA 2005 | During those five years, *we* have undergone ups and downs, made gains and losses, met challenges and experienced changes, just like any other place in the World | 在這五個春秋之中, 特區和任何地方的經歷一樣有起有落, 有得有失, 不斷接受挑戰, 持續發生變化。 | Substitution (replacing the names in the STs with pronouns in TTs) |
| | | *We* will continue to assist them by adopting measures that alleviate their financial difficulties; support their technological, management and systems innovations; and improve the quality of their human resources | 政府將繼續對中小企業採取扶助政策, 致力紓緩中小企業融資困難, 支持中小企業的技術、管理和制度創新, 優化企業人力資源的素質。 | |

(continued)

(continued)

| Year | English text | Chinese text | Translation shift |
|------|-------------|--------------|-------------------|
| CCPA 2010 | We are committed to protecting our people's basic rights and freedoms | 特區政府致力保障居民的基本權利和自由。 | |
| | We are committed to improving employment opportunities, relieving residents' economic hardships, supporting disadvantaged groups and perfecting the social security system | 特區政府致力促進就業, 有效紓解民困, 扶助弱勢社群, 完善社會保障制度。 | |

As shown in Table 4.20, there are different first-person plural pronouns in English translations and with the subject *we* as the majority. The comparative examination between the translated Policy Addresses in English (CHPAE and CCPAE) and the texts in the same discourse type in native English (CSOTU) is conducted, with the subject pronoun *We* as the node word. Table 4.21 summarizes the frequency of the translations in three distinctive corpora. The statistics do not suggest a significant difference in the frequency% of the application of *We* in both translated texts and texts in native English. The examination moves on to the linguistic contexts of *We*.

The colligation of the key pronoun *we* is mostly as collocating with a verb instead of other linguistic constituents, as Pronoun+Verb in both CHPAE and CCPAE. In order to investigate the verbs collocated with this key pronoun, with the setting of *Collocate* search as mentioned, the verbs frequently used with this key word in the two corpora are under examination. In accordance with the colligation of this key pronoun, the range for *Collocates* search is set as 4R, which means four words on the right. As shown in Table 4.22, the *Collocates* attained consist of auxiliary verbs, prepositions, articles etc. To focus on the *Collocates* with apparent meanings, only lexical *Collocates* are selected. Table 4.23 summarizes the lexical Collocates of the key pronoun *we* in the three corpora, which are ordered in accordance with their T-score from high to low.

In the lexical Collocates identified in all three corpora, there are significant ones with common references to **abstract actions of pursuing progress with efforts**, such as *encourage, improve, strengthen, enhance, strive, develop, support* in both CHPAE and CCPAE, *promote, ensure* and *maintain* in CHPAE, *facilitate, expedite, optimize, uphold, perfect* in CCPAE, and *support* and *fight* in CSOTU, as shown in Example 11.1. This particular group of verbs happens in 17% of the *Concordance* of the key pronoun *We* in CHPAE, and 25% in CCPAE, hence, only 1.4% in CSOTU.

| **Table 4.21** Frequency% of *We* in CHPAE, CCPAE and CSOTU | Corpus | CHPA | CCPA | CSOTU |
|---|---|---|---|---|
| | Frequency% | 1.70 | 1.45 | 2.14 |

**Table 4.22** Collocates of *we* in CHPAE and CCPAE

| CHPAE | | CCPAE | | CSOTU | |
|---|---|---|---|---|---|
| T-score | Collocate | T-score | Collocate | T-score | Collocate |
| 24.35467 | Will | 26.67256 | Will | 15.27341 | To |
| 14.72896 | To | 12.91075 | The | 14.68606 | The |
| 14.05114 | Must | 12.3785 | To | 14.03329 | Have |
| 13.2489 | The | 11.9153 | Also | 13.6754 | Will |
| 11.80363 | Also | 10.45247 | Shall | 13.0183 | Are |
| 11.67252 | Have | 9.93536 | Continue | 12.00644 | Must |
| 10.11116 | Should | 9.44719 | Have | 11.52982 | Can |
| 9.91615 | Our | 8.33783 | Are | 10.78441 | ve (have) |
| 24.35467 | Will | 7.53443 | Our | 10.117 | re (are) |
| 14.72896 | To | 7.32158 | A | 9.98012 | Our |

**Table 4.23** Salient Lexical Collocates of *We*

| CHPAE | CCPAE | CSOTU |
|---|---|---|
| Continue, encourage, make, promote, improve, strengthen, enhance, strive, believe, adopt, develop, further, support, ensure, establish, implement, use, increase, raise, maintain, do, build, realise, hope, work, emphasize, give | Continues, further, improve, strive, strengthen, implement, facilitate, enhance, propose, establish, encourage, make, support, expedite, provide, optimise, increase, uphold, perfect, study, complete, conduct, consider, review, commence, develop, understand, build, follow, launch, leverage, introduce | Need, make, know, want, continue, work, take, keep, stand, trust, act, put, support, face, progress, cut, help, afford, believe, set, invest, give, live, show, fight, stop |

**Example 11** Significant lexical Collocates of *We*

| | Year | English text | Chinese text | Category of collocates |
|---|---|---|---|---|
| 5.1 | CHPA 2008 | *We* strongly **support** the development of industrial clusters to diversify our offerings of tourism products by promoting leisure, holidaymaking, sightseeing and shopping | 我們大力鼓勵產業集群的形成, 豐富綜合旅遊的內涵, 推動休閒、渡假、觀光、購物等一系列行業的發展。 | Lexical Collocates with reference to **abstract actions of pursuing progress with efforts** |

(continued)

| | Year | English text | Chinese text | Category of collocates |
|---|---|---|---|---|
| | CCPA 2017 | *We* **encourage** and **support** youngsters to realise their dreams, and will create the space and conditions for their growth and development | 我們鼓勵和支持青年實現自己夢想, 為他們的成長成才創造空間和條件。 | |
| | CSOTU 2016 | [W]e should recruit and **support** more great teachers for our kids | – | |
| 5.2 | CHPA 2004 | Concerning the problems of youth, *we* **believe** Macao has many young people with good potential, but some of them may not be able to fully realise that potential, due to various social factors | 談到青少年問題, 我們認為, 本澳青少年之中, 可造之材甚多, 只不過由於種種環境因素, 令很多人的潛質未能發揮, 以及令少數人的青春, 蒙上陰影。 | Modal lexical words in **epistemic modality** |
| | CCPA 2015 | *We* **understand** the great motherland is always a strong support for a better Macao | 我們清楚, 祖國好, 澳門更好。 | |
| | CSOTU 2012 | *We* also **know** that when students aren't allowed to walk away from their education, more of them walk the stage to get their diploma | – | |
| 5.3 | CHPA 2006 | *We* also **hope** the measures we have outlined today will create a fairer society with a more caring spirit, and encourage people, especially the younger generation, to work hard to raise our quality of life and enhance Macao's all-round competitiveness | 我們亦希望上述措施能更好地體現社會公平, 弘揚人際關愛精神, 鼓勵市民, 尤其是年青一代奮發上進, 提升全體澳人素質, 強化澳門的綜合競爭力。 | Modal lexical words representing **boulomaic modality** |
| | CCPA | – | – | |

(continued)

(continued)

| Year | English text | Chinese text | Category of collocates |
|---|---|---|---|
| CSOTU 2011 | *We* **want** to reward good teachers and stop making excuses for bad ones | – | |

In addition to the verbs with common reference to actions for pursuing progress with efforts, there is another small group of Collocates with salience in common reference, which are the modal lexical verbs in **epistemic modality**, as *believe* in CHPAE, *understand* in CCPAE, and *know*, *trust* and *believe* in CSOTU, as shown in Example 11.2. Table 4.24 summarizes the dramatic differences in the application of these significant *Collocates* in each corpus which act as the significant *Collocates* of the key pronoun in the particular corpus only but not the others. With the explanation provided by *Oxford English Dictionary*, the verb *believe* is with the denotation as to be sure that something is true or possible, while the verb *understand* is with the denotation as knowing or realizing how a fact works, which means having no doubts toward the phenomena in the mental processes and indicates assertation of the proposition. Comparing the denotation of these two verbs, *understand* is the one delivering more confidence about the phenomenon in the mental process than *believe*. *Know* in the State of the Union Addresses means to have information about something, which, same as *understand*, indicates assertation of the proposition while *trust* is with the similar denotation as *believe* to indicate speaker's confidence toward the proposition less than the full epistemic warrant of assertation (Simpson 1993, p. 43). **Thus, in terms of epistemic warranty, while the key pronoun *we* is with the significant *Collocates* with high epistemic warranty, CCPAE and the State of the Union Addresses are with the ones with full epistemic warranty though the one in high epistemic warranty is also with salience in the State of the Union Addresses.**

In addition to epistemic modality, modal lexical words representing **boulomaic modality** are attained in the *Collocate* search, which indicates the wishes and desires of the speaker (Simpson 1993, p. 44). There is one in CHPAE as *hope* (with frequency% in *Collocates* as 0.26%), and one as *want* in the State of the Union Addresses, (with frequency% in *Collocates* as 0.53%). As summarized in Table

**Table 4.24** Significant *Collocates* of *We* representing epistemic warranty

| Collocates | CHPAE | | CCPAE | | CSOTU | |
|---|---|---|---|---|---|---|
| | Rank | T-score | Rank | T-score | Rank | T-score |
| Believe | 27th | 4.7 | 101st | 2.20 | 66th | 3.36 |
| Understand | 159th | 2.1 | 48th | 3.22 | 274th | 1.72 |
| Know | 181st | 1.93 | – | – | 23rd | 6.64 |
| Trust | 872nd | 0.91 | – | – | 42nd | 4.18 |

4.25, likewise, the significant *Collocates* representing boulomaic commitment are with the enormous differences in application. They are with special salience in the particular corpus but not the others. **Thus, while *We* is significantly used in the context representing boulomaic commitment in both CHPAE and the State of the Union Addresses, no considerable salience is identified in CCPAE.**

Example 11.3 presents some instances with this group of Collocates. In those examples, the key word *we* is with the exclusive use as referring to the speaker's own voice on behalf of the Government, which is also the majority of the application of this key pronoun in all of its *Concordance* lines under investigation.

The analysis above reveals that the translation shifts in the translation procedures of the key words with reference to social groups and institutes serve to reposition the target text audience. When tracing the first-person plural pronouns in the English translations, it is found that they are frequently added to the English translations with the translation shifts of addition and substitution to accentuate the governing responsibility and merits of the Government, and meanwhile to build up the relationship between the Government and the public. Among all the first-person plural pronouns in English translations, the subject *we* is the most frequent translation. The study of the linguistic contexts of this particular translation demonstrates the similarities and differences in its application in CHPAE, CCPAE and CSOTU. There are three types of common *Collocates* of *We* in the corpora under investigation, namely (1) the lexical verbs denoting processes with effort, such as *encourage*, *promote* and *optimize*; (2) the model lexical verbs in epistemic modality (concerning with the speaker's confidence of a proposition expressed), such as *believe* and *understand*; as well as (3) the modal lexical words representing boulomaic modality (indicating wishes and desires of the speaker), such as *hope* and *want*. With the first type of common *Collocates*, they contrast in their frequency% in each corpus as 17% in CHPAE, 25% in CCPAE but only 1.4% in CSOTU. In terms of epistemic warranty, while the key pronoun *we* is with the significant *Collocates* in high epistemic warranty in CHPAE, it is mainly with the ones with a full epistemic warranty in CCPAE and CSOTU, though the one in the high epistemic warranty is also with salience in CSOTU. While *We* is significantly used in the context representing boulomaic commitment in both CHPAE and CSOTU, no considerable salience is identified in CCPAE. To summarize, while the key pronoun we collocates with verbs,, such as "support" and "encourage", which are denoting the abstract actions of pursing progress with efforts most significantly in the translated Policy Addresses, in CSOTU, it collocates more frequently with the modal lexical verbs which indicate epistemic warranty, especially full epistemic warranty,, such as "know". Though there are common *Collocates*, they present differently in

**Table 4.25**  Significant *Collocates* of *We* representing boulomaic commitment

| Collocates | CHPAE | | CCPAE | | CSOTU | |
|---|---|---|---|---|---|---|
| | Rank | T-score | Rank | T-score | Rank | T-score |
| Hope | 49th | 3.52 | 160th | 1.67 | 1358th | 0.79 |
| Want | 140th | 2.15 | – | – | 29th | 5.55 |

the three corpora, which suggests that the speaker refers their own voice on behalf of the Government in the Policy Addresses with different language modalities in each corpus.

## 4.4 Multimodal Analysis

As mentioned before, in addition to the verbal modes, non-verbal modes also take a role in the meaning construction of discourse. Though the verbal version of the selected Policy Addresses in this study is the printed verbal texts, they are with visual resources that function in the process of meaning construction as well. In this section, the visual configuration of them is under investigation.

In addition to the visual resources of the verbal versions of the Policy Addresses, as mentioned in the introduction of the data of the present study in Chap. 3, there are infographics of the Policy Addresses released since the beginning of Chui's second term (PA2015 to PA2019) which are the inter-semiotic translations of the Policy Addresses in verbal texts.

Therefore, the visual data of the multimodal analysis is divided into two sections. The first section deals with the visual resources of the selected Policy Addresses in printed verbal texts and the second section works on the visual configuration of the infographics of the selected Policy Addresses. They are the infographics of PA2015 to PA2019 (CCPAP).

The multimodal analysis of the Policy Addresses is conducted with Kress and van Leeuwen's (1996, 2006, 2021) visual grammar. While the investigation of the visual configuration of the printed verbal version of the Policy Addresses focuses on their visual syntax, the use of colors and typography, the examination of the visual configuration of the infographics of the selected Policy Addresses is with the core foci on the represented participants (RPs) and the use of the colors.

### 4.4.1 Analysis of the Visual Presentation of the Policy Addresses

In this section, the visual configuration of the verbal version of the Policy Addresses is under investigation. It is to investigate how the visual resource in the verbal Policy Addresses function in the meaning construction process, and how the visual configuration is arranged in the Chinese-to-English translation process. As mentioned above, the examination focuses on the visual syntax, the use of colors and the typography of the verbal version of the Policy Addresses. In terms of visual syntax, it is analyzed with the three interrelated systems for characterizing the representational and interactive meanings of spatial composition suggested by Kress and van Leeuwen's visual grammar (1996, 2006, 2021), namely *salience*, *information value* and *framing*. A comparison between the visual configuration of the Policy Addresses in Chinese texts and their English translations is drawn to identify how the visual resources function differently in the Chinese and English verbal texts. As a piece of formal printed textual document, the Policy Addresses in printed verbal texts are with the default visual flow as top-to-bottom and left-to-right, due to the actual practice of the languages. With this default visual flow, the structure of their visual presentation are analyzed as follows.

The structure of each piece of printed verbal version of the Policy Addresses demonstrates their visual framing system. In CHPAC, except PA2000c and PA2008c, all other Policy Addresses included start with a content page, as presented in Fig. 4.6. The primary texts of all the ten Policy Addresses in CHPAC are principally divided into three parts, by headings in separate lines. The first part is a general introduction, which is followed by a body text and a conclusion. The body text is with three sections, the review of the Government's work of the previous year, the elaboration of the key administrative policies of the upcoming year, and the summary of the foci and objectives of the policies. They are divided by headings in separate lines. With the introduction and the body text, each Policy Address ends with a conclusion in general. Within all the sections in the body text, only the section for the elaboration of the key administrative policies of the upcoming year is with sub-headings to have the section separated into sub-sections in all the Policy Addresses in CHPAC.

On comparison, PA2008c is with, relatively, a complete structure than all other Policy Addresses in CHPAC. It starts with a cover page, which is followed by a content page, as presented in Fig. 4.7, and the main text of PA2008c is with the three main parts which are divided by the highlighted headings as others. Contrastingly, the first Policy Address in CHPAC (PA2000c) is with a simpler structure when it is compared to all other Policy Addresses within the same corpus. There is no content page included in PA2000c as all other Policy Addresses do, nor a cover page. PA2000c starts with the main text right away, as shown in the first picture in Fig. 4.7. There are also three parts consisted in the main text of PA2000c, the introduction, the body text, and the conclusion separated by headings.

**Fig. 4.6**  Example of visual presentation of policy addresses in CHPAC

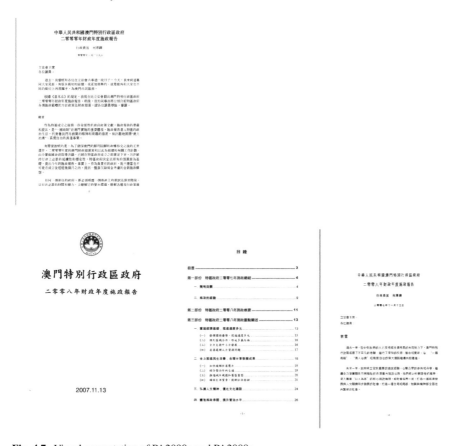

**Fig. 4.7** Visual presentation of PA2000c and PA2008c

In CCPAC, starting from the first Policy Address included in the corpus (PA2010c), each of the Policy Address is with a cover page and a content page, as demonstrated in Fig. 4.8, except PA2012c. In terms of the overall structure of the whole Policy Address, PA2012c, unlike all other Policy Addresses in CCPAC, is presented without a cover page, and starts its presentation with a content page. In the body texts, there is an elimination of an independent part of the summary of the Government's work in the past year in all the Policy Addresses consisted in CCPAC, except PA2011c and PA2012c, comparing to the Policy Addresses in CHPAC. In all other eight Policy Addresses included in CCPAC, the content is primarily divided into three parts, identified by headings printed on the letterhead of the related pages. They all begin with a general introduction to the whole Policy Address, which is followed by the elaboration of the significant policies of the upcoming year, and end with a conclusion in general.

Similar to those in CHPAC, the middle sections are divided into sub-sections with foregrounded headings in the texts. In most of the Policy Addresses in this corpus,

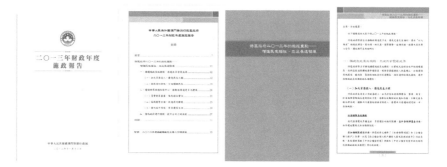

**Fig. 4.8** Example of visual presentation of policy addresses in CCPAC

except PA2011c and PA2012c, the body texts are divided into sub-sections by not only highlighted headings but also headings printed on the letterhead of the related pages and chapter pages as a book does. PA2011c and PA2012c are, to some extent, with simpler structures than others in CCPAC. Figure 4.8 presents an example of the prominent visual presentation in terms of the structure of most of the Policy Addresses in CCPAC.

In terms of visual flow, there are elements applied in the texts to offer different degrees of salience to the items to make them stand out and to have the viewer's attention drawn to them within the long-written texts. In order words, they help to enhance the visual weight of some particular items. With different degrees of visual weight, the items are positioned in hierarchy. As summarized in Table 4.26, diachronically, there is an upward trend in the use of elements applied to different items in the texts to vary the levels of headings.

In CHPAC, contrasting fonts with bolder and/or bigger fonts to provide visual weight, using whitespace before and after, as well as indent to highlight, are the prominent elements applied in the verbal version of selected Policy Addresses in Chinese to divide the texts into different levels of significance. The texts are all in pure black printed in white background. Figure 4.6 presents a typical example of the visual presentation of the Policy Addresses in CHPAC.

However, in CCPAC, more elements are added to contribute to the visual hierarchy of the texts. As summarized in Table 4.26, most of the Policy Addresses consisting in CCPAC are with colors. The use of colors creates contrasts in fonts with font colors as well as contrast in foreground and background colors. As mentioned before, there are separator pages in all the Policy Addresses in CCPAC except PA2011c and PA2012c, which divide the whole texts into chapters. On these chapter pages, there are white texts on a green background to highlight the texts. With all these elements, each Policy Address in CCPAC is clearly divided into sessions, even chapters in some of them, with texts varied in hierarchy, rather than a run-on passage.

**Table 4.26**  Elements provide visual weight to items included in texts

| PA | Chinese | English |
|----|---------|---------|
| 2000 | – Contrasting in **bold and regular form in the same font style**<br>– Contrasting in **font size**<br>– Use of **whitespace** to distinguish headings from body texts<br>– Use of different **alignments** (with indented paragraphs) | – Contrasting in **bold and regular form in the same font style**<br>– Contrasting in **font size**<br>– Use of **whitespace** to distinguish headings from body texts<br>– Use of different **alignments** (with indented paragraphs) |
| 2001 | – Use of **whitespace** | – Contrasting in **bold and regular form in the same font style**<br>– Use of **whitespace** |
| 2002 | – Contrasting in **bold and regular form in the same font style**<br>– Contrasting in **font size**<br>– Use of **whitespace** to distinguish headings from body texts<br>– Use of different **alignments** (with indented headings) | – Contrasting in **bold and regular form in the same font style**<br>– Contrasting in **font size**<br>– Use of **whitespace** to distinguish headings from body texts |
| 2003 | – Contrasting in **bold and regular form in the same font style**<br>– Contrasting in **font size**<br>– Use of **whitespace** to distinguish headings from body texts<br>– Use of **bullet points** to draw viewers' eyes<br>– Use of different **alignments** (with indented lines) | – Contrasting in **bold and regular form in the same font style**<br>– Contrasting in **font size**<br>– Use of **whitespace** to distinguish headings from body texts |
| 2004 | – Contrasting in **bold and regular form in the same font style**<br>– Contrasting in **font size**<br>– Use of **whitespace** to distinguish headings from body texts<br>– Use of **bullet points** to draw viewers' eyes<br>– Use of different **alignments** (with indented lines) | – Contrasting in **bold and regular form in the same font style**<br>– Contrasting in **font size**<br>– Use of **whitespace** to distinguish headings from body texts<br>– Use of **bullet points** to draw viewers' eyes<br>– Use of different **alignments** (with indented lines) |
| 2005 | – Contrasting in **font size**<br>– Use of **whitespace** to distinguish headings from body texts<br>– Use of **bullet points** to draw viewers' eyes | – Contrasting in **font size**<br>– Use of **whitespace** to distinguish headings from body texts<br>– Use of **bullet points** to draw viewers' eyes |

(continued)

**Table 4.26** (continued)

| PA | Chinese | English |
|---|---|---|
| 2006 | – Contrasting in **font size**<br>– Use of **whitespace** to distinguish headings from body texts<br>– Use of **bullet points** to draw viewers' eyes<br>– Use of different **alignments** (with indented lines) | – Contrasting in **font size**<br>– Use of **whitespace** to distinguish headings from body texts<br>– Use of **bullet points** to draw viewers' eyes<br>– Use of different **alignments** (with indented lines) |
| 2007 | – Contrasting in **font size**<br>– Use of **whitespace** to distinguish headings from body texts | – Contrasting in **bold and regular form in the same font style**<br>– Contrasting in **font size**<br>– Use of **whitespace** to distinguish headings from body texts |
| 2008 | – Contrasting in **font styles**<br>– Contrasting in **bold and regular form in font style**<br>– Contrasting in **font size**<br>– Use of **whitespace** to distinguish headings from body texts | – Contrasting in **bold and regular form in font style**<br>– Contrasting in **font size**<br>– Use of **whitespace** to distinguish headings from body texts |
| 2009 | – Contrasting in **font styles**<br>– Contrasting in **bold and regular form in font style**<br>– Contrasting in **font size**<br>– Use of **whitespace** to distinguish headings from body texts<br>– Use of different **alignments** (with indented paragraphs) | – Contrasting in **bold and regular form in font style**<br>– Contrasting in **font size**<br>– Use of **whitespace** to distinguish headings from body texts<br>– Use of different **alignments** (with indented paragraphs) |
| 2010 | – Contrasting in **bold and regular form in the same font style**<br>– Contrasting in **font size**<br>– Contrasting in **font color**<br>– Contrasting **foreground and background colors** (white texts on the green background in chapter pages)<br>– Use of **whitespace** to distinguish headings from body texts | – Contrasting in **bold and regular form in the same font style**<br>– Contrasting in **font size**<br>– Use of **whitespace** to distinguish headings from body texts<br>– Use of different **alignments** (with indented lines) |
| 2011 | – Contrasting in **font styles**<br>– Contrasting in **bold and regular form in font style**<br>– Contrasting in **font size**<br>– Use of **whitespace** to distinguish headings from body texts<br>– Use of different **alignments** (with indented headings) | – Contrasting in **bold and regular form in the same font style**<br>– Contrasting in **font size**<br>– Use of **whitespace** to distinguish headings from body texts<br>– Use of different **alignments** (with indented headings) |

(continued)

**Table 4.26**  (continued)

| PA | Chinese | English |
|----|---------|---------|
| 2012 | – Contrasting in **bold and regular form in the same font style**<br>– Contrasting in **font size**<br>– Use of **whitespace** to distinguish headings from body texts | – Contrasting in **bold and regular form in the same font style**<br>– Contrasting in **font size**<br>– Use of **whitespace** to distinguish headings from body texts<br>– Use of **bullet points** to draw viewers' eyes |
| 2013 | – Contrasting in **font styles**<br>– Contrasting in **bold and regular form in font style**<br>– Contrasting in **font size**<br>– Contrasting in **font color**<br>– Contrasting **foreground and background colors** (white texts on the green background in chapter pages)<br>– Use of **whitespace** to distinguish headings from body texts<br>– Use of different **alignments** (with indented headings) | – Contrasting in **bold and regular form in the same font style**<br>– Contrasting in **font size**<br>– Use of **whitespace** to distinguish headings from body texts |
| 2014 | – Contrasting in **font styles**<br>– Contrasting in **bold and regular form in font style**<br>– Contrasting in **font size**<br>– Contrasting in **font color**<br>– Contrasting **foreground and background colors** (white texts on the green background in chapter pages)<br>– Use of **whitespace** to distinguish headings from body texts<br>– Use of different **alignments** (with indented headings) | – Contrasting in **bold and regular form in the same font style**<br>– Contrasting in **font size**<br>– Use of **whitespace** to distinguish headings from body texts<br>– Use of different **alignments** (with indented headings) |
| 2015 | – Contrasting in **font styles**<br>– Contrasting in **bold and regular form in font style**<br>– Contrasting in **font size**<br>– Contrasting in **font color**<br>– Contrasting **foreground and background colors** (white texts on the green background in chapter pages)<br>– Use of **whitespace** to distinguish headings from body texts<br>– Use of different **alignments** (with indented headings) | – Contrasting in **bold and regular form in the same font style**<br>– Contrasting in **font size**<br>– Use of **whitespace** to distinguish headings from body texts<br>– Use of **bullet points** to draw viewers' eyes<br>– Use of different **alignments** (with indented lines) |

(continued)

**Table 4.26**  (continued)

| PA | Chinese | English |
|---|---|---|
| 2016 | – Contrasting in **font styles**<br>– Contrasting in **bold and regular form in font style**<br>– Contrasting in **font size**<br>– Contrasting in **font color**<br>– Contrasting **foreground and background colors** (white texts on the green background in chapter pages)<br>– Use of **whitespace** to distinguish headings from body texts<br>– Use of different **alignments** (with indented headings) | – Contrasting in **bold and regular form in the same font style**<br>– Contrasting in **font size**<br>– Use of **whitespace** to distinguish headings from body texts |
| 2017 | – Contrasting in **font styles**<br>– Contrasting in **bold and regular form in font style**<br>– Contrasting in **font size**<br>– Contrasting in **font color**<br>– Contrasting **foreground and background colors** (white texts on the green background in chapter pages)<br>– Use of **whitespace** to distinguish headings from body texts<br>– Use of different **alignments** (with indented headings) | – Contrasting in **bold and regular form in the same font style**<br>– Contrasting in **font size**<br>– Use of **whitespace** to distinguish headings from body texts<br>– Use of different **alignments** (with indented headings) |
| 2018 | – Contrasting in **font styles**<br>– Contrasting in **bold and regular form in font style**<br>– Contrasting in **font size**<br>– Contrasting in **font color**<br>– Contrasting **foreground and background colors** (white texts on the green background in chapter pages)<br>– Use of **whitespace** to distinguish headings from body texts<br>– Use of different **alignments** (with indented headings) | – Contrasting in **bold and regular form in the same font style**<br>– Contrasting in **font size**<br>– Use of **whitespace** to distinguish headings from body texts |

Therefore, while the mentioned visual elements provide the text visual hierarchy by using them contrastively to highlight or foreground some items within a composition to make them especially salient to the viewers, they furthermore create connectivity as well as separation visually to the texts by using them cohesively as kinds of visual rhyme to connect different parts of the texts and meanwhile, distinguish different parts of the texts. The chapter pages separate a Policy Address into apparently distinct sections and offer affinity to the pages in between to show that they are associated with each other. With the same font size, font style, font color as well as alignment, the texts will be associated with each other by the viewers, in which rhyme is created in between. Meanwhile, the contrast in the use of these elements indicates the difference of the texts, which likely offers different degrees of importance to the texts. Figure 4.8 presents a typical example of the visual presentation of the Policy Addresses in CCPAC, with the last picture presenting an instance of offering distinct visual weight to different parts of the text with the mentioned non-verbal resources.

Furthermore, the use of color contributes to the meaning potential in its ideational and interactive role. In addition to black and white, green is the other color used in the printed verbal version of the selected Policy Addresses. Green is the color associated with harmony and growth, which is the color of spring, renewal and rebirth (Scott-Kemmis 2009). The Policy Addresses which are filled with this bright and light color create a very different effect on viewers' feelings from the ones with pure black fonts printed in the white background, as the differences presented between Figs. 4.6 and 4.8. In addition, the green color is the representing color of the city, Macao.

Aside from the visual syntax and the use of colors, the typography serves as a type of visual resource which function in the meaning construction process. In terms of font style, the style with serifs, *Arphic Mingti* (文鼎明體) is the only font style applied in PA2000c to PA2007c (see Fig. 4.6 as an example). Serif is a small line or stroke regularly attached to the end of a larger stroke in a letter or a character within a particular font. Font styles with serifs first appeared 500 years ago. Classic literature is mostly printed in this particular type of font style. Due to its history of development, the font styles with serif are associated with history, knowledge and tradition. (Hyndman 2016) Starting from the second last Policy Address in Ho's two terms, PA2008c (see Fig. 4.7), there is no font style with serifs used in the fonts in the body texts of the Policy Addresses. Withal, the font style, relatively, in round shape, as *DFHeiBold-B5* (華康粗圓體) is applied.

In CCPAC, the font style with serif, *DFLiSongBold-B5* (華康儷粗宋), is applied in all the Policy Addresses included, except PA2011C and PA2012C, but on the cover pages and author pages only, and not appeared in the following hundreds of pages in each Policy Address. Some font styles, in which some fonts are with curves rather than straight strokes only,, such as *DFLiShu-B5* (華康隸書體) are used in all the Policy Addresses in CCPAC. The differences in the font styles are also demonstrated in Figs. 4.6, 4.7 and 4.8.

As mentioned before, the visual resources in the printed verbal texts as listed in Table 4.26, provide differences in terms of visual weight to different parts of texts. With those visual resources, a similar level of the visual weight is given to the sub-headings included in the section of the elaboration of the significant policies of the Government in the upcoming year in all the Policy Addresses in CHPAC and CCPAC, and they are all listed in their content pages except PA2000c (which is the only Policy Address without a content page).

How these sub-headings are placed demonstrates the differences in the information value of the meaning delivered by them. With the mentioned visual flow as top-to-bottom and left-to-right, the items within the same frame of the visual presentation take up the top and/or left position are the ones where the viewers' reading starts with. It is termed as the theme position in accordance with visual grammar. When examining the list of the mentioned sub-headings in the content pages, it is found that the majority (66.7%) of the top or the top-left phrases/clauses in CHPAC is with reference to **the Government's administration system**, such as 改善公眾 服務 (Devoting to innovation to match economic restructuring) in PA2002c, 行政 改革循序推行 (Implementing development plans) in PA2003c, and 深入改革吏治 (Intensifying administrative reform) in PA2005c. How the lines with reference to the Government's administration system occupy the majority of the theme position of the content pages in CHPA is presented in Table 4.27, and Fig. 4.9 shows one of the examples in the visual presentation of the content pages in CHPA.

In CCPAC, with the sub-headings which occupy the mentioned theme position, the majority (60%) falls to the ones who are with reference to **people's well-being and livelihoods**, such as 著力保障改善民生 (Improving the people's well-being and fostering the building of a harmonious society) in PA2010c, 持續提升民生素 質 (Continue to improve quality of life) in PA2016c, and 不斷完善五大民生長效機 制 (Continue perfecting the five-long-term mechanisms for people's well-being) in PA2018c. How the lines with reference to people's well-being and livelihood occupy the majority of the theme position of the content pages in CCPA is presented in Table 4.27, and Fig. 4.10 shows one of the examples in the visual presentation of the content pages of CCPA.

Regarding this theme position in the content pages, diachronic changes are identified in the Policy Addresses. In the first term of Ho's Government, 75% of those are with reference to the Government's administration system, which is lowered to 60% in the second term. In Chui's terms, it further descends to 40% in the first term and there are another 40% referring to people's livelihood, which is further raised to 80% in Chui's second term. Figure 4.11 presents the mentioned trend, which shows a relatively stable trend in those with reference to the economy.

The English translations are, likewise, with the visual flow as top-to-bottom and left-to-right, due to the actual practice of the language. With the mentioned visual flow, in terms of the visual syntax, in CHPAE, most of the Policy Addresses start with a content page as the Policy Addresses in CHPAC do, except PA2008e. PA2008c is the only Policy Address in CHPAC with a cover page but it is omitted in its English translation in CHPAE. In CCPAE, most of the Policy Addresses in English experience omission of the cover pages except PA2010e, PA2011e, PA2018e and PA2019e. In these Policy Addresses, the cover pages of their STs (the Policy Addresses of the same year in Chinese verbal texts) were kept.

In terms of the structure of the primary texts, all the English translations follow their source texts (the Policy Addresses in Chinese verbal texts). In both CHPAE and CCPAE, all the Policy Addresses are primarily with three main parts, namely an introduction (or translated into preface) of the full Policy Address, the body text, and a conclusion in general. In terms of the body texts, each of the Policy Addresses in CHPAE and CCPAE is structured as how they do in their source texts.

When comparing the visual configuration of the English translations of the Policy Addresses with the source texts, it is found that only some of the visual elements applied in the source texts are translated into the English versions. As summarized in Table 4.26, the diachronic change of the upward trend in the use of visual elements to different items in the texts to vary their visual weight in the verbal Policy Addresses in Chinese does not happen in the English translations. The visual presentation of

**Table 4.27** Sub-headings of the general policies objectives in theme position on content pages

| Corpus | Year | Sub-headings in Chinese | Sub-headings in English | Category |
|---|---|---|---|---|
| CHPA | 2000 | – | – | |
| | 2001 | 完善市場環境 | Improving market environment and promote economic development | Economy |
| | 2002 | 改善公眾服務 | Devoting to innovation to match economic restructuring | Administration |
| | 2003 | 行政改革循序推行 | Implementing development plans | Administration |
| | 2004 | 行政改革持續 | Intensifying administrative reforms | Administration |
| | 2005 | 深入改革吏治 | Intensifying administrative reform | Administration |
| | 2006 | 調整改革策略 | Strengthening reform strategy | Administration |
| | 2007 | 行政和法律改革 | Administrative and legal reforms | Administration |
| | 2008 | 鞏固經濟基礎 | Reinforcing economic foundations | Economy |
| | 2009 | 調整經濟策略 | Modifying economic strategies | Economy |
| CCPA | 2010 | 著力保障改善民生 | Improving the people's well-being and fostering the building of a harmonious society | Well-being |
| | 2011 | 致力優化民生素質 | Improving people's livelihoods | Well-being |
| | 2012 | 共享發展成果 | Sharing the fruits of development | Economy |
| | 2013 | 構建施政長效機制 | Develop a long-term mechanism for effective administration | Administration |
| | 2014 | 加快建設長效機制 | Accelerate development of long-term mechanisms and press ahead with livelihood projects | Administration |
| | 2015 | 同心協力, 應對內外環境的改變 | Join hands to weather internal and external changes | Economy |
| | 2016 | 持續提升民生素質 | Continue to improve quality of life | Well-being |

(continued)

**Table 4.27** (continued)

| Corpus | Year | Sub-headings in Chinese | Sub-headings in English | Category |
|---|---|---|---|---|
| | 2017 | 落實民生政策措施 | Implementation of livelihood-related polices and measures | Well-being |
| | 2018 | 不斷完善五大民生長效機制 | Continue perfecting the five-long-term mechanisms for people's well-being | Well-being |
| | 2019 | 聚焦民生改善 | Focus on improving people's livelihoods | Well-being |

中華人民共和國澳門特別行政區政府
二零零五年財政年度施政報告

目 錄

前言 . . . . . . . . . . . . . . . . . . . . . . . . . . . . . . . . . . . . . . . . . . 2
第一部分 特區政府二零零四年施政總結 . . . . . . . . . . . . . . . . . . . . . . 3
第二部分 特區政府二零零五年的施政重點 . . . . . . . . . . . . . . . . . . . . 7
　一、深入改革史治，推進服務入微 . . . . . . . . . . . . . . . . . . . . . . . . 8
　二、穩固經濟基礎，確保持續發展 . . . . . . . . . . . . . . . . . . . . . . . 11
　三、加強對外合作，提升平台功能 . . . . . . . . . . . . . . . . . . . . . . . 13
　四、啟動教育改革，力促人文進步 . . . . . . . . . . . . . . . . . . . . . . . 15
第三部分 提升素質，共建未來 . . . . . . . . . . . . . . . . . . . . . . . . . . . 18
結語 . . . . . . . . . . . . . . . . . . . . . . . . . . . . . . . . . . . . . . . . . . 23

Policy Address for the Fiscal Year 2005
of the Macao Special Administrative Region (MSAR)
of the People's Republic of China

CONTENTS

Introduction

Part I    Summary of the MSAR Government's Work in 2004

Part II   Administrative Priorities of the MSAR Government in 2005
1. Intensifying Administrative Reform, Enhancing All Aspects of Service Quality
2. Consolidating Our Economic Foundations, Ensuring Sustainable Development
3. Strengthening External Cooperation, Growing Macao as a Trading and Service Platform
4. Commencing Educational Reform, Striving for Human Development

Part III   Improving Ourselves and Building Macao's Future Together

Conclusion

**Fig. 4.9** PA2005 in Chinese and English

中華人民共和國澳門特別行政區政府
二〇一九年財政年度施政報告

目錄

前言 . . . . . . . . . . . . . . . . . . . . . . . . . . . . . . . . . . . 7
特區政府二〇一九年施政重點——
把握機遇，均衡發展 . . . . . . . . . . . . . . . . . . . . . . . . 9
　一、聚焦民生改善 . . . . . . . . . . . . . . . . . . . . . . . . 10
　二、深化城市建設 . . . . . . . . . . . . . . . . . . . . . . . . 17
　三、促進經濟發展 . . . . . . . . . . . . . . . . . . . . . . . . 22
　四、致力社會善治 . . . . . . . . . . . . . . . . . . . . . . . . 25
結語 . . . . . . . . . . . . . . . . . . . . . . . . . . . . . . . . . . 29
附錄一 澳門特別行政區政府二〇一九年法律提案項目 . . . . . . . 33
附錄二 二〇一九年度各範疇施政主要工作時間表 . . . . . . . . . 35

Translated Copy

The Government of the Macao Special
Administrative Region
Policy Address for the Fiscal Year 2019

Contents

Preface . . . . . . . . . . . . . . . . . . . . . . . . . . . . . . . . . . . 4

1. Focus on improving people's livelihoods . . . . . . . . 6

2. Deepen urban development . . . . . . . . . . . . . . . . . . 14

3. Promoting economic development . . . . . . . . . . . . 19

4. Committed to sound social governance . . . . . . . . 23

Conclusions . . . . . . . . . . . . . . . . . . . . . . . . . . . . . 25

Appendix I: Legal Proposals of the MSAR Government in 2019

Appendix II: Schedule of Major Tasks in Different Policy Domains in 2019

**Fig. 4.10** PA2019 in Chinese and English

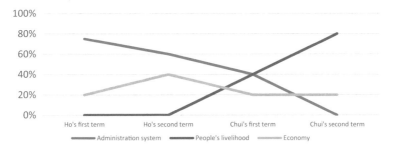

**Fig. 4.11**  The top/top-left headings of general policy objectives

all the Policy Addresses in both CHPAE and CCPAE are identical as purely black fonts printed on white background with contrast in font size and font style as well as the use of whitespace and alignment to offer different visual weight to items. The use of colors and chapter pages in some of their source texts to enhance the visual hierarchy or create separation and affinity is omitted in all English translations.

In terms of the application of colors and typography, the apparent trend in the use of them presented in the Chinese Policy Addresses diachronically does not exist in the English translations. As mentioned, all verbal Policy Addresses in English are with purely black fonts printed on white background. There is no application of other hues of colors. In terms of font style, the typically classic font style with serifs, *Times New Roman*, is used in the last six Policy Addresses in CHPAE (PA2004e to PA2009e). This implementation is kept in the first four Policy Addresses in CCPAE (PA2010e to PA2013e). Others are in *Arial Arabic*, a sans-serif typeface. With the result of the online type-tasting font census done by a well-known graphic designer with a Master's degree in Typography, Sarah Hyndman (Hyndman, 2016), at their interactive role, Times New Roman is associated with tradition, classics, profession, confidence, as well as being honored and neutral. Likewise, Arial Arabic is associated with confidence, reliability, neutrality, and calmness, but modernity.

When examining the list of headings in parallel visual weight on a content page, the order of the items is translated into the English versions in all the selected Policy Addresses. The result of the investigation of the first heading of the primary policy objectives drawing viewers' eyes to each English Policy Address remains the same as how the verbal Policy Addresses in Chinese do. As presented in Fig. 4.11, 75% of those are with reference to government administration system in Ho's first term, which is lowered to 60% in his second. It further descends to 40% in Chui's first term and there are another 40% referring to people's livelihood, which is further raised to 80% in Chui's second term.

Upon the analysis of the visual presentation of the Policy Addresses in Chinese and English, it is found that there are shifts in the Chinese-to-English translation process. Some of the elements applied in the source texts (the verbal Policy Addresses in Chinese) to vary the visual hierarchy and enhance readability are lost in the target texts (the verbal Policy Addresses in English), which present as relatively formal and plain text in terms of composition. The mentioned contrasts between source texts and target texts in terms of visual presentation are illustrated in Figs. 4.9 and 4.10.

To summarize, the multimodal analysis of the printed verbal versions of selected Policy Addresses reveals how the resources contribute to the meaning construction process non-verbally, in Ho's and Chui's Policy Addresses in Chinese, and how the visual configuration of them is translated into the English versions.

In the verbal Policy Addresses in Chinese, there is an upward trend in the application of non-verbal resources as a kind of visual contrast to distinct items of the text, and the cohesive application of non-verbal resources as a kind of visual rhyme to connect different items of a text, from the Policy Addresses in Chinese verbal texts released by Ho's offices to those released by Chui's offices. The visual rhyme and visual contrast meanwhile provide different levels of salience to different parts of the texts which create the visual flow and visual hierarchy. The structures of the selected Policy Addresses get more and more complete from those released in Ho's terms to those released in Chui's terms. Among all the verbal Policy Addresses in Chinese under investigation, starting from the fourth one in Chui's first term (PA2013c), the structure had got to a fix one which is complete as a book does (with a cover page, an author page, the body texts in sections separated by chapter pages and headings and appendix). In contrast, the first one in Ho's terms, PA2000c, is with the structure as a run-on passage without any other elements of a book except the body texts. Diachronically, the structure of the verbal Policy Addresses in Chinese is from printed as a run-on passage functioning as a script to printed as a complete document with elements for enhancing readability as a book does.

When translating the verbal Policy Addresses into English, there is a shift in the translation process in terms of the visual configuration. The elements implemented in the English texts to act as visual rhyme and visual contrast are far less than those in their source texts (verbal Policy Addresses in Chinese). In terms of the layout of the whole document piece, the complete structure as a book does applies in the Chinese versions do not happen in any of the English translations. The layout of all the English translations of the verbal Policy Addresses remains the same throughout the whole investigated period, from the first one released in Ho's terms to the last one released in Chui's terms. The shift happens similarly in the practice of the font size and font styles. In the verbal Policy Addresses in Chinese, there is a noticeable diachronic shift from the application of the classic, traditional typeface to the use of relatively modern and rounded typeface. This trend is not found in English translations. However, when examining the information value to the parallel headings listed in the content pages, the arrangement in the Chinese versions remains the same or is translated into the English translations, with the main trend as emphasizing the information value of the Government's administration system in Ho's terms with the theme position on the content page, but which is with a noticeable decrease throughout the four terms; and emphasizing the information value of the people's livelihood in Chui's last term, which has experienced a considerable rise throughout the four terms.

**Table 4.28** Colors used as visual rhyme in infographics

| COLOR | 2015 | 2016 | 2017 | 2018 | 2019 |
|---|---|---|---|---|---|
| Economics | Pink | Orange | Orange | Orange | Orange |
| People's livelihood | Orange | Blue | Blue | Blue | Blue |
| City environment | Green | N | Green | Green | Green |
| Public administration | Blue | Green | Pink | Pink | Pink |

## 4.4.2 Analysis of the Infographics of the Policy Addresses

After the investigation of the visual configuration of the printed verbal version of the selected Policy Addresses, this section presents the multimodal analysis of the infographics of the Policy Addresses. The infographics of the Policy Addresses has been released by the Government to accompany the verbal version for the public since 2015, the first year of Chui's second term. This section focuses on the investigation of the ideational function, interpersonal function and textual function of the use of color and the represented social actors in the infographics of PA2015, PA2016, PA2017, PA2018 and PA2019.

*Communicative functions of colors*

As mentioned in Chap. 2, colors are considered as one sort of visual resource since they are with their ideational, interpersonal and textual functions. All the infographics of Policy Addresses released in the investigated period are colored with bright colors as red, pink, yellow, and light blue, etc. It is easy to understand that the colorful presentation of the mentioned Policy Addresses has a very distinctive effect on viewers' feelings from the ones with pure black and white. This effect of the use of colors on the viewers is considered as the interpersonal role of colors. In the following, the textual and ideational roles of colors in the infographics of the selected Policy Addresses are under detailed examination.

In terms of the textual role of this sort of visual resource, the cohesive application of colors in the related pages of the infographics provides a connection to some pages and meanwhile distinguishes some pages from other parts of the whole text. In PA2015p, all pages are with the white background but with cohesive colored fonts and character shading for the titles of the pages. Starting from 2016, the pages of the infographics of the Policy Addresses are with page backgrounds in the cohesive application of colors and with consistently colored fonts and character shading for the titles of the pages.

In each page of this group of infographics of the Policy Addresses, the color of the page background, the color of the fonts and the color of the character shading of the page title are consistent, which dominates the use of color of the same page. Figure 4.12 presents some examples of pages consisting of the infographics of the Policy Addresses under investigation. The first picture in Fig. 4.12 is a page from PA2015p, which is with a white background but orange for the font color and character shading of the fonts in the page title. As presented, the whole page is dominated by orange colors. The second picture of Fig. 4.12 is a page of PA2016p, the page is in the green background as well as green character shading for the page title in green fonts. The whole page is dominated by green colors as presented. The third picture is a page of PA2017p. It is a page with blue background and blue character shading for page titles. The whole page is dominated by blue colors. The last picture is a page of PA2018p. It is a page dominated by pink colors, with the page background in pink, color shading for the page title in pink, as well as the fonts in pink for the page title.

With this consistent presentation as mentioned above, some pages are presented with the same dominating color. The cohesive use of the dominating colors of the pages offers them a connection as the same category and, in the meantime, distinguishes them from other pages. Table 4.28 summarizes this application of colours in the pages. These demonstrate the textual function of colors, which serves as the visual rhyme in the infographics. The whole set of the infographics of the Policy Addresses of the same year is divided into categories by the visual rhymes.

In terms of the ideational role of colors, the use of colors on the group of pages presenting different fields of policies serves to associate the policies with particular qualities by the potential meaning delivered by the representation of the colors. In PA2015p, the dominating color of the pages about economics are all in pink. Contrastingly, the dominating color of all the pages of the same topic in PA2016p to PA2019p is orange. In PA2015p, the color orange is used as the dominating color of the pages of people's livelihood. In the following years, the pages of people's livelihood are all with the dominating color of blue. In PA2015p, blue is used as the dominating color of the pages about governmental administration, while green is used in those of PA2016p. In the following years, from 2017 to 2019, all pages about governmental administration are with the dominating color of pink. For the pages about city environment, all those pages of the infographics of the selected Policy Addresses are dominated by the green color.

This presentation of colors shows that colors are applied to represent different areas of policies in the Policy Addresses. In the infographics of the Policy Addresses throughout the investigated period, the aspect of city environment is represented

**Fig. 4.12** The use of colors on pages of the infographics of the policy addresses

by green. With the experience of the color of plants, green is the color of spring, with the meaning potential of growth, renewal, rebirth and harmony (Scott-Kemmis 2009). In all other fields, the application of colors for representing different areas of policies is not consistent throughout the whole period under investigation but gets prominently consistent since 2016. The field of people's livelihood is prominently represented in blue. With the experience of the color of sky, sea and water, blue is the color of trust and peace, with the meaning potential of responsibility, reliability, honesty and calmness (Scott-Kemmis 2009). It is as the reason why the color blue is commonly used in police stations, as well as cars and uniform of police. The field of economics is prominently represented by the color orange. With the experience of the color of sunshine, orange is the color of optimism, with the meaning potential of warmth, happiness, energy and stimulation (Scott-Kemmis 2009). The field of governmental administration is represented prominently by the pink color. With the experience of the color's association with feminine qualities, pink is the color of love and compassion. It is with the meaning potential of nurturing, understanding and intimacy.

The use of colors, as mentioned before, associates the policies of different fields with different qualities. The dominating color of green on the pages associates the policies regarding city environment with growth, renewal and harmony. The dominating color of blue on the pages associates policies regarding people's livelihood with responsibility, reliability, honesty and calmness. By the color orange, policies regarding economics are associated with optimism and energy. And the policies regarding governmental administration are associated with compassion, nurturing and intimacy, by the color pink.

The application of colors not only acts as the visual rhyme to categorize the pages regarding policies of different fields but also associates the policies with particular qualities by the meaning potential delivered by the representation of colors, which presents the ideational role and the textual role of colors.

*Representation of social actors in pictures*

As reviewed in Chap. 2, Kress and van Leeuwen's visual grammar (1996, 2006, 2021, 47) stated that people, places and things (including abstract things) which are represented in semiotic systems are named as RPs, represented participants. The represented participants which are with humanized qualities in visual communication are termed as social actors. The semiotic resources for the depiction of the social actors serve to position the viewers in relation to participants in the pictures, and to encourage the viewers to relate and assess them in certain ways. (Machin 2007, 109) This section presents the results of the examination of the social actors in the infographics of the selected Policy Addresses. Table 4.29 provides a summary of the social actors identified in the infographics under investigation.

This examination which focuses on the depiction of people in the visual communication of the infographics deals with the semiotic resources for aligning the viewers with the experiences of the participants, how visually participants can be categorized and what participants do in the images. (Machin 2007, 107) Similarities and differences are found in the representation of the social actors in the infographics

**Table 4.29** Social actors in infographics

|  | Positioning the viewer | Kinds of participants | Agency and action |
|---|---|---|---|
| PA2015p | – With simple figures without facial expressions and gestures in most of the cases<br>– All presented in same level rather than being raised or lowered<br>– Frontality except two conventional signs for disabled and elderlies | – Depicted as generic ones of specific groups with distinctive features for biological and cultural categorisations: elderlies, the disabled, graduates, employees, civil servants, gaming employees, foreign workers, conventional and exhibition workers, young merchants, security force, governmental committee, committee with general people | – All presented in conceptual processes with iconographical meaning |
| PA2016p | – 6 out of 17 identified figures representing social actors (35.3%) with simple figures without facial expressions and gestures<br>– 11 out of 17 identified figures representing social actors (64.7%) with cartoon figures with facial expression and gestures<br>– 7 of the cartoon ones with gaze engagement with the viewers (in demand visual act), the other 4 in visual act of offer<br>– All presented in same level rather than being raised or lowered<br>– All presented with frontality | – Depicted as generic ones of specific groups with distinctive features for biological and cultural categorisations: elderlies, the disabled, graduates, employees, civil servants, children, governmental committee, merchants, security force, thieves, committee with general people, tourists | – 11 out of 17 identified figures representing social actors (64.7%) in conceptual processes<br>– 6 out of 17 (35.3%) in narrative processes |

(continued)

of different Policy Addresses under investigation. The presentation of the analysis results starts with considering how the social actors are categorized visually in the images. In PA2015p, the social actors are only presented in simple figures (as shown in Fig. 4.13) without facial expressions or even gestures in most of the cases. They are depicted as specific categorisations with the stereotyped group characteristics as well as the standard attributes in culture. For example, in the representation in

**Table 4.29**  (continued)

| | Positioning the viewer | Kinds of participants | Agency and action |
|---|---|---|---|
| PA2017p | – All presented in cartoon figures with gaze, facial expression and gestures<br>– All in visual act of offer (with no gaze engagement with the viewer)<br>– All presented in same level rather than being raised or lowered<br>– Mainly presented with oblique horizontal angles | – Depicted as generic ones of specific groups with distinctive features for biological and cultural categorisations: elderlies, the disabled, graduates, employees, civil servants, children, residents, family, gaming employees, innovative industry workers, merchants, medium-small enterprises owners, young merchants, Portuguese-speaking people, hawkers, employers, medical staff, human resources trainers, students, financial markets practitioners, construction workers, cook | – 4 out of 33 identified figures representing social actors (12.1%) in conceptual processes<br>– 29 out of 33 (87.9%) in narrative processes |
| PA2018p | – All presented in cartoon figures with gaze, facial expression and gestures<br>– All identified figures representing social actors in visual act of offer (with no gaze engagement with the viewer)<br>– All presented in same level rather than being raised or lowered<br>– All presented with oblique horizontal angles | – Depicted as generic ones of specific groups with distinctive features for biological and cultural categorisations: elderlies, the disabled, graduates, employees, civil servants, children, residents, residents with low income, family, governmental committee, innovative industry workers, merchants, medium-small enterprises owners, young merchants, the young, Portuguese-speaking people, civil servants for emergency, tourists, hawkers, medical staff, construction workers, government, caregivers | – All identified figures representing social actors in narrative processes |

(continued)

**Table 4.29** (continued)

| | Positioning the viewer | Kinds of participants | Agency and action |
|---|---|---|---|
| PA2019p | – All presented in cartoon figures with gaze, facial expression and gestures<br>– 34 out of 33 identified figures representing social actors (97.1%) in visual act of offer (with no gaze engagement with the viewer)<br>– All presented in same level rather than being raised or lowered<br>– Mainly presented with oblique horizontal angles | – Depicted as generic ones of specific groups with distinctive features for biological and cultural categorisations: elderlies, the disabled, graduates, employees, civil servants, children, residents, family, gaming employees, foreign workers, governmental committees, conventional and exhibition workers, innovative industry workers, merchants, the young, Portuguese-speaking people, employers, medical staff, students, human resources trainers, students, construction workers, government, athletes, scientists | – 4 out of 35 identified figures representing social actors (11.4%) in conceptual processes<br>– 31 out of 35 (88.6%) in narrative processes |

Fig. 4.13, the actors are with distinctive features for biological and cultural categorizations as the wheelchair for disabled people, the stick and bending gesture for elderlies, the square academic cap for graduates, the working permit for the foreign workforce, and the poker for gaming practitioners. This form of the presentation without facial expressions and gaze reduces the individualization and makes the social actors depicted as generic ones for the specific groups. With the social actors in the images of PA2015p, the specific social groups represented include elderlies, the disabled, graduates, employees, civil servants, gaming employees, foreign workers, conventional and exhibition workers, young merchants, security force, governmental committee, and committees with general people for city development.

As reviewed in Chap. 2, how the viewers are positioned in relation to the people inside the images can be realized by the aspects including the *gaze, angle of interaction* and *distance*. As mentioned before, all the social actors in PA2015p are presented only in simple figures without engaging the viewers by gaze or facial expression. With Kress and van Leeuwen's visual grammar, these are the images with the visual act as *offer* rather than *demand* (1996, 2006, 2021, 129). With this visual act as offer, the readers look at the social actors as spectators instead of being demanded to provide response. In terms of the angle of interaction, except the images for the disabled and the elderly are presented from the side, as shown in Fig. 4.13, all

**Fig. 4.13**  Biological and cultural categorisation of social actors represented in PA2015p

other figures are presented with a frontal angle. And all images are presented at the same level rather than being raised or lowered to the viewers. Therefore, the social actors represented PA2015p position the readers of the infographics as the observers of the information the images offer, with equal power to the represented social actors, instead of being called upon for response. In addition, all the figures in PA2015p are presented in conceptual representation, with no actions involved to convey iconographical meaning.

Different from the infographics of PA2015, starting from PA2016, there are social actors presented by the images with facial expressions and gestures in the infographics of the Policy Addresses. In PA2016p, 35.3% of the social actors represented are presented in simple figures as those in PA2015p, and the rest of them (64.7%) are presented in cartoon figures with facial expressions and gestures. Likewise, regarding the consideration of how participants are categorized visually, for both simple and cartoon figures, the social actors identified in PA2016p are depicted as the generic ones of the specific categorisations with the stereotyped group characteristics as well as the standard attributes in culture. For simple figures, the social actors have distinctive features to represent specific categorisations,, such as those in suit for administrative staff and those with nappies for babies (as presented in Fig. 4.14). For cartoon figures, the actors are, similarly, depicted with richer features for biological and cultural categorizations as the academic cap, the certificate with colored ribbon and the black graduation gown for graduates, the baldness and grey hair for elderlies, the blue uniform for policeman and the conventional zebra stripes for thieves, as presented in Fig. 4.15. With the images representing participants in humanized qualities, the specific social groups represented in PA2016p include elderlies, the disabled, graduates, employees, civil servants, children, governmental committees, merchants, security forces, thieves, the committee with general people and tourists.

As mentioned before, 64.7% of the represented social actors in PA2016p are presented in cartoon figures with facial expressions and gestures. Four of the cartoon figures have no interaction with the viewers by the gaze, with Kress and van Leeuwen's terms, are in the visual act of offer, to present information to the viewers instead of asking for a response. Seven other cartoon figures are with gaze engagement with the viewers, to represent different kinds of demands, together with the facial expression and gestures of the represented social actors. The response operated by the visual act as demand represented with the social actors in PA2016p is divided into two main types, namely inviting the viewers or allowing the viewers to share in the joy moment with their smile together with the gaze as the graduate

**Fig. 4.14**  Simple figures in PA2016p

**Fig. 4.15**  Cartoon figures in PA2016p

and the elderlies represented in Fig. 4.15, and drawing the viewers' attention to the positive information delivered in the particular part of the picture with the pointing gesture together with the smile and gaze, as the elderly in the picture of Fig. 4.15. They are all presented with frontality at the same level rather than being raised or lowered to the viewers.

When investigating what the social actors do in the pictures of the infographics of PA2016, it is found that there are 13 out of 17 (76.5%) identified figures with conceptual representation while the other four are with narrative representation. Two pictures with the social actors introducing narrative representation are with the vector for introducing the mental process as thinking, which is represented by the eye-rolling of the social actors, such as the graduate in the first picture in Fig. 4.15. In addition, one of these four pictures depicting a social actor represents a material process of pointing as the elderly represented in the last picture of Fig. 4.15. In the other one left, as shown in Fig. 4.16, the social actor represented acts as the goal of the material process of watering to suggest the metaphorical meaning as cultivating the youth via education.

Unlike the infographics of PA2015 and PA2016, all social actors identified in PA2017p are presented in cartoon figures with facial expressions and gestures. Corresponding to the infographics of all other Policy Addresses under investigation, the social actors identified in the pictures of PA2017p are depicted as the generic ones of the specific categorisations with the stereotyped group characteristics as well as the standard attributes in culture. They are presented with rich features for biological and

**Fig. 4.16**  Special narrative
representation in PA2016p

cultural categorisations to represent specific social groups. For instance, as shown in
Fig. 4.17, the features which consist of the stick, the baldness, grey hair and wrin-
kles for elderlies; the white coat, the stethoscope and the scrub for medical staff, the
suit for administrative staff, the white uniform and the white chef hat for the cook,
are the non-verbal resources applied in the pictures to depict the particular group of
people. The categorisations of the social actors identified in PA2017p includes elderlies, the disabled, graduates, employees, civil servants, children, residents, family,
gaming employees, innovative industry workers, merchants, medium-small enterprises owners, young merchants, Portuguese-speaking people, hawkers, employers,
medical staff, human resources trainers, students, financial markets practitioners,
construction workers and the cook. Contrasting to PA2016p, all the pictures with
the depiction of social actors are in visual art of offer, having no contact with the
viewers by gaze, to present information to the viewers. They are mainly presented
with oblique angles but in same level rather than being raised or lowered. With these
forms of presentation, the actors are positioned as the observers of the information
the pictures offer, with equal power to the represented social actors.

In all the images in PA2017p, the social actors are involved in narrative representation to represent reaction processes and action processes. Figure 4.17 presents
examples of the mentioned processes. When introducing the subsidies to different
groups of residents, as presented in the first two pictures in Fig. 4.17, there are social
actors to present the reaction process by looking at the description as reactors to react

**Fig. 4.17**  Narrative representation in PA2017p

to the subsidy given by the Government with a smile of approval. Action processes are also represented in some pictures. The third and fourth pictures in Fig. 4.17 are the instances. In the third picture, there is a staff stretching out his hands to depict the staff as a social actor in the non-transactional vector of welcoming. In the fourth picture, it is the action process with symbolic representation that first appeared in PA2016p. Rather than being presented as an Event (representation of actions which include only a Goal, which is to show something happening to someone without mentioning who or what makes it happen (Kress and van Leeuwen 1996/2006/2021, 60)) without an actor as in PA2016p (Fig. 4.16), there is a senior person who is watering the graduates in PA2017p (Fig. 4.17). It suggests the metaphorical meaning of cultivating the young. In some other pictures, there is a combination of action and reaction processes, as presented in the fifth and sixth pictures in Fig. 4.17. In the fifth picture, the medical staff talks to the kid as the actors and the little girl reacts to them as a reactor with a smile of approval again to represent the positive connection in between. The sixth picture presents a cook, an administrative staff and a cultural and creative professional who are talking together as the interactors to each other with the vector of talking. In all the mentioned action processes, the actors or the interactors meanwhile act as the reactors to the others by looking at them with the joyful facial expression to react with approval.

As mentioned before, starting from PA2017p, the depiction of people in the info-graphics of the Policy Addresses are all presented in cartoon figures with facial expression and gestures. They are depicted as the generic ones of the specific groups. With the rich resources presenting the distinctive features for biological and cultural categorisations, the social actors represented in PA2018p consist of elderlies, the disabled, graduates, employees, civil servants, children, residents, residents with low income, family, governmental committee, innovative industry workers, merchants, medium-small enterprises owners, young merchants, the young, Portuguese-speaking people, civil servants for emergency, tourists, hawkers, medical staff, construction workers, caregivers and government. Figure 4.18 presents some examples.

There is a social actor in the special depiction which does not exist in the previous ones, with the potential signified as the Government. It is found that there is a heart appearing in every page of the infographics of PA2018. This is the only social actor in the infographics that does not depict a human being but with humanized qualities. It is a personified heart character with facial expressions and gestures, as shown in Fig. 4.18. With the humanized qualities, the heart character presents action and reaction to have engagement with other social actors represented in the pictures. With the processes the heart character delivered, the heart character is depicted as taking up the role of the Government to interact with other participants of the society. The details of the processes are elaborated in the following. Corresponding to PA2017p, all social actors in PA2018p do not engage the viewers with gaze but represent the visual art as offer to deliver information to the viewers. Likewise, all of them are presented in the same level rather than being raised or lowered to the viewers. With these forms of presentation, the viewers are positioned, with equal power to the represented social actors, as the observers of the information they offer.

**Fig. 4.18** Narrative representaion in PA2018p

When investigating what the represented social actors do in the pictures, similar to PA2017p, the social actors in PA2018p are with narrative representation. Figure 4.18 presents some relevant examples. When introducing the subsidies offered by the Government, instead of the pure reaction process presented only with their gaze and smile as presented in PA2017p (see the first and the second picture of Fig. 4.17), the social actors in PA2018p present action processes. As shown in the first and the second pictures in Fig. 4.18, the social actors not only react to the announcement of the subsidies with their gaze and smile, but also present the actions of putting their hands up and leaning their bodies on the announcement board with joy. There are other action processes represented in the infographics of PA2018p, such as the non-transactional process shown in the third picture of Fig. 4.18 with the social actor as the actor to present the action, and the transactional process shown in the fourth picture with the two social actors as the interactors to present the interaction in between.

As mentioned before, there is a unique social actor which is not with the visual depiction of a human being in shape but with humanized qualities. It is with the potential representation of the Government presented in a personified heart character on each page of PA2018p. As presented in the first and the fifth picture in Fig. 4.18, the heart character presents the verbal process with the bubble to announce the subsidies to students offered by the Government. In some other pictures, the heart character even maintains interaction with the other social actors. For instance, in the last picture of Fig. 4.18, there is a social actor with very simple clothing and an unpleasant facial expression. The heart character presents the action process to hold this social actor to invite him to the announcement board of the financial support for residents with low income. It is found that the heart character takes the role of announcing the Government policies as well as inviting other represented social actors to the Government's supports for residents. With this particular depiction, this personified heart character serves as a social actor with the potential signified of the

Government to announce the policies and engage with different participants in the society, on each page of the infographics of PA2018p.

Similar to PA2017p and PA2018p, the infographics of PA2019 are with the social actors in cartoon figures with facial expressions and gestures. They are all depicted with distinctive features for biological and cultural categorizations as elderlies, the disabled, graduates, employees, civil servants, children, residents, family, gaming employees, foreign workers, governmental committees, conventional and exhibition workers, innovative industry workers, merchants, the young, Portuguese-speaking people, employers, medical staff, students, human resources trainers, students, construction workers, the Government, athletes and scientists.

Comparing with PA2015p, PA2016p, PA2017p and PA2018p, there are more social actors identified in the infographics of PA2019, such as scientists and athletes, which do not exist in the infographics of the Policy Addresses of all previous years. In addition to the distinctive ones, corresponding to PA2018p, there is a personified heart character on each page of PA2019p with the potential signified as the Government. This character is depicted as the role of announcing the policies and interacting with other characters in the pictures. The details of the specific processes are elaborated in the following.

When investigating how the viewers are positioned in relation to the people inside the images of PA2019p, it is found that all the represented social actors are not with the gaze engagement with the viewers, but with the visual act as offer to present information to the viewers instead. Regarding the angle of interaction, they are shown at the same level to the viewers, and our viewing position is not raised or lowered when looking at these social actors. With these forms of presentation, in the infographics of PA2019, the viewers are positioned, with equal power to the represented social actors, as the observers of the information they offer.

When examining what the social actors do in visual communication, it is found that they are mainly with narrative representation in the pictures of PA2019p, as how they do in PA2017p and PA2018p. With the narrative representation, the social actors are depicted as doing actions in the pictures. In terms of the actions represented, there are transactional and non-transactional action processes, as well as reaction processes, which are similar to the pictures of the two previous years. However, more interaction between the personified heart character and other social actors are identified in PA2019p. Figure 4.19 presents some relevant examples.

**Fig. 4.19**  Narrative representaion in PA2019p

As presented in the first picture of Fig. 4.19, the family with the smile on each member's face is brought together by the heart character with an action process. In the second picture, the heart does the same to deliver an action process to bring the disabled and the employee together, both of whom react with a smile. In the third picture, the heart character acts in the role of delivering the letters. The social actor underneath presents a non-transactional action process of jumping joyfully with the letter in hand. His pleasant reaction serves as the response to the letter delivered by the heart character. In the fourth picture, the heart character puts up the umbrella for the merchant, and he reacts with joyful facial expressions and gestures. In these pictures, it is found that all other social actors react with pleasant facial expressions and gestures to the materials processes of the heart character. With these forms of presentation, and engagement with other social actors, the heart character in PA2019p is further depicted as the role to deliver joy to other participants in the society.

In the multimodal analysis of the infographics of the Policy Addresses, how the unique key word, 博彩 (LT: gambling), in the present study is translated in the inter-semiotic translation process is under investigation. As one of the key words referring to the policy foci identified in this study and the one with the unique presentation when compared to the others in the same category, the representation of "gaming" in the infographics of the Policy Addresses is worth examination. Figure 4.20 presents the relevant images in the infographics of the Policy Addresses. It is found that, as shown in the pictures in Fig. 4.20, the gaming industry "collocates" with other kinds of entertainment,, such as cable cars, hot air balloons and carousels, which are neutral and suitable for any types of customers even families with children and tourists for sight-seeing. It is also attached to the representation of "international" by being placed in the context of the buildings representing other foreign countries, as presented in the third picture of Fig. 4.20. In spatial composition, the representation of the gaming industry is carnival-related, diversified, and international.

To summarize, this section investigates the infographics of the Policy Addresses released in the investigated period, with a special focus on the use of colors and the represented social actors. It is found that the dominating colors of the pages are presented cohesively as the visual rhyme to connect pages related to the policies in the same field. Meanwhile, they distinguish the pages about particular policy from the others.

In addition to its textual role, the dominating colors of the pages are with their ideational role to associate different categories of policies with particular qualities by the potential meanings they signify, as green for growth and renewal; blue for

**Fig. 4.20**   Images related to gaming industry in infographics of the Policy Addresses

harmony, reliability, honesty; orange for energy; and pink for understanding and compassion. In the examination of the represented social actors in the infographics, it is found that they are prominently represented with narrative representation to present action processes as the harmonious interaction among represented social actors and reaction processes as the positive response to the policies of the Government. In PA2018p and PA2019p in particular, there is harmonious interaction between the Government and other participants of the society represented by the depiction of the social actors in the pictures.

Comparing to the verbal analysis to the selected Policy Addresses in verbal texts, translation shifts in the inter-semiotic translation process are identified. The results of the analysis of the verbal version of the Policy Addresses of CCPAC reveal that there are more policy foci, more specific governmental measures, schemes for continuously developing and putting the planned goals into effect, as well as new goals for diverse development raised by Chui's second office. The discourse semantics of CCPAC corresponds to the discourse semantics of CCPAP. Though the analysis shows that the two modes work together to present the Government with their semiotic configurations with common discourse semantics, the variations in between are somewhat stable. The infographics of the Policy Addresses represent not only the governing policies, development schemes and directions of the Government, but also the harmonious society with the pleasant governing in the city. While verbal semiosis is basically informative, the appellative qualities of the verbal texts are enhanced in the infographics of the Policy Addresses, which responds to the nature of the two modes of resources.

## 4.5  Summary of Finding

This chapter conducts a corpus-assisted analysis of the key words of the Policy Addresses from Ho's two offices and Chui's two offices, with the multimodal analysis in terms of spatial composition of the selected Policy Addresses and the multimodal analysis of the infographics of the Policy Addresses under investigation, in the particular focus of the use of colors and the represented social actors in the pictures. With the corpus tool, the key words of CHPAC and CCPAC are identified. It is found that the denotation of the key words can be classified into three major categories, namely policy foci, actions, and social groups.

In the examination, diachronic changes are found in the distribution of the key words. While there is no key word referring to the policy foci appearing in the *Keyword* search of CHPAC, there are three key words attained from CCPAC with reference to this category. These three key words are with very different distribution in both corpora as rocketing in the application in the Policy Addresses of Chui's first term. Among these three key words referring to policy foci, 博彩 (LT: gambling) presents a similar distribution as others, but there is also an increase in the application of its opposite, "non-gaming" in the investigated period.

For the key words with reference to the Government's actions, in addition to the common key verbs which introduce the processes of improving and refining, there are distinctive key verbs identified in both Ho's and Chui's Policy Addresses. While there is the one conveying the mental process of making promises in CHPAC, there are the ones conveying material processes of creating new goals, putting goals into effect, as well as the action of giving in CCPAC.

For the category of the key words with reference to social groups, a first-person plural pronoun is far more frequently used in CHPAC for labeling the voice of the Policy Addresses, while it is labeled with the name of the Government per se more often in CCPAC.

In addition to the distribution of the key words, similarities and differences are found in their contextualization and translation in CHPAC and CCPAC as well. **For the key words with reference to policy foci**, throughout the investigated period, diachronically, three of them present correspondingly in their linguistic contexts that they form word groups with their *Collocates* **to deliver meaning from being consistent to more diverse and from being general to more specific**.

For 博彩 (LT: gambling), while the word groups which denote the general gaming industry are with salience in CHPAC, the word groups which denote not only the general industry but also the specific companies of the industry are with particular salience in CCPAC; while the word groups which denote the growth and the change of the industry are with salience in CHPAC, there are word groups which denote not only the growth and the change of the industry but also healthy and long-term development of the industry are with particular salience in CCPAC; while the word groups which refer to managing the industry are with salience in CHPAC, particular salience are put to the word groups which denote the meaning not only controlling but also observing and checking the progress and qualities of the development of the industry in CCPAC.

For 民生 (LT: people's lives), while there are word groups denoting the meaning as removing unwanted elements and making minor changes to improve the people's lives in the city with salience in CHPAC, the word groups referring to not only removing unwanted elements and making minor changes but also perfecting the relevant measures are with particular salience in CCPAC; while the noun groups denoting the general public system of the Government in terms of people's lives are with salience in CHPAC, there are noun groups, more specifically, denoting the Government's plan or course of action as well as different sorts of policies and measures for the lives of people in the city with salience in CCPAC. In CCPAC, salience is also put to the word groups with reference to making positive process toward people's livelihood and well-being in a non-stopping manner.

For 多元 (LT: diversification), while salience is put to the word groups with reference to the diversification of the economic system of the city in both CHPAC and CCPAC, the word groups with reference to making the diversification of the economic system of the city happen earlier and faster are also with salience in CCPAC.

**For key words denoting the Government's actions, though there are common key verbs in both corpora, contrasts in the goals of the key verbs are identified**. Salience is put to the key verbs in both corpora with common reference to improving and refining. The goals of these key verbs in their linguistic contexts of the Policy Addresses are similar in general, with the economy, people's livelihood, public administration, regional cooperation and population quality as the top five and with the first two ranked the same in both CHPAC and CCPAC. In addition, the goals with reference to legal environment appear in CCPAC with a certain proportion, which does not exist in CCPAC.

While the goals related to economics are represented by the word groups which denote the recovery of the economic system of the society as well as the coordinated economic development in CHPAC, they are the ones denoting adequate diversification of the economic system, coordinated economic development, economic environment, as well as the continuation of socioeconomic development in CCPAC.

While the goals referring to people's livelihood are represented by the word groups which denote the residents' living quality and education in CHPAC, they denote the more specific living qualities and aspects to education in CCPAC.

While the goals related to public administration are represented by the word groups denoting the quality of governing and civil servants, the cooperation among departments, and the consultation and complaint mechanism in CHPAC, they are the ones denoting not only the quality of governing and civil servants, but also the response mechanism to emergency in CCPAC. **They present the changes from dealing with essential elements to diverse development, from recovering to further continuously developing**.

For the distinctive key verbs, with their significant *Collocates*, they represent the meaning **from promising the stability and harmony of the society, as well as citizens' living quality in CHPAC, to introducing new goals for tourism development, and putting the goals with reference to people's livelihood into effect, with education as one of the primary foci in particular, as well as sharing the fruitful financial results with the public in CCPAC**.

For the category of **social groups and institute**, the key words identified are in common as the nouns denoting the name of the speaker, the audience and other participants of policy addresses but with a most distinctive one in CHPAC, the only personal pronoun obtained from *Keyword* search, 我們 *(we, us, our, ours)*, which is with similar reference to other key words in the same group as 政府 *(government)*, 特區政府 *(SAR government)* or 特區 *(SAR)*, all of which are different labeling of the government in the Policy Addresses.

**For the personal pronoun, in the linguistic contexts in CHPAC in particular, salience is put to the *Collocate* s reflecting a positive attitude and speaker's high confidence toward the propositions. This particular significance does not exist in CCPAC**. And the mentioned personal pronoun is prominently with exclusive use to denote the Government only, which is with the same reference to the other two key words in this category, the names of the Government.

**The names of the Government**, with their significant *Collocates*, corresponding to the presentation of the other naming of the Government---the personal pronoun, offer salience to speaker's positive attitude toward the propositions throughout the investigated period. In addition to the contexts in common, the key word forms a word group to label the Government as a clean and open administration for a new age in CCPAC.

When investigating the English versions of the Policy Addresses, translation shifts are identified. For **the key words with reference to policy foci**, it is found that translation takes a role in constructing the change in meaning in the English version. Specifically, the three key words representing three significant political fields present differently in the translation.

For 博彩 (LT: gambling), with the translation shifts of diction, substitution and omission, there is the primary trend in translating the key word with the word choice in neutral reference. The word choice with negative reference has been used in different relevant contexts after 2004, which are with the representation of disadvantages of the risking activities and getting away from the related bad influences. Given the primary trend of translating 博彩 (LT: gambling) into *gaming*, the translations reframe the key word 博彩 (LT: gambling) as the more general and neutral concept for entertainment.

For 多元 (LT: diversification), it is found that the key word is translated dynamically with the shifts as *diction, substitution, omission* and *conversion*, and prominently with *diction* and *conversion*. Nominalization is widely applied in the presentation of this key word in both Chinese and English versions. It is noticeably frequent in the application of the word groups with reference economy. With the translation shifts of *diction* and *conversion* (translating a word in other word forms into a noun), the implementation of nominalization is even enhanced in English translation.

For 民生 (LT: people's lives), it is found that the key word is translated inconsistently throughout the whole investigated period with the shifts of diction and specification. With the most frequent word choice, which occupies more than half of the translations of the key word, the key word is specified into materials lives rather than the abstract well-being in the English translation, throughout the investigated period.

**For the common key verbs, the translation also presents in common**. Throughout the investigated period, the translation shift identified in the process of translating this group of key verbs in Chinese into English is *diction*. Moreover, the word choices and proportion of the word choices are similar in both corpora. However, though the common key verbs are with very high *Keyness* in the Policy Addresses under investigation, the considerable significance of these verbs does not exist in the texts in this particular discourse type in native English. Instead, it is the distinctive feature of this Chinese-to-English translated text in particular.

**For the translations of the key words with reference to social groups and institutes**, the first-person-plural pronouns as the only key pronoun attained in this study and with the theoretical foundation to prove that they are considered as one type of linguistic resources which covey language modality, this study focuses on the investigation of all first-person plural pronouns in the English translations.

The analysis of the first-person plural pronouns in the English version of the Policy Addresses reveals that the translation shifts in the Chinese-to-English translation process serve to reposition the English texts' audience. When tracing the first-person plural pronouns in English translations, it is found that they are frequently added to the English texts via the translation shifts of addition and substitution to accentuate the governing responsibility and merits of the Government, and meanwhile, build up the relationship between the Government and the public.

Among all the first-person plural pronouns in English translations, the subject *we* is the most frequent one. The contextualization of this particular translation demonstrates the similarities and differences in its application in CHPAE, CCPAE and the State of the Union Addresses. There are three types of common *Collocates* of *We* in all three corpora, namely the lexical verbs denoting processes with effort, such as *encourage, promote* and *optimize,* model lexical verbs in epistemic modality (concerning with the speaker's confidence of a proposition expressed), such as *believe* and *understand*, as well as modal lexical words representing boulomaic modality (indicating wishes and desires of the speaker), such as *hope* and *want.*

With the first type of common Collocates, they contrast in their frequency in each corpus as 17% in CHPAE, 25% in CCPAE but only 1.4% in the State of the Union Addresses. In terms of epistemic warranty, while the key pronoun *we* is with the significant *Collocates* in high epistemic warranty, CCPAE and the State of the Union Addresses are with the ones with full epistemic warranty though the one in high epistemic warranty is also with salience in the State of the Union Addresses.

While *We* is significantly used in the context representing boulomaic commitment in both CHPAE and the State of the Union Addresses, no considerable salience is identified in CCPAE. Though there are common *Collocates*, they present differently in the three corpora, suggesting that the speaker refers their own voice on behalf of the Government in the Policy Addresses with different language modalities in each corpus.

For the translations of all these identified key words, when using them as the node words to search in the corpus with selected the State of the Union Addresses, it found that these translations are with evident difference in their linguistic presentation in the contexts. The translations are not only with distinctive frequency in application but also with unique collocations in Macao Policy Addresses, compared with the texts in the same discourse type in native English, which suggests their special significance in Macao contexts.

The textual analysis of the verbal resources is moved forward to **a multimodal analysis of the non-verbal resources of the verbal version of the selected Policy Addresses**. Diachronically, the structure of the Policy Addresses in Chinese is from printed as a run-on passage functioning as a script, to a complete printed document with elements enhancing readability as a book does. When translating into English, there is a shift in visual presentation as well the translation process. The layout of all the selected English translations remains similar. The elements implemented in the English texts to act as visual rhyme and contrast are far less than those in the Chinese texts. The complete structure as a book applied in the Chinese versions does not happen in any of the English translations.

A similar trend appears in the shift of the application of the font style. In the verbal version of the Policy Addresses in Chinese, there is a noticeable shift from the application of the classic and traditional typeface to the use of a relatively modern and rounded typeface throughout the investigated period. However, this trend is not found in the English versions. Furthermore, with the multimodal analysis, it is found that with non-verbal resources in both Chinese and English versions, a considerable decrease in the significance is attached to the field of public administration and a noticeable rise appears in the salience attached to the field of people's livelihood.

Having analyzed the verbal version of the selected Policy Addresses, the study moves forward to the analysis of the infographics of the Policy Addresses released in the investigated periods, which include the infographics of the Policy Addresses from Chui's second office (PA2015 to PA2019). It is found that the colors, with their textual role, are used as the visual rhyme to classify pages of the infographics into categories; meanwhile, the use of colors attaches the qualities of growth, renewal, harmony, reliability, honesty, energy, understanding and compassion to the presentation of the Government with the ideational role of colors.

In addition, with the social actors in the infographics, it is found that the ideational role of the Policy Addresses not only represents the policies but also harmonious society with their narrative representation, which consists of the depiction of the pleasant interaction among social actors and the Government. With the interpersonal role of pictures, the colorful infographics of the Policy Addresses have created the distinctive effect on viewers' feeling from the ones purely in black and white.

The verbal analysis reveals that the Policy Addresses from Chui's two terms are with the representation of more policy foci, more specific governmental measures, schemes for continuous development and putting the planned goals into effect, as well as new goals for diverse development, which corresponds to the results of the multimodal analysis toward the infographics of Chui's Policy Addresses in his second term to a certain extent. However, in terms of the general function of the texts, while the verbal semiosis is basically informative, the appellative qualities of the verbal version of the Policy Addresses are enhanced in the infographics. This analysis shows that the two modes work together to present the Government with their semiotic configuration. The two modes vary in terms of function due to the nature of the two modes of resources.

The similarities and differences of the semiotic constructions of Ho's and Chui's Policy Addresses are identified in the above corpus-assisted multimodal analysis, which reflects the changes in the ideologies of society in the first two decades of the Macao SAR Government which are interpreted and discussed in the next chapter.

# References

Anthony, L. 2018. AntConc (Version 3.5.7). [Computer software] Tokyo, Japan: Waseda University. Retrieved from http://www.laurenceanthony.net/software

Baker, Paul. 2006. *Using corpora in discourse analysis.* London: Continuum.

Durrant, P., and N. Schmitt. 2009. To what extent do native and non-native writers make use of collocations? *IRAL-International Review of Applied Linguistics in Language Teaching* 47: 157–177. https://doi.org/10.1515/iral.2009.007.

Ellis, N.C., R. Simpson-Valach, and C. Maynard. 2008. Formulai language in native and second language speakers: Psycholinguistics, and TESOL. *TESOL Quarterly* 42: 375–395. https://doi.org/10.1002/j.1545-7249.2008.tb00137.x.

Gablasova, D., Brezina, V., and McEnery, T. 2017. Collocations in Corpus-Based Language Learning Research: Identifying, Comparing, and Interpreting the Evidence. Language Learning, 67(S1), 155–179. https://doi.org/10.1111/lang.12225.

Granger, S., and Y. Bestgen. 2014. The use of collocations by intermediate vs. advanced non-native writers: A bigram-based study. *International Review of Applied Linguistics in Language Teaching* 52: 229–252. https://doi.org/10.1515/iral-2014-0011.

Halliday, Michael, and Christian Matthiessen. 2004. *An introduction to functional grammar*, 3rd ed. Great Britain: Hodder Arnold.

Hu, Kaibao, Tao Li, and Ningzi Meng. 2018. *Introducing corpus-based critical translation studies.* Beijing: Higher Education Press.

Hyndman, Sarah. 2016. *Why fonts matter*. UK: Penguin Random House.

Kjellmer, G. 1990. Patterns of collocabiltiy. In *Theory and practice in corpus linguistics*, ed. J. Arts and W. Meijs, 163–178. Amsterdam: Rodopi.

Kress, Gunther, and Theo van Leeuwen. 1996/2006/2021. *Reading images: The grammar of visual design*. 3rd ed.

Lakoff, Robin Tolmach. 1990. *Talking power: The politics of language in our lives*. New York: Basic Book.

Machin, David. 2007. *Introduction to multimodal analysis*. 1st ed. London & New York: Bloomsbury Academic.

Scott-Kemmis, Judy. 2009. Empower-yourself-with-color-psychology.com. https://www.empower-yourself-with-color-psychology.com/meaning-of-colors.html. Accessed 20 Feb 2018.

Simpson, Paul. 1993. *Language, Ideology and point of view. Interface*. USA and Canada: Routledge.

Sinclair, John. 1991. *Corpus, concordance, collocation*. Oxford: Oxford University Press.

Siyanova-Chanturia, A., and R. Martinez. 2015. The idiom principle revisited. *Applied Linguistics* 36: 549–569. https://doi.org/10.1093/applin/amt054.

Zhu, Xiaomin. 2011. A corpus-based critical discourse analysis of the English translation of report on the work of the government: First person plural pronouns. *Foreign Languages Research* (3): 73–78+112. https://doi.org/10.13978/j.cnki.

# Chapter 5
# Discussion

This chapter discusses the results of the case analysis. The previous chapter has examined the linguistic and semiotic configuration as well as the translation shifts in the interlingual translation between the verbal version of the Policy Addresses in Chinese and English in the first two decades of the Macao SAR Government, and the inter-semiotic translation between the verbal version and the infographics of Chui's Policy Addresses.

The analysis in the previous chapter provides the description of the existing semiotic phenomena of the selected Policy Addresses. With Fairclough's *Critical Discourse Analysis* as the macro-analytical framework, after the text analysis, this chapter goes further into the discursive practice dimension and social practice dimension.

With the quality of the selected Policy Addresses as a specific communicative event, the chapter process the description attained in the previous chapter to interpret the textual phenomenon within the particular discursive context of the selected Policy Addresses with the specific production, distribution and consumption. In addition, this chapter further discuss the social and cultural factors influencing the discursive construction and the interplay between the discourse and socio-cultural context in the dimension of social practice.

The following presents the discussion on how the ideological effects of discourse are constructed in the Policy Addresses announced by Macao Chief executives and the role of translation in the meaning construction process, as well as the relationship between the discursive construction of Policy Addresses as a particular discourse type and the society of Macao. It is to explore how the Policy Addresses function in the social changes of Macao, in a role of institutional discourse which is with Ho's and Chui's offices as the discourse producer, and the relevant social agents as the discourse consumers.

© The Author(s), under exclusive license to Springer Nature Singapore Pte Ltd. 2023     143
M. Lam Sut I, *A Corpus-assisted Multimodal Analysis to Policy Addresses of Macao SAR Government*, Corpora and Intercultural Studies 11,
https://doi.org/10.1007/978-981-99-1195-0_5

## 5.1  Ideology Constructed in Discourse

Taking from Fairclough (1992, p. 64), discourse contributes to the constitution of different dimensions of social structure. Discourse is not only a practice representing the World, but also a practice signifying the World, constituting and constructing the World in meaning, which contributes first to the construction of social identities and subject positions, social relationships as well as a system of knowledge and belief.

As a particular type of institutional discourse, the Policy Addresses of Macao SAR Government are with ideological effects on the city. They serve as the necessary documents produced by the institution that governs the city, which provides them with the quality of the discourse type, demonstrating the correlation among discourse, power and the institution.

As mentioned in Chap. 1, Policy Addresses are the documents produced by the consultants of the Office of the Chief Executive of Macao SAR Government with the chief executive at the time, who presents them to the public as a leading figure of the Government on behalf of the whole team of the administrations. The relevant addressees of the Policy Addresses will take action accordingly to get the Policy Addresses into practice after the chief executives' presentation. In this chapter, within the specific discursive context and socio-cultural context, the ideologies the Macao SAR Government constructed in the first two decades of the new Government reflected in the description of the textual phenomenon of the Policy Addresses of the investigated period is further discussed to reveal the social realities and social structure of the city in the first two decades of the SAR Government, to explore the relationship between the discursive construction of the Policy Addresses and the socio-cultural context of the city.

The following section elaborates on the social realities and social structure of Macao reflected in the linguistic and semiotic realization of the selected Policy Addresses, which include changes of the condition for governance, changes of the image of the gaming industry, changes of the economic system and changes of the image of the Government in the investigated period. The role of translation in the mentioned discourse constructive effect is elucidated in detail in the following.

### 5.1.1  Discourse Constructing Changes of the Condition for Governance

The investigation of the selected Policy Addresses as a particular discourse type reveals the changes of the condition for governance in the first two decades of the Macao SAR Government, which is evident in their linguistic and semiotic phenomena.

As described in the previous chapter, when identifying the key words of the Policy Addresses under investigation, no key word with reference to policy foci appears in Ho's but three appear in Chui's. The examination of their linguistic context in the selected Policy Addresses reveals a diachronic change in the word groups formed by their significant *Collocates*, delivering from consistent to more diverse meaning, from general to more specific meaning. For instance, while the key word 民生 (people's lives) forms word groups with its significant *Collocates* which denote the general public system of the Government in terms of people's lives, such as 民生服務 (services with respect to people's wellbeing) in Ho's Policy Addresses, it forms the ones which denote, more specifically, the Government's plans or course of actions as well as different sorts of policies and measures for the lives of people in the city, such as 民生政策措施 (livelihood-related policy measures) in Chui's Policy Addresses, which represents the relatively more general governing schemes of Ho's administrations and the governing schemes of Chui's administrations with more specific and detailed actions.

Moreover, in the analysis of the key verbs, the linguistic configuration reflects Chui's administrations' specific governing schemes as introducing new goals for tourism development and putting some existing goals relevant to people's livelihood into effects, with the distinctive key verb, such as 建設 (to build/construction) and 落實 (to implement) as well as their linguistic context. In terms of key verbs, there are common ones, such as 提升 (to increase/increase) and 優化 (to optimise) in both Ho's and Chui's which signify the action of refining and improving. They, yet, contrast in the goals they introduce, such as 提升教學質素 (enhance the teaching quality) and 提升師資的素質 (improve teachers' quality) in Ho's and 優化持續教育 (optimize continuous education) and 加強校園愛國愛澳教育 (enhance patriotic education) in Chui's; 提升居民生活素質 (enhance residents' living quality) in Ho's and 優化居民的出行環境 (improve commuting conditions) in Chui's. The examination of these goals shows the diachronic change from Ho's terms to Chui's terms in the goals for refining and improving from dealing with general and basic elements to diverse development, with the trend from general to more specific, from simple to more diverse, from recovering to further continuously developing with diverse opportunities.

As a particular discourse type as the significant governmental documents to announce to the public the work plan set for the coming year by the Government, the results of the analysis, as the examples mentioned above, reveal the changes in the condition of governance of the administrations in different periods of time. As reflected in the linguistic and semiotic realization mentioned above, Chui's administrations can focus on more topics and introduce new elements to be developed. They are able to deal with more details of different aspects by taking more specific actions to work on various issues. All these reveal the improvement of the governance conditions from Ho's terms to Chui's terms. Under the change of the general governing condition, changes in other specific facets are represented in the discourse as elaborated in the following.

### 5.1.2  Discourse Constructing Changes of the Image of the Gaming Industry

In addition to the changes of the condition for governance, the investigation of the selected Policy Addresses as a particular discourse type reveals the changes of the image of the gaming industry of the city in the first two decades of the SAR Government, which is evident in their linguistic and semiotic construction.

The corpus-assisted analysis of the selected Policy Addresses identifies 博彩 (LT: gaming/gambling) as one of the key words with reference to the Government's policy foci, which has its distribution different from the other two key words in the same category. While the other two are with their *Keyness* rocketing in Chui's first term, 博彩 (gaming/gambling) has its *Keyness* started rocketing in Ho's second term which remains identical in Chui's first term. The word group with its opposite reference 非博彩 (non-gaming) is found in Chui's Policy Address with an increase of its *Keyness*, which does not exist in any of Ho's Policy Addresses. These linguistic phenomena indicate the significance of both 博彩 (gaming/gambling) and 非博彩 (non-gaming) in Chui's terms.

When examining the linguistic context of this key word, the author identifies the diachronic change of its linguistic contexts as with word groups denoting meaning from general to specific, which suggests the changes in the role of the gaming industry throughout the investigated period. The differences in the relevant word groups foregrounded in Ho's and Chui's Policy Addresses make the representation distinctive. When the general gaming industry was the concern in Ho's terms, the Policy Addresses focuses more on the specific gaming enterprises in Chui's terms, as reflected in the salient word groups, such as 博彩業 (gaming industry) in Ho's Policy Addresses but 博彩業 (gaming industry) as well as 博彩企業 (gaming enterprises) in Chui's Policy Addresses. While the general growth and change of the industry is a significant concern in Ho's terms, Chui's offices transpose the focus to the growth and change in the healthy and long-term way, as reflected in its significant *Collocates* as 發展 (to develop/development) in Ho's Policy Addresses but 健康發展 (healthy development), 有序發展 (development in orderly manner) and 長遠發展 (long-term development) in Chui's Policy Addresses. When Ho's offices concerned generally on the management of the industry, Chui's administrations put an eye on the specific management as controlling, observing and checking the industry, as suggested in the salient *Collocates* of the key word as 管理 (management) in Ho's Policy Addresses but 監管 (monitor) and 調控 (facilitate and control) in Chui's Policy Addresses.

The change of the image of the gaming industry is further enhanced in the translation process. As mentioned in the description of the textual phenomena in the previous chapter, the key word 博彩 (LT: gaming/gambling) is prominently translated with the shifts of diction and with a few cases of omission. It is worth noting that the word choices include the ones with neutral and negative references, but with the ones with neutral references as the majority. And there is also a decrease in the application of word choices with negative references throughout the investigated period. The translations with negative references are gradually used in the contexts which refer to the disadvantages of the risking activities and the actions of getting away from the related bad influences of this activity.

In addition, the multimodal analysis reveals that the representation of the gaming industry in infographics of the Policy Addresses is carnival-related and international. In spatial composition, the gaming industry "collocates" with other entertainment, such as cable cars, hot air balloons and carousels, which are neutral and suitable for any type of customer, even children. It is also attached to the representation of "international" by being placed in the context of the buildings representing other foreign countries.

With the role of the Policy Addresses as a discourse type to announce the political actions of the coming year to the public and offer instructions for the related participants to follow and put the policies into practice, the results of the analysis as the examples mentioned above reveal the changes in the image of gaming industry throughout the investigated period. As evident in the linguistic and semiotic realization, the discursive construction of the Policy Addresses reveals the Government's attempt to construct the image of gaming industry as a neutral one with its unavoidable negative references which are under the Government's control.

### 5.1.3 Discourse Constructing Changes of the Economic System

Related to the changes in the depiction of the image of the gaming industry, the investigation of the selected Policy Addresses as a discourse type reveals the changes of the economic system in the first two decades of the SAR Government, which is reflected in their linguistic and semiotic phenomena.

The description of the textual phenomena of selected Policy Addresses signifies a change in the economic system of the city within the discursive context of the Policy Addresses. For instance, in the examination of the linguistic context of one of the key words with reference to policy foci, 多元 (LT: diversification), it is found that there is an increase in the application of this key word throughout the investigated period. The statistics show that the *Keyness* of this key word rocketed in Ho's second term, as four times higher than the previous, and maintained a considerable increase in Chui's first term as 2 times higher than the previous. It then leveled off in Chui's second term. This diachronic change in the application of this key word in the four terms of the Macao SAR Government represents that "to diversify" is one of the significant political actions in the governing scheme on which the Government has been enhancing the salience put in this period of time.

Its linguistic context in the selected Policy Addresses further discloses the close association between this key word and the economic system of the city. The analysis of the linguistic context shows that 適度 (adequate) and 經濟 (economy) are its common significant *Collocates* with the highest frequency in both Ho's and Chui's Policy Addresses. With these most significant *Collocates*, the key word forms word groups with the reference to the diversification of the economic system of the city, such as 經濟多元 (diversified economy) and 經濟適度多元 (adequate economic diversification), which occupies 69.2% of all the *Concordance* of this key word in the selected data.

These textual phenomena, more specifically, represent that diversifying the economic system is one of the policy foci of the Government, which is offered noticeably increasing significance by the administrations from Ho's terms to Chui's terms.

In addition, the contextualization of the common key verbs in Ho's and Chui's Policy Addresses signifies a similar representation. As mentioned in the previous chapter, there are common key verbs in Ho's and Chui's Policy Addresses which represent the processes of improving and refining, such as 提升 (to increase/increase), 優化 (to optimise), 促進 (to reinforce), 加強 (to enhance). Similarly, in both Ho's and Chui's Policy Addresses, in over 30% of their *Concordance*, these key verbs form salient word groups with reference to the economy, which is the majority in the proportion of the goals introduced by this group of key verbs.

Withal, contrasts are identified in the detailed examination of this common goal. While they are prominently with the representation of the recovery of the economic system of the society, such as 經濟復甦 (recovery of economy) in Ho's Policy Addresses, they are more commonly with the representation as the economic environment of the society, such as 營商環境 (business environment), the continuation of socioeconomic development, such as 經濟社會可持續發展 (sustainable socioeconomic development) and the adequate diversification of the economic system of the society, such as 經濟適度多元 (adequate economic diversification) in Chui's Policy Addresses, with the last representation accounting for more than 50% of all the mentioned goals.

These linguistic phenomena identified in the analysis reveal that generally refining and improving the economic system is always one of the important aims of the Government, yet, the specific goals for improving or enhancing in terms of the economy are changed diachronically. Developed from aiming at attaining the recovery of the economy of the city in the early years of the Macao SAR Government, Chui's administrations turned to developing more opportunities for diversifying the economic system of the society for the continuation of socioeconomic development.

This aim of diversifying the economic system of the society for the continuation of socioeconomic development, and the change of the gaming industry as the increase in the involvement of non-gaming elements correlate to each other, which suggests modifying the role of the gaming industry in the city as the major engine of the economic growth to the role to motivate the growth of non-gaming elements.

The salience put on the policy "to diversify" is further enhanced in the translation process. For instance, the case analysis shows that nominalization is widely implemented in the translations of the key word 多元 (LT: diversification) and more frequently applied when dealing with the word groups with reference to the field of the economy via the translation shifts of diction and conversion. More than 50% of its translations in both Ho's and Chui's Policy Addresses are in noun forms. For instance, 經濟適度多元發展 (LT: the economic adequately diverse development) is translated as *optimum diversification of the economy*. The adjective 多元 (LT: diverse) in the source text is translated into a noun *diversification* in the target text. The implementation of nominalization enhances the objectivity and formality by nature. It positions the process as a "thing" by the deletion of the agents of actions and other participants, temporal, spatial and modal adjuncts of the processes. The widely use of nominalization in the translation of the key word 多元 (LT: diversification), while it is involved in the word groups with reference to the economy in particular, discloses the Government's solid attitude toward the political action of diversifying the economic system.

In addition, the representing color of the field of economy in the intersemiotic translation, orange, associates the economic system of the city with energy and stimulation to suggest the pleasant situation in the time period of the last few years of the first two decades of Macao SAR Government.

With the related evidence provided by the textual phenomena of the Policy Addresses as the examples above, the Government presents to the public the economy of the city from the status with the need to be recovered to the status with energy and opportunities for long-term development, which reflects a change in the economic system of the city throughout the first two decades of Macao SAR Government.

### 5.1.4  Discourse Constructing Changes of the Image of the Government

In lines with the changes of the condition for governance, the changes of the image of the gaming industry, as well as the changes of the economic system, the corpus-assisted multimodal analysis to the selected Policy Addresses as a discourse type reveals the changes of the image of the Government in the first two decades of Macao SAR government, which is evident in their linguistic and semiotic phenomena.

As described in the case analysis, distinctive key verbs are identified in Ho's and Chu's policy addresses, which represent various political actions in different terms of the Government. While there are the key verbs introducing mental processes of making promises for the public as 確保 (to ensure) identified in Ho's Policy Addresses, there are key verbs introducing the material processes of sharing fruitful financial results with the public as 發放 (to grant/to offer/to provide) identified in Chui's Policy Addresses. The contrast in the distinctive key verbs reveals that the attitudinal status of the Government is changed, diachronically, from the intention of Ho's administration to help the public to build up confidence toward the new government, to the intention of Chui's administration to showcase the merits of the Government in social development so as to present the administrations' ability and power to the public. This difference is further evident in other parts in the analysis.

More instances are provided in the examination of the key pronoun. The analysis identifies only one key pronoun from the selected data, which is a first-person plural pronoun applied with considerable high frequency and *Keyness* in only Ho's Policy

Addresses. It is found that, when labeling the speaker of the Policy Addresses, the names of the Government per se, i.e., 特區 (LT: SAR), 特區政府 (LT: SAR Government) and 政府 (LT: the government), are used more often in Chui's, while the first-person plural pronouns are the more frequent choice in Ho's instead. As mentioned in the case analysis, in Ho's Policy Addresses, the first-person plural pronoun is frequently applied in the context with the lexical modals in high epistemic modality, such as 相信 (believe) and the lexical verbs for the actions of pursuing progress with effort as 加強 (strengthen/enhance) and 鼓勵 (encourage), to represent the speaker's positive attitude toward the propositions, at which Ho's administrations' intention to foster solidarity is further evident.

When analyzing other labeling of the Government, a significant *Collocat*e of 政府 (LT: the government), 陽光 (sunshine), is identified, which does not exist in any of Ho's Policy Addresses. It is a word that first appeared in Chui's first Policy Address and with the only collocation as 陽光政府 (sunshine government). It is used to label the Government with the representation of a clean and open administration for a new age.

The aforesaid results suggest Ho's administration's intention to display and motivate solidarity in general, while there is no considerable salience put in this aspect in Chui's Policy Addresses in contrast. Instead, Chui's administrations put effort to present the Government to the public with a governing team that is clean and open and is ready for a new age.

The multimodal analysis toward the visual resources reveals the change in the relationship between the Government and the public. In the analysis of the visual resources of the verbal version of Policy Addresses, the diachronic change in visual presentation is identified. In the verbal version of the Policy Addresses in Chinese, there is a noticeable change in typography throughout the investigated period, from the application of the classic, traditional typeface to the use of relatively modern and rounded typeface. As van Leeuwen (2006) believes, typography can also be used ideationally to represent qualities and express attitudes to what is being represented. Thus, the change of the application of the typography signifies the change of the role of the Government as the authority to the more approachable institution welcoming the participation of the public.

In terms of the visual presentation in the structure of the Chinese Policy Addresses, it is changed from a run-on passage functioning as a script to a complete printed document with elements to enhance readability as a book does. In addition, the infographics of the Policy Addresses are released along with the verbal version of the Policy Addresses in Chui's second term, which is to further enhance the readability of the Policy Addresses.

The visual configuration of the Policy Addresses suggests the change in the distribution of this critical type of government document. By enhancing the readability, the target readership would be, very likely, changed from reaching the specific groups with the text type as the formal governmental documents to reaching the public with the readable presentation to showcase the development of the Government. With the represented social actors and the use of colors, the visual configuration of the infographics identified in the detailed multimodal analysis suggests the representation of a healthy society with a harmonious relationship between the public and an accomplished, considerate and nurturing government.

Again, as a particular discourse type as the significant governmental documents to announce to the public the policies formulated by the Government, the Policy Addresses construct the image of the Government in different period of time. The change of the textual phenomena of the Policy Addresses throughout the investigated period, such as the relevant evidence mentioned above suggests the change of the different administrations' attitudinal status in governing. While an image of the Government is constructed in Ho's terms as to display and motivate solidarity from the public, the image of the Government in Chui's terms is constructed as the accomplished one with merits and power, which is clean and open to invite more involvement from the public.

### 5.1.5  The Role of Translation in Ideology Construction

The corpus-assisted multimodal analysis toward the verbal version of the Policy Addresses in Chinese and their English translations as well as their inter-semiotic translations as the infographics uncovers the role of translation in ideology construction, with the ideological effect of the Policy Addresses. This is evident in their linguistic and semiotic phenomena, as in some of the instances mentioned above.

As mentioned before, in this study, there are two sorts of translation activities: interlingual translation and inter-semiotic translation. They are the translation process from the verbal version of the Policy Addresses in Chinese to the verbal version of the Policy Addresses in English produced by Ho's two administrations and Chui's two administrations, as well as the translation process from the verbal version of the Policy Addresses to the infographics of the Policy Addresses produced by Chui's second administration. The case analysis reveals that the translation processes function in the discourse construction as amplifying the meaning constructed in the discourse and reinforcing the salience of some concepts in the Macao context with the translation shifts.

*Reframing a Concept with Translation Shifts*

The investigation of the interlingual translation processes reflects that translation functions in amplifying the meaning constructed in discourse. This function of translation is demonstrated in different examples in English translations of Policy Addresses. The translation of key word 博彩 (gaming/gambling) is one of the examples. This example demonstrates how translation processes contribute to amplifying the meaning constructed in discourse by reframing a concept with translation shifts. As mentioned before, it is found that the change of the image of the gaming industry is further enhanced in the translation process with the translation shifts in the interlingual translation process as *diction*, *substitution* and *omission*. With the shifts, there is the primary trend in applying the translations with neutral references for the key word 博彩 (gaming/gambling) in the English Policy Addresses. Though there are translations with negative references as *gambling* and *casino*, they have been gradually used in different relevant contexts with the representation of the specific environment of this risking activity, disadvantages of this risking activity and prevention of the bad influences of this risking activity, such as *problem gambling*. These translation processes label this concept with different references in different contexts. The translation process which labels this concept with the neutral and general reference related to games instead of risk discards the negative association of the signified of the key word in the English texts, which reframes the concept as generally neutral entertainment. The unavoidable negative association of this key word remains in the labeling of the specific risking activities which are consisted in the signified of this key word and is framed by the translations with negative reference. With these translation processes, the gaming industry is framed as neutral, with its unavoidable negative association under control for prevention.

*Specifying the ST Signified with Translation Shifts*

In addition to reframing the concept, this study demonstrates that translation contributes to amplifying the meaning constructed in discourse by specifying the ST signified in the translated texts. For instance, as mentioned in the case analysis, the key word 民生 (people's lives) is translated inconsistently throughout the whole investigated period with the shifts of diction and specification. With the most frequently used word choice, *people's livelihood*, which occupies more than half of the translations of the key word, the key word is specified into the material lives rather than the abstract well-being in the English translations. With the translation shift, this board concept in the source texts is specified to the recipients of the Policy Addresses in English. The specific signified in the English translations correlates to the economic development of the city and reveals the constant salience that administrations put on the economy of the city.

*Enhancing the Determination of the Voice of the Discourse with Translation Shifts*

Translation's function in amplifying the meaning constructed in discourse is also evident in its function in enhancing the determination of the voice of the discourse with translation shifts. As one of the examples mentioned above, nominalization is widely applied in the translations of 多元 (LT: diversification) and in the word groups with reference to the economy in particular to enhance the Government's solid attitude toward the related political action toward the economic system of the city. In the verbal Policy Addresses in English, the key word 多元 (LT: diversification) is translated dynamically with the shifts as *diction, substitution, omission* and *conversion*, and prominently with *diction* and *conversion*. With these frequent translation shifts, the application of nominalization is widely used in the English translation. With the nature of nominalization to strengthen the objectivity and formality, and to present the idea as a "thing", the determination toward the political scheme is enhanced by the English translations. The translation with the frequent application of nominalization intensifies the speaker's determination of the mentioned propositions to the recipients of the verbal version of the Policy Addresses in English.

*Intensifying the Power, Authority and Social Affinity of the Voice of the Discourse with Translation Shifts*

Withal, in this study, translation presents its function in amplifying the meaning constructed by intensifying the power and authority, as well as the social affinity of the voice of the discourse, which is evident in the application of first-person plural pronouns in the English translations. In the investigation of this group of translations, it is found that the first-person plural pronouns are frequently added to the English translations via the translation shifts of addition and substitution. They act as the linguistic realization of different kinds of representation in the discourse. For instance, as the examples mentioned above, "*our*" is frequently added to the nouns relating to the governing responsibilities and merits, to emphasize the Government's administrative experience and their governing strategies in the English translations. By adding the pronouns as the modifiers of nouns, the translations function to accentuate the governing responsibilities and merits of the Government.

In addition, this type of translation shifts also suggest the offices' intention in creating social affinity. As mentioned in some of the examples above, adding "*our*" to *people* and *space* to translate 保障居民的基本權利和自由 (LT: protecting residents' basic rights and freedoms) into *protecting our people's basic rights and freedoms* and adding "*our*" to translate 拓展發展空間 (LT: expand space for development) into *expand our space for development* are the examples to shorten the distance between the Government and the recipients of the Policy Addresses in English by the inclusive use of the pronouns to involve the recipients. With the inclusive and exclusive use of the pronouns as well as the concept "royal we" (Lakoff 1990, 190), the offices' power and authority are enhanced by accentuating the Government's responsibilities and merits as well as its social affinity as demonstrated in the instances provided in the case analysis.

The investigation of the contextualization of the subject pronoun *We* in the English translations of Policy Addresses further demonstrates the translations' role in amplifying the power and authority of the speaker of the discourse. As mentioned, the analysis shows that the subject *We* saliently collocates with the lexical verbs which refer to the processes of pursuing progress with efforts in the English translations of both Ho's and Chui's Policy Addresses to represent the Government's ambition. This is the significant collocation of *We* in the translated Policy Addresses as 17% of all its *Concordance* lines in Ho's and 25% in Chui's, but with considerably lower frequency in the State of the Union Addresses as only 1.4% of all *Concordance* lines of *We*. The features of the contextualization of the subject *We* in the English translations suggest the reinforcement in the power and authority of the speaker of the discourse by the representation of the Government's ambition with the linguistic context.

In addition, in the English translations, the subject *We* also collocates with the modal lexical verbs indicating epistemic modality in both Ho's and Chui's translations to present the public with the Government's confidence toward their propositions. While Chui's offices present their high confidence to the public with the significant Collocates in full epistemic warranty in absolute certainty as those in the

State of the Union Addresses, such as *understand* and *know*, Ho's offices present their confidence with the salient Collocates in high epistemic warranty in relatively lower certainty, such as *believe*. This responds to the change in the governing condition of the Government from Ho's terms to Chui's terms, as mentioned above. All the aforesaid results of the examination of the first-person plural pronouns in the English translations demonstrate the role of translation in ideology construction as accentuating the Government's power, authority as well as its social affinity with the discourse construction of the English translations. This noticeable contrast between the translated texts and the texts in the same discourse type in native English enhances their significance to the English communities in the Macao context.

*Reinforcing the Salience of Concepts in the Macao Context with Translation Shifts*

Last but not least, as mentioned, this study demonstrates that translation functions in ideology construction by reinforcing the salience of some concepts in the Macao context. This is evident in various examples of the textual phenomena of the Policy Addresses under investigation. For instance, in the analysis to the translation of the key verbs in this study, though the translated verbs are with considerably high *Keyness* in the English version of the Policy Addresses of Macao SAR Government under investigation, the noticeable salience of these verbs does not exist in the texts of the same discourse type in native English. Moreover, they are not only with specific frequency in the selected English translations but also with unique collocations which do not exist in the texts of same discourse type in native English as well. The distinctiveness reveals that these textual phenomena are the features of the translated texts rather than the linguistic features of the language, which represents their uniqueness in the Macao context and, meanwhile their particular salience in the Macao context.

This is further evident in other features identified in the selected translated texts. When comparing the English versions of Ho's and Chui's Policy Addresses in the last two decades with the State of the Union Addresses, more distinctive features in the linguistic configuration of the translated English policy addresses are figured out. For instance, as mentioned, while *gaming*, *gambling*, *casino* and *diversification* do not exist in any of the selected State of the Union Addresses and *livelihood* exist very rarely, they act as the translation of the key words in Macao's policy addresses. While *improve* acts as one of the verbs without considerable high application in the State of the Union Addresses, it is with the normalized frequency 100 times higher and acts as the most frequent word choice in the translations of a particular group of key verbs in the translated Policy Addresses of Macao and appears in the linguistic context which does not even exist in the State of the Union Addresses. An ordinary verb in the texts of the same discourse type in native English having distinctly high frequency and unique collocations in the translated texts amplifies the noticeable salience of its representation to the recipients of the English translations of Macao's Policy Addresses. All mentioned above are the instances of the translation features of the verbal version of Macao's Policy Addresses in English. The distinctiveness in the translated Policy Addresses when compare to the texts of the same discourse type in native English, emphasizes their significance in the Macao context to the English communities.

*Amplifying the Meaning Constructed in Discourse with the Translation Shifts by Visual Resources*

In addition to the interlingual translation, the inter-semiotic translation also plays a role in ideology construction as well. This is evident in the application of the visual resources of the verbal version and the infographics of the Policy Addresses.

In terms of the visual presentation of the verbal version of the Policy Addresses in Chinese and English, a dramatic shift is identified in the translation process. The layout of all the selected English translations remains similar. The elements implemented in the English texts to act as visual rhyme and contrast are less than those in the STs. The complete structure as a book applied in the Chinese versions do not happen in any of the English translations. Thus, the readability enhanced diachronically in the verbal version of the Policy Addresses in Chinese is absent in the English translations. While the presentation of the verbal version of the Policy Addresses in Chinese is gradually shaped as to invite the public's involvement by more non-verbal resources to enhance the readability, the English version remains plain and formal in visual presentation. It is framed as the formal governmental documents rather than the materials to be read by the public.

The differences in the Government's intention in inviting the involvement of Chinese-speaking communities and English-speaking communities are revealed. The hierarchy of languages in the society is also suggested, with Chinese as the more important choice comparing to English, which is further evident in the choice of language in different version of Policy addresses as well, with both Chinese and English in the production of the verbal version of the Policy Addresses but Chinese only in the production of the infographics.

In the infographics of the Policy Addresses, as mentioned above, the carnival-related and international representation attached to the gaming industry of the city by the visual resources further enhances the construction of meaning of 博彩 (gaming) without negative reference. In addition, with the use of colors in the infographics, the Government is associated with the qualities of growth, renewal, harmony, reliability, honesty, energy, understanding and compassion. With the social actors and processes represented, a harmonious society with a pleasant relationship between the public and the Government is shaped. The visual configuration mentioned above further intensifies the intention of Chui's second administration to present a clean, open, and accomplished government with merits and authority.

These are the instances of how the inter-semiotic translations play a role in the ideology construction of discourse. All of the above demonstrate how the case analysis provides evidence for the translation role in the discourse construction of social ideologies. It functions in amplifying the meaning constructed in the discourse by reframing the concept, specifying the ST signified, enhancing discourse producers' determination, intensifying the power and authority of the voice of the discourse and reinforcing particular salience in Macao context with translation shifts.

To summarize, investigating the key words as well as the contextualization and the translations of the key words in the Policy Addresses of the first four terms of the Macao SAR Government reveals the ideologies constructed in the investigated period. The linguistic and semiotic realization, as well as translation shifts of the Policy Addresses reflect the social changes in the condition for governance, the role of gaming industry, the economic system of the city, the image of the Government as well as social relationships among different social communities. In what way these constructive effects of the selected Policy Addresses correlate to the socio-cultural context of Macao is further elaborated in the following.

## 5.2  Dialectical Relationship Between Policy Addresses and Society

*Critical Discourse Analysis* is to study discourse as social practice, which is to investigate the correlation between discourse and other facets of social life. With this core concept, Fairclough (2006, p. 10) describes the process of discourse production metaphorically as designing for a new automobile "engine" as "internalized and materialized", which is to illustrate the way how a change in discourse turns into actions taken place in the society. With the interconnection between discourse and other aspects of the social life, changes in discourse are "operationalized" into more general change, and meanwhile the production of discourse is influenced by the social contexts. (Fairclough 2006, 9–10) This is termed the "dialectical relation" as that discourse is socially constituted and socially constitutive (Fairclough 1992, 2001).

Fairclough's theory applies to the effect of the selected data of this study. Policy addresses are produced by the Governmental authorities in relation to the social contexts at the time; and meanwhile, with their verbal and visual presentations, the Policy Addresses shape the ideological framework of their recipients who would turn what the discourse represents into things really happen in the society.

With the theoretical basis of the dialectical relation between discourse and social realities, in the following of this section, within the relevant socio-cultural context, it is to explore the factors behind the production, distribution and consumption of the Policy Addresses within the socio-cultural context of the city in the first two decades of Macao SAR Government.

### 5.2.1  Discourse and General Social Background

The general social background of the city throughout the investigated period acts as one of the social factors which correlate to the discursive construction of the Policy Addresses of Macao SAR Government.

As mentioned in the previous section, the discourse construction of the Policy Addresses contributes to the changes of the condition for governance of the Macao SAR Government throughout the investigated period. From the more general governing scheme of Ho's administration to the more specific governing schemes of Chui's administration; from the significant goals of refining essential elements of the city in Ho's terms to the aims of further development in different facets in Chui's terms; from the recovery of the economy as one of the significant tasks of Ho's offices to seeking for further continuous development with diverse opportunities in this field as the one of the main objectives of Chui's offices. All these changes in the first two decades of the Government are reflected in the diachronic changes in the textual phenomena of the Policy Addresses as mentioned above. This representation of the selected data corresponds to the changes of the social realities in the city during the same period of time.

Macao is a city with a special political background as a former Portuguese colony. Mr Edmund Ho Hau Wah is the Chief Executive of the first term of the new SAR Government. Before the start of this new Government, there were problems in the social order of Macao. Cases, such as shootings, explosions, arson, kidnapping, robbery, and intimidation constantly happened in society, which became the serious concern of society (Guo 2003; Zheng 2004). The social condition creates the need for Ho's offices to strive for "recovery" and "steady development". In order to achieve the goals, there would not be many other objectives to be achieved in the first term of the new Government, but the primary task of the administration is to deal with social security. The new Government is with the social needs which are evident in the case analysis with the textual phenomena of the selected data, for instance, as Ho's administration's goals for refining being more general than those in Chui's.

After the sovereignty of Macao returned to China in 1999, the social security of the city has apparently improved. Ho's aims in the Policy Addressees as "recovery" and "steady development" have turned into social realities, which creates a better social basis for Chui's offices. As mentioned in the case analysis, Chui's Policy Addresses focus on more topics and even introduces new elements to be developed, which reveals that the social context at the time allows Chui's administrations to deal with more details of different aspects by taking more specific actions to work on different issues.

All these unfold the interrelation between the change of the social conditions and the production of Ho's and Chui's Policy Addresses. While the social background provides a change in the governance conditions to Ho's and Chui's administrations, their Policy Addresses respond to the change of the social context, which leads to the change of the social condition throughout the investigated period.

## 5.2.2  Discourse and Socio-Economic Structure

More specifically, the socio-economic structure of Macao is another significant social factor having effect on the production of the Policy Addresses and meanwhile, the Policy Addresses are operationalized into changes in the socio-economic structure throughout the investigated period. How they correlate to each other is elaborated in the following, in terms of two aspects: the uniqueness of the pillar industry of the city and the overall socio-economic context of the city.

### 5.2.2.1  Uniqueness of the Pillar Industry

The discursive construction of the selected Policy Addresses contributes to the representation of the changes in the role of the pillar industry of the city, the gaming industry. As mentioned in Sect. 5.1.2, the related textual phenomena shape the diachronic changes in the role of this pillar industry of the city. While generally the industry itself, the overall growth of the industry and the Government's generic concern on the management of the industry are foregrounded in Ho's Policy Addresses, more specifically the gaming enterprises, the growth and change of the industry in a healthy and long-term way, the Government's management with specific actions as controlling, observing and checking, as well as the neutral and even positive elements, such as being international and welcoming family customers are foregrounded in Chui's Policy Addresses.

The Government's attempt to shape the role of the gaming industry, which is neutral and welcoming children and families, with its negative reference under the Government's control, is reflected by the textual phenomena as well as the translations as demonstrated above. This change in the image of the pillar industry of the city constructed in the selected Policy Addresses corresponds to the social context related to the uniqueness of this pillar industry of the city.

The gaming industry, which has the determining role in the economy of Macao, is a controversial industry with its uniqueness in development. As a particular type of industry, its unavoidable negative external association causes certain social cost. (Huang 2019; Liu 2016) There are possible social problems in association with the gaming industry. As studied, the gambling activities with the highest stake and profit in Macao is VIP gambling tables in casinos, however nearly 70% of the gaming profits are from slot machine (which involves gambling activities with a small amount of stake) in Las Vegas. (Gu and Zhuang 2017, 157) It is obviously shown that, different from Las Vegas, the principal business of Macao's gaming industry is the gambling activities with a large amount of stake rather than the entertainment with a small amount of stake as another great gaming hub does in the market.

Furthermore, as recounted in Chapter One, the gaming tax was 40.2% of the Government's fiscal revenue in 2002, which increased to over 70% in 2006 and approached 80% in 2019 (statistics from DSEC). The dominating role as well as its unavoidable negative reference due to the nature of the industry itself, offer the Government the need to reframe the industry's image for long-term social development. As a discourse type with special political status, the discursive construction of the Policy Addresses responds to this social need and put the related governing goals into actual governing actions.

The results of the analysis as mentioned reveal that the Government has been striving to construct Macao's gaming industry as the one with neutral association rather than negative, under their close control on the negative effects caused by the nature of this special type of activity, to respond to the social need of the development of the city with this special type of industry as the pillar industry. With the role as the significant governmental document with ideational effects on the city, the Policy Addresses shape the gaming industry as an industry which is more diversified, controlled and with long-term growth.

### 5.2.2.2 Overall Socio-Economic Context

In terms of the socio-economic structure of the city, apart from the uniqueness of the pillar industry of Macao, the overall socio-economic context of the city acts as the relevant social factors to explain the discursive construction of the selected Policy Addresses.

With the rapid development of gaming industry as described above, Macao is well-known all over the World as the most extensive gaming hub. Its gaming revenue surpasses Las Vegas' as the top in the market. However, the city had gone through the years with depressed economy before the handover of the sovereignty in 1999. Starting from 1996, the GDP grew negatively in the four consecutive years that followed. The unemployment rate was high and up to 6.4% in 1999 and the employed population was with significant fall in income in these years. The monthly income of the employed population in 1999 is even lower than 1996. The flagging economy provided the new Macao SAR Government with a big challenge. (Cheong 2009; Kwan 2019).

The challenges provided by the social realities at the time correspond to the production of Ho's Policy Addresses. As discussed, the goal of the recovery of the economy is foregrounded in Ho's Policy Addresses by the discursive construction with different textual phenomena, such as the contextualization of the key verbs as mentioned before. The production of Ho's Policy Addresses, hence, responds to the social need regarding the socio-economic context at the time. Meanwhile, the Policy Addresses take their political function to put the goals into actual actions to instruct changes in the socio-economic situation at the time.

The Government's goal of recovery of the economy in the early years of Macao SAR Government offers the historical background to the gaming liberalization in 2003. (Cheong 2009; Kwan 2019) The gaming liberalization brought the gaming industry and the city the enormous adjustment with blooming economy. The unemployment rate was down to under 4% throughout the years starting from 2006 and falls to 1.7% in 2019. The gaming tax rocketed from 47 billion MOP in 1996 to 1,367 billion MOP in 2014, which as a percentage of the Government revenue rose year by year, from 37% in 2000 to over 64% in 2004 and up to 81% in 2011. The domination of the gaming industry in Macao' economy reveals the potential risk in the economic development of the city, which arouses the need of the policy of diversifying the economic system for long-term development. (Che 2018; Liu 2016).

The results of the analysis in the previous chapter reflect that the production of the Policy Addresses responds to the social context in terms of this particular field by foregrounding the Government's intention in providing changes to the economic system of the city at the time. For instance, the production of the Policy Addresses from Ho's second term and onwards put salience on the word groups which refer to reinforcing the non-gaming elements when stabilizing the pillar industry (gaming industry).

The Government's objective of fostering synergy between gaming and non-gaming elements is not just to make changes to the gaming industry but the whole economic system of Macao from depending on one single industry to motivating the growth of other economic activities with the help of the strong financial basis of the pillar industry so as to achieve the adequate economic diversification. As revealed in the case analysis, the Government associates Macao's gaming industry with the concepts, such as entertainment, family and tourism, through the non-verbal resources in the translation shifts; and foregrounds the diversification of economy throughout the investigated period but Chui's terms in particular, with the wide application of nominalization in the translation of the related word groups. These are the instances of how the production of the Policy Addresses respond to the socio-economic situation of the city at the time and meanwhile drive the social change in terms of socio-economic aspects of the city.

With its political function, the Policy Addresses put this into social practice, as evident in the continuous rise of the non-gaming revenue in society. The annual reports of the gaming enterprises state that the non-gaming income as a percentage of the total revenue has been rising continuously, as from 5.76% in 2013 to 7% in 2016 in Wynn Macao's, from 11.26% in 2013 to 16.23% in 2016 in Venetian Macao's, from 5.91% in 2013 to 13.28% in 2016 in Melco Resorts & Entertainment Limited, etc.. (Liu 2018, 121) A consecutive increase in the proportion of the non-gaming revenue is presented. These records reflect the operationalized role of the Policy Addresses, while the production of which is influenced by the social need aroused by the socio-economic context at the time.

### 5.2.3  Discourse and Political & Cultural Identities

Macao is a city with a special political background. It provides the social contexts for the construction of unique and complicated political and cultural identities. The political and cultural identities hence apparently influence the production of the Policy Addresses of Macao SAR Government, and meanwhile, the political and cultural identities are changed by the political actions instructed by the operationalized role of the Policy Addresses in the four terms of the Government throughout the first two decades of the new Government.

### 5.2.3.1   General Political and Cultural Background

The historical root of the city creates complicated formation and fluidity of Macao's identity, which poses challenges to the first term of the Macao SAR Government in building the relationship between the brand-new government and the public.

Different from some other regions which have experienced a difficult period of time because of colonialism, the history of colonization is a complicated experience for people in Macao and the perception of decolonization is vague. (Ng 2019, 9) The key historical event, "123 incident" triggered anti-colonial protests and finally shaped the "Portuguese local regime-Chinese state relationship" in colonial history (Kaeding 2014, 184). The Luso administration diminished its rule over Macao, and the Chinese local groups took over many services from the Luso administration to become the dominant local force. Hence, afterward, Macao people did not undergo suppression due to the invasion of governance by Portuguese colonialization in actual practice but "enjoyed" the blending of cultures caused by the colonialization.

Portuguese arrived in Macao in the sixteenth century and their long stay in this city with different political statuses over time created the long-established interaction of cultures, which makes the coexistence of Chinese and Western cultures with mutual respect, tolerance, and harmony rather than conflict in the city. This builds the unique cultural identity of Macao as evident in the cultural hybridization in architectural heritage, cuisine, and language, etc. In addition, since 1951, the imposition of border controls has severely limited the once intimate interface between Macao and Mainland China, and the cross-border contact between Macao and Mainland China leads to a perception of differences in between.

In addition to the complicated political and cultural identity of Macao before the handover of the sovereignty in 1999, the economy of the city, was not buoyant in 1990s, and the social order was not well preserved as described before. The city at that time caused considerable concern for the future development. With this socio-economic background, in the time period right before the transfer of sovereignty over Macao from Portugal to China, many people in Macao had different degrees of fear because of the uncertainty of the future of the city.

As mentioned above, the analysis of the selected discourse reflects a change of condition for governance and a change of the image of the government, which is evident in the semiotic configuration of Ho's and Chui's Policy Addresses. Contrasting to the textual phenomena of Chui's Policy Addresses, Ho's Policy Addresses are with the linguistic and semiotic configuration, such as the frequent use of the lexis for making promises and the frequent use of the only key pronoun 我們 (we, our, ours, us) as well as its contextualization with lexical modal in high epistemic modality and lexical verbs for actions of pursuing progress with effort to display and motivate solidarity, which reflect Ho's offices' attempt in refining the basic social elements in their governing scheme and building up confidence for the citizens toward the brand-new government. This is the evidence that the production of Ho's Policy Addresses responds to the socio-cultural context at the time; meanwhile, Ho's Policy Addresses instruct the social actions to create social changes.

Having governed by Ho's administrations for ten years, there is an apparent improvement in the public order and the economy of Macao, which is the evidence of the change in the social realities caused by the relevant political actions operated by Ho's Policy Addresses which acts as the engine for the change in social realities. With the merits of Ho's offices, most people in Macao enjoy a better economic environment as well as other favorable conditions offered by the rapid development of society. Chui's administrations are eased from the significant attempt of Ho's offices to earn the trust of the public for the new government in a society filled with social problems. Instead, they are responsible for showing power and authority to a certain extent. Though the social condition with existing problems is apparently improved in Chui's terms, Chui's administrations are not free from dealing with social problems but with another sort of social challenges.

The rapid development causes a revolutionary change in social structure and economic system, which brings dramatic difference to people's lives and create some potential social problems. For instance, there has been a growth in the middle class in the city due to the economic development. They are the group of the population with more demands toward the Government, which leads to the higher political participation of the public. There is also the import of a large amount of people outside Macao due to the vital need for a workforce and the flourishing growth of tourism, which creates possible conflicts with the lives of local people. In addition, the blooming gaming industry forges social problems with its unavoidable risking nature, etc. (Yang, Wei, & Zhang, 2016) In this social context, the Government is actually in the need of the better governing power and ability to deal with the potential risks, in terms of economic problems and social development. This socio-cultural context influences the production of Chui's Policy Addresses.

As evident in the case analysis, Chui's Policy Addresses, with the linguistic and semiotic resources, present a clean and open governing team as 陽光政府 (sunshine government) and suggest a healthy society with the harmonious relationship between the public and the accomplished considerate and nurturing government which is clean and open to welcome more involvement from the public. All these linguistic and semiotic realizations in Chui's Policy Addresses represent the change in condition for governance and the government's image, from Ho's Policy Addresses to display and motivate solidarity, to Chui's Policy Addresses to construct and present authority and ability, which responds to the social need due to the socio-cultural context. This is the evidence to demonstrate how the production of Chui's Policy Addresses is influenced by the change of the socio-cultural context at the time and meanwhile, with the political function of Policy Addresses, they turn the discourse into social actions to influence the social realities.

The semiotic configurations represent that Chui's administrations are the accomplished offices which is clean and open to welcome public involvement. With the ideologies constructed in the Policy Addresses, Chui's offices present to the World their governance ability and power.

### 5.2.3.2  Application of Languages

As mentioned above, translation plays a role in the ideology construction in the Policy Addresses. The analysis reflects that the translation process of Ho's and Chui's Policy Addresses functions in amplifying the meaning constructed in discourse and reinforcing the special salience of some concepts in Macao social contexts, through translation shifts to reframe the concepts, specify the signified meaning in source texts, intensify the power, authority and social affinity of the voice of the discourse, etc. These effects on discourse provided by the translating processes reflect the application of the two languages involved in the present study in Macao.

Macao's unique and complicated cultural identity is also revealed in the language use in the communities. This is a city with rich language resources and its complicated multilingual phenomenon which has aroused research interest from scholars. (Yan 2012, 151) As mentioned in Chapter One, as a museum of languages (Wong 1998), Macao is with a multi-lingual community where Cantonese has an absolute advantage, English has practical value, Mandarin has potential space, and Portuguese has a historical origin (Su 2014). Since the present study focuses on Chinese and English, the elaboration in the following focuses on these two languages only.

Chinese has become one of the official languages of the city since the transitional period between the date of the entry into force of the Joint Declaration on Question of Macao. Though English is not given the official status in Macao, it is always with its social role. English has been with its surprisingly high application before 1999 and is widely used in various fields, such as politics, economy, education, media, etc. which enjoys a "de facto status" within government agencies in the city (Moody 2008, 4). In accordance with the detailed results of the population by-census 2016 released by Statistics and Census Service of Macao (DSEC), Macao is always a city dominated by a Chinese-speaking community with 80.1% of the population aged three and above, while the corresponding proportion for English is 2.8%. The results of the present study coincide with the social realities in terms of language use of the city.

As evident in the comparison of the textual and discursive phenomena of the different versions of the Policy Addresses of the first two decades of the Macao SAR Government, the Chinese versions (both verbal version and infographics) and English translations deliver some common representation, but heterogeneous text types are found to be utilized across discourse in different languages (and in different modes). The analysis reveals that the Chinese Policy Addresses are somehow more operative, which offers communication of content with a persuasive character. They serve not only to inform the governing actions but also to present a harmonious society to the public for developing the social affinity of the Government with different sorts of visual resources to enhance the readability and create the emotional appeal.

In contrast, the visual presentation of the English translation is relatively plain and formal with fewer non-verbal resources to create social affinity. The distinctiveness in the presentation of different language versions is apprehensible as targeting different recipients. Instead of taking up the role of "de facto status" in other situations as Moody (2008) suggested, with the particular discourse type of the Policy Addresses, the English translation apparently addresses different target readerships for different communication purposes when compared to the Chinese versions. Rather than aiming mostly the general public, as well as the related offices and journalists, the English version, more reasonably, functions as only the formal governmental documents which aim presumably at publicizing the city by presenting the governing schemes to the outside World.

## 5.2.4   Discourse, Knowledge and Power

The correlation between the discursive phenomena and the social background, socio-economic structure as well as political and cultural identities of the city demonstrates the interplay among discourse, knowledge and power. With Foucault's view of knowledge and power (Foucault 1998), the social approach to discourse concerns the way which discourse is used to bind to issues of what we believe to be correct and wrong, who has power over whom, and what we have to do and say to conform to the social context. (Jones 2012/2019, 36) The interpretation of the textual phenomena and the explanation of the discursive phenomena of the Policy Addresses under investigation within the socio-cultural context of Macao demonstrates the concerns above.

As described in Chapter Two, according to Foucault (1980, 1988), knowledge creates power in the way that what we know governs how we can shape something via discourse practice; however, power creates knowledge in the way that we only know what we are allowed or offered to know. Following this line of thought, the discursive construction of the Policy Addresses is considered as a vehicle for social and political process which reveals the interplay among power, knowledge and discourse.

Policy addresses, as a particular discourse type, not only are the materials that reflect the Government's work plan, but also are as empowered as a political practice to define or shape the city as how the authority would like it to be presented to the recipients, which is to create knowledge as how the city is to the audience whom the discourse addresses. In other words, the social ideologies constructed by the discursive construction of the Policy Addresses reveal how the administrations would like to present the city to the public and the outside World.

As mentioned in the case analysis, the infographics of the Policy Addresses represent not only the governmental policies and development schemes and directions, but also a harmonious society under the effective governorship. While verbal semiosis is basically informative, the appellative qualities of the verbal texts are enhanced by the visual resources of the infographics of the Policy Addresses. In other words, when the verbal version of the Policy Addresses is relatively more informative and prominently serves to provide facts, the infographics of the Policy Addresses are more operative in essence which incorporate visual resources to create emotional appeals that are wrapped in aesthetic forms to reinforce the social affinity. This approach to using heterogeneous communication materials by Chui's administrations is apprehensible, as the verbal materials target narrow audience, whom are mostly the relevant social agents to assist in putting the Policy Addresses into actions. Whereas, the infographics of the Policy Addresses are basically advertising materials which target presumably at the general public, to invite them to know more about the effectiveness of the governance of the Government by presenting the Policy Addresses in a more readable measure.

This heterogeneity in the presentation of the Policy Addresses could be construed with Foucault's idea of discipline while exercising power. For Foucault, discipline is a set of strategies or procedures employed to regulate the behaviors of individuals within certain context. This study reveals that the Government exercises its power in presenting the work plans, conforms to the "norms" in crafting and distributing the Policy Addresses, i.e., to present the comprehensive work plan to the legislative council so as to address the relevant sections of the administration to take actions; to present the outside World how Macao is with the formal government work plan in English, while feeds the public or, more specifically, the residents, with the more abridged, more emotion-laden presentation of the Policy Addresses in pictorial form to appeal to them, with the merits of the Government, for admitting the administrations' governance. As mentioned above, with the constitutive function of discourse, the Government is constructed as the accomplished one with merits and power which is meanwhile clean and open enough to invite more involvement from the public in Chui's terms by the discursive construction of different versions of the Policy Addresses.

In addition, in line with the idea of exercising power relationships while distributing discourse, the presentation of Macao's Policy Addresses demonstrates the power hierarchy in the society since most of the work plans set by the Macao SAR Government respond to the strategic scheme of the Chinese Central Government. For instance, as revealed by the case analysis, Macao SAR Government has been striving to associate Macao's gaming industry with the concepts, such as entertainment, family and tourism, via the linguistic and semiotic configuration, such as attaching the pictures representing gaming industry with carnival-related pictures of facilities welcoming children and landmarks of foreign countries. The foregrounding of the non-gaming elements of the industry responds to official announcements from the Chinese Central Government.

As mentioned in Chapter One, the development of the economic diversification of Macao was first announced as the strategic planning and deployment of Macao's development in the 11th Five-Year Plan for National Economic and Social Development of the People's Republic of China (one of a series of social and economic development initiatives) in 2006. In 2008, the Plan for the Reform and Development of the Pearl River Delta released by the National Development and Reform Commission positioned the development of Macao as a World Centre of Tourism and Leisure, which was then mentioned in the 12th Five-Year Plan in 2011. Afterward, the positioning was further reassured in the 13th Five-Year Plan in 2016, as the strategic objective of the development of Macao. These are some of the related policies toward the economic development of Macao announced by the Chinese Central Government.

Regarding the discursive construction of the Policy Addresses under investigation, as mentioned in Chapter Two, the key word 多元 (LT: diversification) presents an upward trend in its application in the Policy Addresses throughout the investigated period and is with a noticeably increase in PA2007, which is the Policy Address released right after the announcement of the 11th Five-Year Plan from Chinese Central Government. The salience put on the word groups with denotation related to economy and the diversification of the economic system afterward are the instances in the textual phenomena of the Policy Addresses in the same vein. The correspondence reveals the power relationship as the influence of China's political schemes on the production of Macao's Policy Addresses. This is to show how Macao SAR Government's policy responds to the announcement of the Chinese Central Government. The connection in between reveals the power relationship between Macao SAR Government and the Chinese Central Government.

All of the above in Sect. 5.2 elaborate on the interplay between Macao's social realities in different periods of time and the textual and discursive phenomena of the Policy Addresses with examples. The elaboration demonstrates the correlation between the socio-cultural context of the city and the discursive construction of the Policy Addresses. The socio-cultural context with the influences given by the general social background, the socio-economic structure, the political and cultural identities of the city in particular, provides the rationale for the production of Policy Addresses, which demonstrate the interplay between discourse, knowledge, and power with the role of the Policy Addresses as a special discourse type of institutional discourses.

## 5.3  Summary

This chapter further processes the textual phenomena identified in the corpus-assisted multimodal analysis presented in Chapter Four, with the discursive context of the Policy Addresses and the particular socio-cultural context of Macao. The chapter starts with the constitutive effects of the Policy Addresses to elaborate on the representation of discourse realized in the linguistic and semiotic configuration, which reveals the changes of some core ideologies of the society in the first two decades of the SAR Government, as a change of the condition for governance, a change of the image of the gaming industry, a change of the economic system, a change of the image of the Government.

These changes of core social ideologies are further discussed to explore the correlation between discourse and other facets of social life, which illustrates the dialectical relationship between the discourse and the socio-cultural context as how the Policy Addresses are produced to respond to the general social background of Macao, the socio-economic structure of Macao, and the special political and cultural identities of Macao; and how the Policy Addresses take their specific political role to operationalize the discourse into social practice. In between, the discussion argues how translation plays a role in the ideological construction of discourse. The interplay among discourse, knowledge and power is explored to uncover the authorities, the social and political factors behind the production, distribution and consumption of the Policy Addresses.

# References

Che, Sei Tak. 2018. Problems in the industrial structure of Macau and the path of optimization. *Journal of One Country Two Systems Studies* 4: 176–183.

Cheong, Chok Man. 2009. Insist on its own way: The direction of the future economic development of Macau. *Journal of One Country Two Systems Studies* 1: 158–163.

Foucault, Michel. 1980. *Power and Knowledge.* Translated by Robert Hubley and Others. Edited by James D. Faubion.

Foucault, Michel. 1988. *Power and Knowledge: selected interviews and other writing,* Colin Gordon. New York: Pantheon Books.

Foucault, Michel. 1998. *The History of Sexuality: The Will to Knowledge.* London: Penguin.

Fairclough, Norman. 1992. *Discourse and Social Change.* Cambridge, England: Polity.

Fairclough, Norman. 2001. The discourse of new labour: Critical discourse analysis. In: *Discourse as Data: A Guide for Analysis,* Margaret Wetherell, Stephante Taylor and Simeon J. Yates. London: The Open University.

Fairclough, Norman. 2006. *Language and globalisation.* London: Routledge.

Guo, Jiading. 2003. The past and the future of Macao. *Administration* 60: 367–370.

Gu, Xiangwei, and Jinfeng Zhuang. 2017. On the construction of world tourism and leisure center and the transformational development of gaming industry in Macao. *Journal of One Country Two Systems Studies* 1: 152–158.

Huang, Guihai. 2019. The Review and Prospects of the Twenty Years of Tourism Gaming in Macao. *Macao News,* 2019.

Jones, Rodney H. 2012/2019. *Discourse AnalysisL A Resource Book for Students.* 2nd edition ed.*Routledge English Langugae Introductions.* Milton Park, Abingdon, Oxon; New York, NY: Routledge.

Kwan, Fung. 2019. The two decades of change in the economic growth of Macao. *Macao News* 2019, Economic Development.

Kaeding, Malte Philipp. 2014. Post-Colonial Macao's Changing Identity. In *China's Macao Transformed: Challenge and Development in the 21st Century,* Eilo W. Y. Yu and Ming K. Chan. Hong Kong: City University of Hong Kong Press.

Lakoff, Robin Tolmach. 1990. *Talking power: The politics of language in our lives.* New York: Basic Book.

Liu, Shuang. 2018. The cultivation and development of non-gaming elements of Macau gaming companies. In *Blue Book of Macau--Annual Report on Economy and Society of Macau (2017–2018),* C. L. Ng and Yufan Hao, 114–131. Beijing: Social Sciences Academic Press (China).

Liu, Jinglian. 2016. The future of the gaming and tourism industry. *Academic Journal of One Country* 27: 125–130.

Moody, Andrew. 2008. Macau English: Status, functions and forms. *English Today* 24 (3): 3–15.

Ng, C.L. 2019. Macaology and Macao's development path. *South China Quarterly* 9 (1): 4–12.

Su, Jinzhi. 2014. The socio-cultural meaning and its theoretical value of "Research on the application of Mandarin in Macao". *Applied Linguistics (Yuyan Wenzi Yingyong).*

Wong, L. 1998. *Macao: Language Museum.* Hong Kong: Hoi Fong Press.

van Leeuwen, Theo. 2006. Towards a semiotics of typography. *Information Design Journal* 14 (2): 139–155.

Yan, Xi. 2012. A Study of Language use and Multilingual Ability of Macao Population Before and After the Handover.*Journal of One Country Two Systems Studies* 13 (3): 150–157.

Zheng, Kuen. 2004. Merits on the fifth year after Macao's handover: The scan of Macao Security. *people.cn,* 2004.

# Chapter 6
# Conclusion

This chapter concludes and presents the concluding remark of the study—Two Decades of Change in Macao: a corpus-assisted multimodal analysis to Policy Addresses of Macao SAR Government. This concluding chapter starts with a summary of the research, which is followed by the implications as well as the reflection on the limitation of the present study. The chapter ends with suggestions and perspectives for relevant future research.

## 6.1 Summary of the Research

This study, with Fairclough's three-dimensional *Critical Discourse Analysis* model as the macro framework, examines the Policy Addresses of the first two decades of the Macao SAR Government. The analytical framework is integrated with corpus analysis and multimodal analysis under the theoretical root of Halliday's *Systemic Functional Grammar*, to explore the relationship between the discursive construction of the Policy Addresses and the socio-cultural context of Macao with the discourse prosodies and translation shifts.

This study starts with defining the scientific background to position the study as discourse analysis in Translation Studies with corpus-assisted multimodal approach, which is followed by describing the specific research background about the social and cultural context of Macao, Macao's stories in academic research and Macao's stories in Policy Addresses, to set the scene of the study. With the scene set, the theoretical framework of the study is built with Fairclough's three-dimensional model of discourse analysis as the macro-analytical framework and Halliday's systemic functional linguistics as the theoretical root of the analytical system to provide guides for the description, interpretation and explanation of the selected data.

© The Author(s), under exclusive license to Springer Nature Singapore Pte Ltd. 2023    169
M. Lam Sut I, *A Corpus-assisted Multimodal Analysis to Policy Addresses of Macao SAR Government*, Corpora and Intercultural Studies 11,
https://doi.org/10.1007/978-981-99-1195-0_6

In the analysis, firstly, it deals with the large set of verbal resources for the examination of key words and their contextualization with the relevant corpus tools. With the objective of identifying the discourse prosodies, the word denotations and connotations, the representation of word groups, as well as modality conveyed by the textual resources in the verbal version of the selected Policy Addresses in Chinese and their English translations, are investigated in detail, based on the theoretical foundation with Halliday's meta-functions of language. The linguistic presentation of the verbal version of the Policy Addresses in Chinese and English is compared to identify the shifts in the interlingual translations.

Secondly, as mentioned, to avoid discounting codes of different modes in meaning making process, visual presentation of the verbal version of the Policy Addresses is also under examination, based on Kress and van Leeuwen's visual grammar with special attention put on the spatial composition of the verbal version of the Policy Addresses and the meta-functions of the use of colors and represented social actors in the infographics of the Policy Addresses included in the selected data. After the description of the semiotic presentation of the infographics, the shifts in the inter-semiotic translation process between the verbal version and the infographic of the Policy Addresses are identified.

The corpus-assisted analysis identifies the key words of the selected data, and diachronic changes in the application of the key words, which consists of the distribution of the key words, their contextualization and their English translations. The multimodal analysis finds out the diachronic change in the visual presentation of the verbal version of the Policy Addresses, as well as the semiotic phenomena of the infographics. The translation shifts in the inter-lingual translation process and the inter-semiotic translation process are identified in between. All these textual phenomena and discursive phenomena identified reveal the salience put on the respective aspects in the Policy Addresses in different periods of time. Changes of the condition for governance, changes of the image of the gaming industry, changes of the economic system and changes of the image of the government., in the first two decades of Macao SAR Government, are represented within the communicative event finished by the production, distribution, and consumption of the Policy Addresses, in which the Government distributes the discourse to the public and relevant social agents to consume.

Lastly, the discursive phenomena of the different versions of the selected Policy Addresses are explained within the particular socio-cultural context of Macao. The explanation illustrates the dialectical relationship between the discourse and the socio-cultural contexts as the general social background of the city, the socio-economic structure of the city which includes the uniqueness of the dominant industry of the city, the special political and cultural identifies of the city which includes the application of languages in the communities of Macao.

In short, the findings reveal that the discursive construction of the Policy Addresses, as well as translations, play a role in the constitution of social ideologies which reflects the social changes of Macao. Meanwhile, the historical background, socio-economic structure, as well as the political and cultural identities directly and indirectly shape or constrain the production of the Policy Addresses. The findings of the study serve as evidence of discourse constitutive and constructive effects as well as the dialectical relationship between discourse and socio-cultural context.

## 6.2  Implications

After a brief summary of the study, this section elaborates on the implications of the study from three aspects: the theoretical implications, the empirical implications, and the practical implications.

### *6.2.1  Theoretical Implications*

The theoretical implications of this study consist of but not limit to the following facets:

(1)  The study presents an integrated model for the investigation of social changes from the perspective of discourse analysis, which should be applicable to the studies with similar research interests. The analysis which is conducted in this study is with the theoretical foundation integrated with relevant theories from different fields. The theoretical framework is built based on Fairclough's three-dimensional *Critical Discourse Analysis*, Halliday's Systemic Functional Linguistics, Multimodality and Corpus linguistics. They invite the involvement from linguistics to semiotics, from qualitative to quantitative approaches, from language-based perspectives to sociology. The study demonstrates the applicability of this integration of relevant theories from different disciplines to deal with a large set of data with verbal and non-verbal resources for investigating the discursive construction and exploring the factors influencing the production, distribution and consumption of the discourse within socio-cultural context behind.

(2)  This study enriches the entry points of research in Translation Studies in terms of theoretical basis. Firstly, the study indicates the significance of the discourse analytical approach in Translation Studies. The findings of this study serve as evidence that translation plays a role in the ideological effects of discourse, which can be revealed and explored from the perspective of discourse analysis. Thus, the implementation of discourse analysis into Translation Studies enables researchers to probe into the investigation of translation process beyond the linguistic level but the social-cultural level to examine the role of translation in social change and how the production of translations is constrained by the socio-cultural context. Secondly, the analysis conducted in this study is

a translation-based analysis consisting of different sorts of translations: inter-lingual translation and inter-semiotic translation, which demonstrates the importance of inviting multimodal analysis to Translation Studies. Thirdly, to investigate the change in social ideologies over two decades, this study presents the demand for corpus-assisted analysis to deal with a large set of data in Translation Studies. As mentioned in the previous chapters, there is existing literature involving the relevant theories into Translation Studies. However, this study serves as the one to demonstrate the applicability of marrying all these relevant theoretical concepts with Translation Studies in particular.

### *6.2.2   Empirical Implications*

In addition to the theoretical implications, this study is with its empirical implication attained from lining up multimodal analysis to quantitative examination. As mentioned at the beginning of the book, having recognized the high threshold of the multimodal corpora, with reference to the existing alternative approaches to multimodal translated discourse studies, this study proposes an alternative to the line-up corpus approach and multimodal approach.

Firstly, to ensure the alignment of modes, draw on the same theoretical basis across different modes, i.e., *Systematic Functional Grammar* (SFG) (Halliday 2016, 1994, 1985; Halliday and Matthiessen 2004). Specific steps include an initial corpus-assisted analysis with the verbal resources to offer insights for a subsequent multimodal analysis toward the visual resources and to uncover how the information of verbal mode is translated to different modes for creating meanings and to explore the interplay between modes.

Secondly, to systemize the tagging system for different modes with the same theoretical basis as *Systemtic Functional Grammar.* While lexicogrammar developed by Halliday is to analysis linguistic configurations systematically, visual grammar evolved from it by Kress and Van Leeuwen (1996/2006/2021) can be applied to the analysis to the visual modes.

### *6.2.3   Practical Implications*

This study investigates the Policy Addresses of Macao from 2000 to 2019. It identifies changes in the presentation of this important type of governmental document from the different administrations of the Government in first two decades of the Macao SAR Government, which are interpreted and explained within the discursive context and socio-cultural context to reveal the social changes of the city in the first two decades of Macao SAR Government and how the Policy Addresses as a type of discourse function in "operationalizing" the social changes of the city.

The study demonstrates the dialectical relationship between the Policy Addresses and socio-cultural context, as how the Policy Addresses are produced to respond to the general social background of Macao, the socio-economic structure of Macao, and the unique political and cultural identifies of Macao. In addition, the study made an attempt to demonstrate the interplay among power, knowledge and discourse, which is to uncover the authorities behind the production of the Policy Addresses. Thus, this study, to a certain extent, contributes to the production of Policy Addresses by providing scientific reference for the policy making.

On the other hand, with the position of falling into the research field of discourse analysis to Translation Studies, this research offers implications to practitioners in the translation field as well. This study also demonstrates the importance of the role of translation in the ideological effect of discourse via the investigation of the translation shifts in both inter-lingual and inter-semiotic translation processes. It is found that translation functions in the semantics construction in discourse production as amplifying the meaning construction by specifying the signified, enhancing the determination of the user of language, etc., to respond to the social contexts of the consumers of translations. The translation is not just a process of transferring the signified in the ST to the TT. It involves the ideological effects on the socio-cultural context of the target language as well. Translation, including inter-semiotic translation, plays a role in the ideological effects of discourse, which should offer insight for translators in the production of translations with both linguistic and semiotic resources.

## 6.3 Perspectives for Future Work

In this paper, a corpus-based discourse analysis is applied to investigate the linguistic and semiotic configuration of the Policy Addresses of the first four terms of the Macao SAR Government and to explore how the Policy Addresses as a type of discourse functions in the social changes of Macao, such as the shaping the image of the Government, the shaping of the image of the gaming industry, and the "operationalization" of the changes in the economic system of the society. To deal with the large set of data, corpus tools are used to study the "aboutness" of the selected Policy Addresses. It is found that how the Government positions itself by different administrations and the governing directions of different administrations are revealed in the discourse construction of the Policy Addresses.

It is hoped that this study can give some implications that a corpus-assisted multi-modal investigation can better reveal how production of Policy Addresses is influenced by the change of social practice of Macao in the post-colonized period and how they are produced to operationalize social changes of the city, as well as how they are used to contribute to the relationship construction between the Government and the public.

However, this study presents an analysis only at a general level to show the overview of a Keyword analysis. If more research with detailed analysis on particular sorts of keywords is carried out in the future with specific foci, that would further enrich the literature and give more implications to the research in the similar vein.

# References

Halliday. 2016. *Aspects of language and learning*. Ed. Chenguang Chang Guowen Huang. *The M.A.K. Halliday Library Functional Linguistics Series*, ed. Jonathan J. Webster. London: Springer

Halliday, Michael, and Christian Matthiessen. 2004. *An introduction to functional grammar*, 3rd ed. Great Britain: Hodder Arnold.

Halliday,. 1994. *An introduction to functional grammar*, 2nd ed. London: Edward Arnold.

Halliday,. 1985. *An introduction to functional grammar*, 1st ed. London: Edward Arnold.

Kress and Van Leeuwen 1996/2006/2021. *Reading images: The grammar of visual design*, 3rd ed

# *Uncited References*

AntConc 3.5.7. Waseda University, Tokyo, Japan

Bestgen, Y., and S. Granger. 2014. Quantifying the development of phraseological competence in L2 English writing: An automated approach. *Journal of Second Language Writing* 26: 28–41. https://doi.org/10.1016/j.jslw.2014.09.004.

Corpus Word Parser 3.0.0.0. Institute of applied linguistics ministry of education. Beijing, China

Dayrell, Carmen. 2007. A quantitative approach to compare collocational patterns in translated and non-translated texts. *International Journal of Corpus Linguistics* 12 (3): 375–414.

Dijk, Teun A., and van,. 2008. Critical discourse analysis and nominalization: Problem or pseudo-problem? *Discourse & Society* 19 (6): 821–828.

Fairclough, Norman 1995a. *Critical discourse analysis: The critical study of language*. ed. 1st. London and New York: Longman

Fairclough, Norman 1995b. *Media discourse*. London and New York: Edward Arnold

Fairclough, Norman. 2009. A dialectical-relational approach to critical discourse analysis in social research. In *Methods of critical discourse analysis*, ed. by Ruth Wodak and Michael Meyer, 162–186. Los Angeies, London, New Delhi, Singapore, Washington DC: SAGE

Forceville, Charles J. 1996. *Pictorial metaphor in advertising*. London: Routledge.

Forceville, Charles J., and Eduardo Urios-Aparisi. 2009. *Multimodal, metaphor*, Ed. Gitte Kris-tiansen, Michel Achard, Rene´ Dirven and Francisco J. Ruiz de Mendoza Iba´n˜ez. *Applications of cognitive linguistics*. Berlin New York: Mouton de Gruyter

Fowler, Roger. 1996. On critical linguistics. In *Texts and practices*, ed. Carmen Rosa Caldas-Coulthard and Malcolm Coulthard, 3–14. London and New York: Routledge

Gablasova, Dana, Vaclav Brezina, and Tony McEnery. 2017. Collocations in corpus-based language learning research: identifying, comparing, and interpreting the evidence. *Language Learning* 67 (S1): 155–179. https://doi.org/10.1111/lang.12225.

Lim, Fei V. 2004. Developing an integrative multi-semiotic model. In *Multimodal discourse anal-ysis: systemic-functional perspectives*, ed. Kay L. O'Halloran, 220–244. London & New York: Continuum

Lu, Xiaojun. 2016. *National image and Chinese-English translation strategies for china's global communication*. Shanghai: Foreign Language Teaching and Research Press.

Munday, Jeremy. 2016. *Introducing translation studies: theories and applications. The fourth.* Ediction. London and New York: Routledge.

O'Halloran, Kay L. 2004a. Mathematical discourse: language, symbolism and visual image. In *Multimodal discourse analysis: systemic functional perspectives*, ed. Kay L. O'Halloran, 109–130. London and New York: Continuum

O'Halloran, Kay L. 2004b. *Multimodal discourse analysis: Systemic-functional perspectives*. London & New York: Continuum.

O'Toole, Michael. 1994/2011. *The Language of displayed art*. London: Leicester University Press

Scollon, Ron, and Suzie Wong Scollon. 2003. *Discourse in place: Language in the material world*. New York: Routledge.

Stubbs, Michael. 2001. *Words and Phrases: Corpus Studies of Lexical Semantics*. London: Blackwell Publishing.

Wodak, Ruth. 2006. Dilemmas of discoruse. *Language in Society* 35: 595–611.

Printed in the United States
by Baker & Taylor Publisher Services